D0208271

CÉCILE CHAMINADE

Cécile Chaminade. Undated Photograph by H. S. Mendelssohn. Reproduced with the kind permission of Madame Colette Lorel-Savard.

CÉCILE CHAMINADE

A Bio-Bibliography

MARCIA J. CITRON

BIO-BIBLIOGRAPHIES IN MUSIC, NUMBER 15
Donald L. Hixon, Series Adviser

Greenwood Press
New York • Westport, Connecticut • London

012.78092
C44c

Library of Congress Cataloging-in-Publication Data

Citron, Marcia J.
    Cécile Chaminade, a bio-bibliography / Marcia J. Citron.
      p.   cm. — (Bio-bibliographies in music, ISSN 0742-6968 ; no.
15)
    Bibliography: p.
    Discography: p.
    Includes index.
    ISBN 0-313-25319-6 (lib. bdg. : alk. paper)
    1. Chaminade, Cécile, 1857-1944—Bibliography. 2. Chaminade,
Cécile, 1857-1944—Discography. 3. Chaminade, Cécile, 1857-1944.
    4. Music—Bio-bibliography. I. Title. II. Series.
    ML134.C425C6 1988
    016.78'092'4—dc19   88-21315

British Library Cataloguing in Publication Data is available.

Copyright © 1988 by Marcia J. Citron

All rights reserved. No portion of this book may be
reproduced, by any process or technique, without the
express written consent of the publisher.

Library of Congress Catalog Card Number: 88-21315
ISBN: 0-313-25319-6
ISSN: 0742-6968

First published in 1988

Greenwood Press, Inc.
88 Post Road West, Westport, Connecticut 06881

Printed in the United States of America

The paper used in this book complies with the
Permanent Paper Standard issued by the National
Information Standards Organization (Z39.48-1984).

10 9 8 7 6 5 4 3 2 1

To Madame Colette Lorel-Savard,
a woman of
great nobility and wisdom

University Libraries
Carnegie Mellon University
Pittsburgh, Pennsylvania 15213

Contents

Preface

This volume is the first scholarly book on Cécile Chaminade (1857-1944), once a very popular composer and pianist. It includes the first thorough listing of her prolific creative output, of pertinent discography and bibliography, as well as the first extended biography based on a significant collection of primary sources, in the possession of her heirs.

The biographical account occupies the first chapter. Compared to its counterpart in other volumes of Greenwood's Bio-Bibliography series, this biography is relatively long. This is no accident. It is, rather, a calculated attempt to present the most basic information on the what, when, and who of this neglected composer. These facts have either never been published or else have appeared countless times in erroneous form. The narrative goes well beyond a mere recital of facts, however: it poses questions and offers hypotheses for several knotty historical and aesthetic issues inherent in her life and career, and also delves into her musical style.

The second chapter, "Works and Performances," lists each composition and selected performances. A "W" number is assigned each piece; each performance is affixed a lower-case character. For example, the *Concertstück* is catalogued as W58, its premiere in Anvers is W58a, its next performance is W58b, etc. For some compositions no performances are given. This means either that no bibliography was found to detail a performance, or, less likely, that the work was intended mainly for publication and was not presented in a professional setting. The chapter is organized in four sections. The first, published works with opus numbers, proceeds by opus number. The second lists published works without opus numbers, which consist almost entirely of songs (*mélodies*); it proceeds chronologically by date of publication. The third section is a modest selection of published collections of her works; the prefix "WC" is applied to each. The last, unpublished works, appends the prefix "WU" to each item. It embraces pieces never published as well as important unpublished arrangements of published works. Throughout the chapter the reader is referred to relevant items in the "Bibliography" chapter, which have the prefix "B." The location of the autograph is provided when known. Because of the numerous arrangements of many compositions, both by Chaminade and others, this catalogue presents only the most important versions, which in almost every case are by the composer. Paris is the place of publication unless stated otherwise.

The "Discography" constitutes the third principal division. It attempts to list every commercially made recording of Chaminade's works, both in and out of print. The latter category makes up the lion's share of the over 200 items and includes recordings as old as 1903, piano rolls, and a large number of 78s. Each recording is given a "D" number. The chapter is divided into three sections: recordings of individual works, recordings of more than one Chaminade work (anthologies), and recordings by Chaminade. The first section is organized alphabetically by title of composition. Under each title the ordering of entries is alpabetical by record label and then by performing artist. The reader will note that some entries contain more information than others, such as matrix number or date or place of recording. The author thought it preferable to include the information if available rather than omit it for consistency of format. As much as possible the author filled in first name of a performer if absent or abbreviated. Some entries, especially of songs, list only one performer, omitting the piano accompanist. As in other areas, the presence or lack of such information is dependent upon the source utilized.

The "Bibliography" chapter is an annotated listing of over 475 pertinent sources. Each entry is affixed a "B" number. The emphasis is on contemporary reviews but the list also embraces a variety of other materials, such as magazine features, newspaper interviews, stylistic analyses, essays by Chaminade, entries in selected dictionaries and encyclopedias, and biographies. The organization is chronological rather than alphabetical so that the chapter can serve as an alternate or supplemental biography. A brief section at the end, however, isolates Chaminade's prose works. Access to the authors is provided through the index. Chronological subheadings reflecting the several periods in her career define the chapter's internal organization. The annotations exhibit an approach that is sometimes summary, sometimes critical, sometimes a combination. A substantial proportion extract passages from the source. When these come from a foreign-language instrument only the translation is given (all translations are by the author), without the original text. Considerations of limited space and of ease of use on the one hand, and of scholarly rigor on the other, were weighed very carefully by the author, who finally decided that ease of use was of paramount importance for the intended user. All French sources originate in Paris unless stated otherwise. The author made every reasonable attempt to provide full bibliographic citations, but because many items were encountered as loose clippings with sparse or no bibliographic information, and because many sources are unobtainable in the United States or even in France, there are still some entries that lack some bibliographic component. Brackets surround dates that are approximate rather than certain as well as bits of information that are fairly certain but not stated explicitly in the source.

Three appendices round out the volume. The first two furnish additional access to Chaminade's compositions: an alphabetical list, and a classified list by genre. The third appendix supplies summary information on important archival resources for Chaminade research.

The "Index" lists all names, all compositions, and other significant categories, such as performing series. Items located in chapters 2, 3, and 4 ("Works and Performances," "Discography," "Bibliography") are identified with the relevant mnemonic and catalog number. References to the "Biography" and "Appendix III" are indicated by the actual page number, e.g. "26."

Acknowledgments

My deepest gratitude is extended to the descendants of Cécile Chaminade: Madame Colette Lorel-Savard, great niece of the composer; and her daughter, Madame De Cornulier. Their generosity in permitting me to view and photograph documents in their substantial collection knew no bounds. I am also very appreciative of their innate understanding of scholarship and its value. One could not have worked in a more supportive atmosphere.

In addition, two individuals in Paris were of key importance in the early stages. Gérard Condé, music critic of the Parisian daily *Le Monde*, provided substantial background information as well as functioning as a local liaison. Madame Denis, administrative assistant at the music publishing firm of Enoch et Cie, told me of Madame Savard and went out of her way to assist me as I looked through a few hundred Chaminade compositions at the firm's Paris office.

There are several others in France whom I would like to thank for their assistance: Jacques Enoch, director of the publishing firm; Mme. Francony-Sablayrolles, of Neuilley sur Seine, a distant cousin to the composer; the music publishing firm of Hamelle, in Vernouillet; Madame Langloes, of the Société des Auteurs, Compositeurs et Editeurs de Musique, in Paris; Jean Leduc, of the music publishing firm of Heugel, in Paris; François Lesure, director of the Département de la Musique of the Bibliothèque Nationale, Paris; Wilfrid Maggiar, pianist, of Aix-en-Provence; Catherine Massip, assistant director of the Département de la Musique of the BN; Jean Mongrédien, professor of music at the Université de Paris-Sorbonne, Paris IV; P. Montelèon, director of the Centre des Arts et Loisirs, in Le Vésinet; Patrick Vazeilles, of the Archives in Le Vésinet; Odette Vidal of the music publishing firm of Durand S. A., in Paris; and Roxanna Patterson of Eze-sur-Mer, for helping to establish Chaminade's date of death.

I wish to express sincere appreciation to the numerous individuals in North America who contributed to the bibliographic component of the study: J. Richard Abell, head of the History Department of the Public Library of Cincinnati and Hamilton County; Elmer Booze, music specialist at the Library of Congress; Ralph Clayton of the Enoch Pratt Free Library in Baltimore; Mark Dimunation, rare books librarian of the Stanford University Library; Timothy Dodge of special collections at the University of New Hampshire Library; Don Ellinghausen of reference services of The Newberry Library, Chicago; Louise Goldberg, head of rare books and special collections at the Sibley Music Library of the Eastman School of Music; Nancy N. Gootee of the music room of the Indianapolis-Marion County Public Library; Sidney Grolnic, music librarian at the Free Library of Philadelphia; Alma Hyslop, music librarian of the Metropolitan Toronto Reference Library; Rodney H. Mill, music specialist at the Library of Congress; Laura V. Monti, keeper of rare books & manuscripts, Boston Public Library; Myrna Nachman, associate professor of music at Nassau Community College in New York; Mary Natvig, reference assistant at the Sibley Music Library of the Eastman School of Music; Daniel Olivier, department head of the Salle Gagnon of the Bibliothèque Centrale, Montreal; Diane O. Ota, curator of music at the Boston Public Library; Harold E. Samuel, librarian at the Yale University Music Library; Richard Schwegel, head of the music information center at the Chicago Public Library; Joan L. Sorger, head of the main library, Cleveland Public Library; Mimi Tashiro, assistant librarian at the Music Library of Stanford University; Judy Tsou, of the women's collection of the University of Michigan Music Library; J. Rigbie Turner, Mary Flagler Cary Curator of Music Manuscripts and Books, at the Pierpont Morgan Library; and John R. Ward, in the Kentucky division of the Louisville Free Public Library.

Several persons gave generously of their discographical expertise. They are Richard Cole, authority on piano rolls, in London; Morgan Cundiff, piano archives librarian at the University of Maryland; Michael Gray, chief discographer at Voice of America, and discographical series adviser for Greenwood Press; Sidney Grolnic; Deborah Hayes, associate professor of music at the University of Colorado; Frank Holland, MBE, of the British Piano Museum, in Middlesex; Eric Hughes, of the National Sound Archive of the British Library, London; Wilfrid Maggiar; Don McCormack, curator of the Rodgers and Hammerstein Archives of Recorded Sound at the New York Public Library; Dominique Villemot, director of the Phonothèque Nationale, in Paris; and Richard Warren, Jr., curator of historical sound recordings at Yale University.

Generous financial support was furnished by the National Endowment for the Humanities (summer 1986) and Rice University (1987). A special word of thanks to Don Hixon, series adviser, and Marilyn Brownstein, editor at Greenwood Press.

And finally, to my husband, Mark Kulstad, deep gratitude for his assistance in matters computorial, and even more important, for his continued enthusiasm through the myriad stages of detective work.

CÉCILE CHAMINADE

Biography

Cross-references with a "W" pertain to entries in "Works and Performances," with a "D" to entries in the "Discography," and with a "B" to entries in the "Bibliography."

"Who Was Cécile Chaminade?" Such is the title of an article published in 1982 in the local magazine of Le Vésinet, the Parisian suburb where the composer spent a good part of her life, where today a street bears her name.[1] Yet the posing of this basic question is reflective of the general obscurity surrounding her. Except for the ubiquitous *Concertino* for flute and orchestra her music is mostly silent. The silence is reinforced by the absence of any reliable, comprehensive study of her life or works; there is no complete list of her compositions. It is all the more surprising when one considers Chaminade's extraordinary fame around the turn of the century, especially in England and the United States. Why the marked change? The reasons are complex and will be taken up at the conclusion of the biographical narrative.

Cécile Louise Stéphanie Chaminade was born in Paris on 8 August 1857. The date has served as the source of considerable confusion, as virtually all writings during her lifetime listed 8 August *1861* as her date of birth. A likely reason is that she herself wanted to conceal her true age and thereby profit from a youthful appearance. Her parents were musical: her father, a violinist; her mother, a pianist and singer who gave her daughter her first lessons on the keyboard. The family was fairly well-to-do. Hippolyte managed the Paris office of the British insurance firm, Gresham. His forebears include one Reverend Father Chaminade, founder of the Marianite Order. The maternal lineage embraces Naval officers. Cécile was the third of six children, of whom the next two died in childhood. Of note were her older brother, Henri, whose daughter and granddaughter tended her in her declining years and inherited her estate; and her younger sister, Henriette, who married Moritz Moszkowski, a member of Chaminade's artistic circle.

In the early 1860s the family lived in Paris, on the Rue Brochant. For holidays they would travel to their villa, Château de la Farge, in Périgord. In 1865 land was purchased in Le Vésinet, a village west of Paris, where the family began to spend their vacations. Except for a few rooms retained in

Paris for after-concert use, it would become Chaminade's year-round home ca. 1890. In Le Vésinet the young Chaminade made the acquaintance of Georges Bizet, a neighbor, who is said to have admired her musical gifts when he visited on 28 August 1869. At any rate Chaminade was beginning to compose in the mid 1860s. Various accounts pinpoint various pieces as her first works. In a 1908 interview the composer singled out some mazurkas, published in a French magazine. In the posthumous biography written by her niece, Antoinette Lorel, *La Pastorale Enfantine* is credited as earliest, composed at age seven. Other sources designate sacred pieces intended for a childhood Communion at Le Vésinet.[2]

Reliable information about Chaminade's music education is sketchy at best. Few dates emerge. Lorel's biography--the most detailed, thorough, and accurate account of Chaminade--states that in 1867-68 Cécile was taken to see Le Couppey, on the faculty of the Conservatoire, for an assessment of her talent. His reaction was enthusiastic and he advised that she enter the institution for theory instruction. Hippolyte was firmly opposed to the suggestion: it ran counter to his views on proper decorum for young women of their class. He did, however, permit his daughter to study privately with Le Couppey. Cécile also received instruction from Marmontel and Savard (counterpoint), two other members of the Conservatoire faculty. At some point she became a pupil of Benjamin Godard.[3]

Three musical experiences of her early years are noteworthy. Chaminade attended her first opera performance on 14 December 1868, Meyerbeer's popular *Les Huguenots*. Second, sometime in the late 1860s she supposedly played for Liszt, who found her style similar to that of Chopin.[4] And last, Chaminade was present at the disastrous premiere of *Carmen*, on 3 March 1875. Her deep, bitter feelings about the great pain Bizet suffered at the hands of the musical establishment would be expressed later in her essay on the composer.[5] The experience left an indelible mark and probably had a profound impact on her own opera-writing career.

The Franco-Prussian War ushered in the 1870s. The Chaminades, like many a Parisian family, took refuge in safer territory, in Angoulême; they returned to Paris after the termination of hostilities. Chaminade seems to have continued her musical studies in composition and piano. Her first review appeared in 1875 and assessed a performance of a Mozart *Violin Sonata* with her friend, Marsick, at Le Vésinet (see B1), which had been the site of regular *salons* for several years. In 1877 she made her professional playing debut, at the Salle Pleyel in Paris (see B2-3). Around the same time her *Etude*, Op. 1, was published, to favorable reviews (see B4). But her true *entrée* into composition came with a recital of 25 April 1878 devoted to her own works.[6] It took place at the residence and under the auspices of Le Couppey. Widely reviewed and well received (see B5-8), the program would serve as a model for the typical Chaminade recital some twenty years later: repertoire consisting entirely of her works, a mixture of piano solos and songs, and the composer at the keyboard.

Regarding sources for this period we are indebted to Chaminade's mother, who began a scrapbook of clippings in 1875 that continued through c. 1890. Many notices were also retained during Chaminade's subsequent career but unfortunately were not mounted; few were provided with source or date.[7] According to Lorel, Mme. Chaminade also kept a diary during her daughter's younger years and even incorporated some of Cécile's letters.[8] Such personal documents, as well as the diary Chaminade herself wrote over a period of forty-two years but requested be destroyed after her death, help form the basis of Lorel's unpublished narrative.

Chaminade's next major musical event took place on 8 February 1880, a successful recital of her works at the Salle Erard (see B12-15). The *Trio* No. 1, Opus 11, was featured in addition to various piano pieces and *mélodies*. Her first published chamber work, Opus 11 would be followed in a few years by the more well-known second *Trio*, Op. 34, and by a *Capriccio* for violin and piano, Op. 18. Throughout her career, transcription from one medium to another, by her own hand or that of another, was common. Thus a work like the *Sérénade Espagnole*, Op. 150, which became popular in Kreisler's arrangement for violin and piano, existed previously as the song *Chanson Espagnole*, and may have originated in a version for piano. An unpublished piece, *Marche Hongroise* for two pianos, also graced the Salle Erard program--one of the rare instances of a piano work performed in public but never issued in print.

A year later, on 4 April, Chaminade ventured into symphonic literature with the four-movement *Suite D'Orchestre*, Op. 20, presented on a program of the Société Nationale de Musique. Of three available reviews one was positive, one was mixed, and one was negative (see B18-20). The orchestration in general was praised, although *Le Ménestrel* had harsh words for the repeated use of cymbals in the Chorale. Jules Ruelle, of the rival *L'Art Musical*, criticized all the works on the program. Still, the daily *Petit Journal* predicted a bright future for the young musician, a sentiment echoed, for example, in the *Gil Blas* notice of the publication of the *Trio* two months later (see B22).

Meanwhile, Chaminade began to perform publicly on a steady basis: in chamber concerts, often with Marsick and associates; and in recitals in which her compositions occupied at least a major portion of the program. She soon branched out into opera. On 23 February 1882 she directed a private performance of her *opéra comique*, *La Sévillane*, at her parents' residence in Paris. Invitations were issued to a broad spectrum of the press and musical establishment, including Ambroise Thomas, head of the Conservatoire. Rendered with Chaminade at the piano, the one-act drama garnered plaudits across the board (see B26-39) and gave rise to speculation regarding its mounting at the Opéra Comique. But the work, whose locale was influenced by *Carmen*, was never staged. Perhaps Chaminade was fearful of pursuing a public performance because of the fiasco of *Carmen*, and also because she sensed that as a woman she would encounter greater obstacles in obtaining a performance and in achieving a success. Because of its separability as a concert number, only the overture was published (Op. 19). But the opera did not disappear completely from public view. It was kept alive through vocal excerpts that would appear on concerts from time to time, for example on 25 February 1884 and 4 April 1889 (see W18b and W18f).

Chaminade's career was gaining momentum. Later in 1882 the *Suite D'Orchestre* was performed twice. The press responded warmly to the 19 March event (see B43-52) and praised the orchestration. Melody also attracted the attention of a few writers, such as Charles Darcours in *Le Figaro*:

> Mlle. Chaminade comes from a school in which melodic invention is not considered the mark of the inept. It has grace and infuses the phrases with a contour that is in no way banal.[9]

Continued iteration of this stylistic affinity would approach an *idée fixe*. The other 1882 performance of the *Suite* occurred on 17 December, on the Concerts Populaires series of Jules Pasdeloup. Once again the evaluations were positive (see B62-65) and singled out the orchestration. One reviewer remarked:

> How many in the audience were far from realizing that this symphony [sic], which reveals an uncommon talent in orchestration, was written by a young lady![10]

Variations on the gender theme were to follow Chaminade throughout her career. We shall explore the issue later.

The middle years of the decade saw a continuation of the chamber and soloistic activity, mainly in her own compositions. Of note is the premiere of the *Trio No. 2*, Op. 34, on 4 February 1886 at the Salle Erard. Chaminade detailed the early history of the work in a letter probably from the late 1890s, and probably addressed to Joseph Bennett, London music critic:

> It was performed for the first time at the Salle Erard in February 1886. The year after it was played in every Parisian quartet society, and since [then] everywhere, particularly in Brussels at the [Cercle] Artistique, at the Société Philharmonique in Geneva and in Lyon. And it's worked on every day in classes at the Paris Conservatoire.[11]

Her name surfaced regularly on orchestral programs: repeat performances of orchestral works, such as the 29 March 1885 presentation of the *Suite* at Les Concerts Modernes; and orchestral arrangements of piano pieces, such as the *Menuet*, Op. 5, and *Zingara*, Op. 27 No. 2.[12]

Two important personal events colored this period. The first was the engagement of her younger sister Henriette to Moritz Moszkowski, a musical colleague, in 1886. According to Lorel it caused deep strife within the family. Hippolyte is reported to have severed all ties with his daughter. He objected to her marrying a Jew and a German.[13] Like many a military Frenchman, Monsieur Chaminade had not recovered from the humiliation of the defeat of 1872, the latest in a long history of Franco-German confrontations.

The second event was Hippolyte's sudden death in 1887.[14] The tragedy had consequences beyond the grief of losing a loved one: it placed the family's financial security in jeopardy. In addition to the loss of current income, the Chaminades sustained an intersection of bad investments and an estate that would now be divided. These difficulties necessitated the selling of the large house in Paris in order to retain the property at Le Vésinet.[15] The more significant consequence for Chaminade, however, was the marked change in her artistic activities around 1890. She veered away from composition in the large forms (symphony, opera, concerto, chamber music) in favor of virtually exclusive cultivation of the small, more marketable genres of solo piano and song.

Meanwhile, however, the last years of the eighties yielded arguably the greatest artistic triumphs of Chaminade's long career. She later attributed the start of her public career--read *performing* career--to her *Concertstück* performance in Paris in January 1889:

> In 1889, I at last came before the public at one of the Lamoureux, with a *Concertstück* for piano and orchestra. . . . It was a success, and, to tell a long story in few words, it was the beginning of my public career. My reputation had commenced.[16]

This event, however, was not the first but the third in a cluster of important orchestral successes for Chaminade the composer. It is telling that two of the three took place in the provinces rather than Paris, the undisputed center of French cultural life.

With her score to the full-length ballet *Callirhoë* Chaminade spread her creative wings yet again. The work was originally to have been composed by Benjamin Godard, but because he was busy on another project, the opera *Jocelyn*, he offered it to Chaminade. She finished it within six weeks.[17] After its completion she decided to have it performed in Marseille. As Lorel asserts, she needed the money and no offer was tendered from Paris.[18] *Callirhoë* premiered on 16 March 1888 and was accorded the kind of pre- and post-performance publicity not possible in the capital. Several of the local journalists displayed their obvious pride in having such a major work debut in the provinces. As one reviewer noted, "The success of the work is without precedent in Marseille."[19] Its many repeat performances attest to its popularity.[20] *Callirhoë* would go on and be performed in most major French cities, often numerous times, within the next twenty years. It seems

to have disappeared from the stage after 1910. Curiously, of
the hundreds of sources consulted not one has mentioned the
striking fact that *Callirhoë* was never performed in Paris.
Many sources, however, make the undocumented claim that the
ballet was performed some 200 times. No evidence substanti-
ates the associated claim that *Callirhoë* was presented at the
Metropolitan Opera in New York.

The scenario was written by Elzéard Rougier, a native
son. Thus the added pride of the city. The story was inspired
by a poem by Anacreon, and the locale, as expected, is an-
cient Greece. The remote and exotic qualities of that setting
touched off an aesthetic discussion in local newspapers concerning the representational capabilities of music.[21]

As was customary, a piano arrangement was later issued,
probably in the second half of 1888. In addition, a few movements became separate piano pieces. These include some of
Chaminade's most well-known compositions, such as *Pas Des E-
charpes* ("Scarf Dance") and *Pas Des Amphores*. A remark in the
Parisian journal *Le Progrès Artistique* after the tenth performance was probably prophetic rather than retrospective
when it asserted, "We are persuaded that an arrangement of
the principal sections of this work into a suite will be very
succesful at the Colonne or Lamoureux concerts."[22] Two years
later, on 23 November 1890, the *Callirhoë Suite* bowed to the
public, at the Colonne concerts. The four-movement work
proved popular and played in cities such as Lille (1893) and
Geneva (1894).

Chaminade followed the brilliant premiere of her ballet
with a dual triumph: the introduction of *Concertstück*, her
only piece for piano and orchestra, and of *Les Amazones*, her
only symphony.[23] Both were performed on 18 April 1888 in Anvers (Antwerp). Several aspects of this premiere are of note.
First, once again the location was *not* Paris, but the provinces. Second, the *Concertstück* premiere in Anvers antedated by
nine months the Lamoureux performance of January 1889 generally cited as the work's debut. Third, *Les Amazones*, a dramatic symphony deploying large choral forces and several vocal
soloists, was never performed again--at least, no evidence
has surfaced regarding any other performances. Another astonishing bit of information is that the work, perhaps in an
earlier version, was apparently intended to be performed in
1884-85, in Paris.[24] Did a Paris performance fall through?
Did Chaminade decide not to have the work performed in order
to modify it?

Both of the available local evaluations of *Les Amazones*
praised the flight of Himris and Gandhar, one of the component numbers. The Flemish source, *Het Handelsblad* (see B129),
compared it to Wagner's "Ride of the Valkyries." The French
organ also noted a resemblance to Berlioz's "Ride to the
Abyss" in *The Damnation of Faust*:

> In this time of musical troubles and compli-
> cations, in which every new arrival strains
> to imitate Wagner, Mlle. Chaminade's music
> provides a character that is fundamentally

> French, faithful to its nature . . . . This
> "flight" is indeed a French "ride."[25]

Chaminade was probably attempting to publicize the symphony when she sent a few autograph lines of the score to the popular Parisian weekly, *L'Art Musical*, that summer.[26] Unfortunately, however, the work failed to capture the interest of the powers-that-be of the major concert series.

In contrast, Chaminade's only work for piano and orchestra, *Concertstück*, would boast numerous performances and thus take on a life of its own. At its Anvers debut it was ignored by *Het Handelsblad* but drew the following commentary in *L'Escart*:

> It contains nice ideas, elegantly and naturally developed. We heard a remarkable series of scales, linked successively with truly original harmonies ["tonalités"], blending with the solo instruments and complementing them.[27]

Nine months later Chaminade introduced the work to Paris, on Sunday afternoon, 20 January 1889, at a Lamoureux concert. The event was reviewed by several prominent newspapers, including *Le Figaro*, *Le Progrès Artistique*, and *Le Soleil*, and the weeklies *Le Ménestrel* and *La Semaine Artistique et Musicale* (see B139-43). Every report of substance commented on the orchestration. The critiques spanned the gamut--from an attack on the brutal handling of brass and percussion in one section of the piece, to praise for its incomparable handling of orchestral color.[28] Two reviewers mentioned its brevity. Overall, however, critical reception was favorable. Its next performance in Paris was probably that of 4 March, on a Colonne concert, with Louise Steiger as soloist. A year later, 30 January 1890, Chaminade marked the anniversary of the Paris debut with a rendition at the Salle Erard.[29]

In the 1890s *Concertstück* was presented throughout Europe and even in the United States. In 1892 it was performed in Marseille by Louis Livon, a local pianist of repute. A perceptive reviewer in the *Journal de Marseille* discerned the work's affinity with the fantasy or rhapsody, and pointed out "an expansive theme, like a leitmotif, [which] permeates the score."[30] A few months later, in London, Chaminade performed the piece in a two-piano version. Occasionally she would play this arrangement, perhaps believing it preferable to perform the piece this way than not at all if an orchestra were unavailable. Furthermore, she may have been attempting to prompt additional sales of the music by showing by example that the piece was also suitable for non-professional situations. In 1894 *Concertstück* traveled to Geneva. Chaminade was scheduled to perform but exchanged roles with the conductor, Willy Rehberg, at his request.[31] And perhaps most interesting was its inclusion--possibly its American debut--on a program of the Theodore Thomas Orchestra, in Chicago, in December 1896. It would receive another American presentation when Chaminade played it with the Philadelphia Orchestra on 6-7 November during her 1908 tour. By c. 1910 it reached its peak and only sporadic performances ensued, such as that of Israel Vichnin, in Philadelphia, on 7 December 1919.

As mentioned above, the decade of the 1890s inaugurated a new era in Chaminade's creativity in which small forms pre-dominated to the virtual exclusion of large forms. The only exception would be the *Concertino*, Op. 107, for flute and or-chestra, of 1902, which resulted from rather special circum-stances: a commission from the Conservatoire (her only one) for a competition piece. Intimately linked with this change was her embarking on a full-fledged round of tours throughout Europe, and to England as well, over the next twenty years. As we have seen, she and her mother were in poor financial health after Hippolyte died, and performing her own composi-tions in public figured as a reasonable and socially accep-table means of earning a living. Another goal was to make money from the sale of music. The performing and the sales went hand in hand: new pieces were composed for performance on recitals, and the recitals generated greater sales. Des-pite this practical analysis, however, it is likely that other, less tangible forces also played a role, such as dis-couragement or lack of interest from the Parisian musical establishment.

We have hardly spoken about Chaminade's *mélodies*--works for voice and piano. Well suited to the criteria of perform-ability and marketability, they only began to gain prominence in the 1890s. The following statistics indicate her activity in this genre:

1870s	8 songs
1880s	15 songs
1890s	64 songs
1900-09	41 songs
1910-19	10 songs

These numbers, based on year of publication, reflect fairly accurately the date of composition, for Chaminade seems to have had new works published fairly quickly. We may recall that particularly after 1890, publication, because of its potential financial remuneration, served as a prime reason for composing. In any case, the numbers above speak for them-selves. The 1890s produced the greatest outpouring of *mélo-dies*, with the next decade not far behind. After 1910 there was a marked drop, representative of a general creative de-cline.

Songs and solo piano music formed the backbone of her touring repertory. Occasionally, depending upon available forces, other types of music would be offered, such as the *Concertstück* or the *Trio No. 2*. Chaminade herself performed the piano part in her songs. The singers sometimes were local, sometimes part of the entourage, and sometimes a com-bination. Some of her most famous songs originated in the 1890s, such as *L'Anneau D'Argent* (1891), *Viens, Mon Bien-Aimé* (1892), *Si J'Etais Jardinier* (1893), and *Viatique* (1895).

In June 1892 Chaminade made her first visit to England.[32] The foray across the Channel became practically an annual event. Even though she could not speak English, Chaminade and the British public developed a special mutual affection. She certainly did not receive that degree of attention and support from her native city. Chaminade would cross the Channel in early summer, performing one or more recitals in June or July, sometimes returning in October. She gave a recital in St. James's Hall in London annually from 1892 to 1895, and in 1897 and in 1899. In addition, reviews appeared for two rounds of London concerts in 1907 (late June and late October) and for a recital in September 1922. *Madame* magazine mentioned her successful series of recitals in London, Sussex, and Surrey in fall 1902.[33] Chaminade wrote to a friend in May 1908 that she would be traveling to London in June.[34] She is also known to have visited London in the summers of 1913 and 1914 to record piano rolls for the Aeolian company. At least on the first trip she performed in Aeolian Hall, in early July, doing duets with the Pianola rolls she had recorded.[35] Furthermore, the family's documents include two undated reviews from Manchester, which I estimate were around the year 1894 (see B231-32). Her last trip to England, accompanied by her niece Antoinette, took place in 1924.[36]

The reviews of the first tour were numerous and extremely favorable. One could extract so many positive comments from so many different sources that the London branch of her publisher, Enoch, devoted the entire inner cover of at least one of her compositions to critical excerpts. The review in *The Times* was the most negative. But even here the writer identified some good qualities (in the *Trio No. 2*), although the *Concertstück*, in its two-piano version, was "of no great originality." Over the next two years the *Times* reviewer bewailed a lack of stylistic variety. In 1895 the paper unveiled a new image: the notion of Chaminade disposing of her latest creations just as painters might do at small exhibitions. In 1897 the tone was biting and condescending. The works were trivialized by being compared to the newest fashions in apparel from Paris. Two years later the reviewer pointed to the lack of anything new in her style.[37] This string of negative reports, however, ran contrary to the enthusiastic response of the audience--no doubt the main reason Chaminade was asked to return year after year.

Queen Victoria was an ardent fan and invited Chaminade to Windsor Castle on at least one occasion.[38] The composer dedicated a song, *Reste*, to Princess Beatrice, Victoria's daughter. Chaminade also witnessed the festivities of the Diamond Jubilee, in 1897, and later received a Jubilee Medal and a signed photo from the Queen. At Victoria's funeral, in 1901, Chaminade's organ *Prélude*, Op. 78, was heard.

Because this bio-bibliography is the first systematic investigation into Chaminade's life, a complete picture of her extensive and intensive touring--one that can provide exact dates for all her concert activity--is impossible. The problem is exacerbated by the lack of newspaper indexing for this period, the incompleteness of the holdings of potential lending institutions, and also the extremely fragile state of those sources. We can nonetheless sketch the general outline and fill in several details.

Every indication points to Chaminade having led a full concert life, especially in the 1890s. This meant tours all throughout the Continent in addition to England. She visited Germany regularly. Perhaps her earliest trip there was in the 1886-87 season, as reported in advance in the *Berliner Tageblatt* of 16 February 1886. Another indirect reference placed her in Germany in 1889.[39] Eighteen ninety-six found her performing in Berlin's Bechsteinsaal; Chaminade considered the audience very critical.[40] *Le Ménestrel* reported her in the same hall during the 1897-98 season.[41] A European correspondent for *The Etude* reviewed Chaminade's Berlin program of fall 1899.[42]

Vienna was another main stop on the concert circuit. Chaminade probably presented concerts there on several occasions, but the only specific date that can be ascertained is 28 February 1899, in the Grosser Musikvereins-Saal.[43] Typically, the program was devoted entirely to her compositions. In the same year, and possibly on the same trip, Chaminade made her first concert tour of Eastern Europe and the Balkans. Among the countries visited were Poland (two concerts in Lenberg, one in Cracow), Hungary, Romania (Bucharest, Craiova, Iasi), Bulgaria, Serbia, Greece, and Turkey.[44] She returned to some of these countries in 1901.

Belgium played host to Chaminade on a regular basis. We know she performed in Brussels on 1 December 1895, sponsored by Schott.[45] In January 1894 she visited Tournai. The biographical typescript of c. 1930 (p. 60) states, without documentation, that she toured Belgium in 1904.

Because of the existence of relatively ample documentation, the year 1893-94 can serve as an example of the scope of Chaminade's concertizing activity:

June 1893	London
November 1893	Lille (includes the *Concertstück*)
January 1894	Tournai
February 1894	Geneva (3 concerts, one conducting the *Concertstück*)
March 1894	Reims (includes the *Concertstück*)
April 1894	Paris
May 1894	Lyon
June 1894	London

In the waning years of the century, Chaminade became involved in another opera project. It never reached fruition. As early as 1897 it was mentioned in the Chaminade literature. The account described how she is presently completing a "drame lyrique" in collaboration with Armand Silvestre.[46] Over the next three years essentially the same report surfaced in various articles (see, for example, B270 and B272). In January 1903 the story changed somewhat. Now, as reported in the British magazine *Madame*, Chaminade "hopes soon to finish her lyric drama, which was delayed by the death of Armand

Silvestre, her collaborator" (in February 1901).[47] Four years
later an extended article in *New Idea Woman's Magazine* (New
York) stated that Chaminade thought Silvestre's libretto too
long (four acts), and it would be difficult to find a libret-
tist willing to cut it to the desired three acts. In addition, she was loathe to do the mammoth work necessary to complete an opera without a definite performance prospect.[48] In
November 1908, during the American tour, she mentioned the
incomplete work in an article in *The Washington Post*:

> I have written but one opera. That one was
> never finished. The librettist . . . died,
> and I have never had the heart to complete
> the music. I doubt if I ever shall; but parts
> of it--the overture and some of the choruses-
> -have been separately published.[49]

It is unclear what Chaminade meant by published excerpts--
perhaps they were pieces with no titular relationship what-
soever with the opera. Also, whether or not intentionally,
she seemed to have forgotten *La Sévillane*, her *opéra comique*
from 1882.

Lorel's informative biography mentions an operatic project based on a libretto of Silvestre, but the circumstances
strongly suggest that it was a completely different undertak-
ing.

> The short libretto of Griselidis was written
> for her, but when Massenet read it, he was so
> enthusiastic about it that Cécile, hearing of
> this, at once took it to the great composer,
> for whom she had a great affection. She
> would, nevertheless, much have liked to han-
> dle it herself. The melody *L'Ondine du Léman*
> [W384] had been written for Griselidis.[50]

Massenet's opera *Grisélidis*, a "conte lyrique" based on a
libretto by Silvestre and E. Morand, premiered at the Opéra-
Comique on 20 November 1901. One can only wonder what Chaminade's setting would have been like, what its fate would have
been, and how it would have affected her career and her reputation.

In the next few years Chaminade's personal life under-
went a major change. She married the Marseille music publisher Louis-Mathieu Carbonel, on 29 August 1901, in Le Vésinet. From then "Mme." replaced "Mlle." as her title of address. Sometimes she signed her name Carbonel-Chaminade or
added a "C" before Chaminade. According to Lorel, Chaminade
had become close to Carbonel in 1899 when Cécile's mother
asked him, an old friend, to take her place in accompanying
Cécile on an extended tour (probably the Eastern European
trip). In July 1901 Chaminade announced their marriage plans.
Her family was bewildered and upset by the news. Carbonel was
more than twenty years Cécile's senior, and it was clear that
the prospective bride was proposing a platonic match. Lorel
describes Chaminade's conditions: each would reside in his or
her former home, she near Paris and he in Marseille; he could

visit her periodically and accompany her on her travels; and there were to be no sexual relations between them.[51] On one of the tours--to Ostende, in 1903--Carbonel contracted a lung disease that eventually caused his death, in early 1907.[52] Chaminade's family believes that the marriage caused her to sacrifice professional momentum and precious creative years to the nursing of a sick man. The composer confirmed this in part, in an interview of October 1908 with the New York *Sun*, where she was paraphrased as stating that in the last two years she had not done much composing. A glance through the "Works and Performances" chapter corroborates her assertion; only three *mélodies*, for example, were published in this period (W379-81).

Why did Chaminade enter into such a marriage? The actual reason probably disappeared with the destruction of her diary. Nevertheless we can speculate, based on evidence at hand. Chaminade was aware that her mother was concerned about her being without a mate, although Mme. Chaminade never promoted the cause of Carbonel as a suitor. From Cécile's point of view, marrying someone older and well established, in a marriage of convenience, would allow her to preserve her professional independence. She expressed her views in two interviews of 1908:

> Marriage must adapt itself to one's career. With a man it is all arranged and expected. If the woman is the artist it upsets the standards, the conventions, the usual arrangements and, usually, it ruins the woman's art. . . . Tho' I have been married and am a widow now, I feel that it is difficult to reconcile the domestic life with the artistic. A woman should choose one or the other.[53]

> [The artist] must have freedom, not restraint, she must receive aid, not selfish, jealous exactions and complaints. When a woman of talent marries a man who appreciates that side of her, such a marriage may be ideally happy for both.[54]

Paternal identification also figures in a relationship with an older man. Perhaps Chaminade was somehow attempting to recapture her relationship with her father. Lorel claims that Cécile avoided romantic relationships in general because she did not want to be subjected to male authority; her father had been extremely autocratic, especially in his last years.[55] Nonetheless, Lorel relates that in summer 1888 Chaminade had fallen in love and become engaged with a "Dr. L.," but because of a tragedy in the man's family marriage was an impossibility.[56]

Chaminade, meanwhile, was cultivating an enormous following in the United States. Sales of her music were extremely brisk, articles were appearing regularly in popular outlets such as *Century Magazine* (March 1898), *The Etude* (November 1899), and *The Ladies Home Journal* (February 1900). Fea-

tures were seen from time to time in newspapers, such as the
Boston Evening Transcript (11 December 1901) and *The Brooklyn
Daily Eagle* (14 July 1907). This attention was echoed in England (<u>see</u> B273, B281), where her piano pieces and songs were
as popular as in America. But a phenomenon unique to the United States was the Chaminade clubs. Initiated sometime near
the end of the nineteenth century, these clubs grew up in
tandem with the burgeoning National Federation of Music
Clubs. An acceptable musical outlet for amateurs, almost entirely women, such clubs had diverse performing purposes and
would probably choose to name their club "Chaminade" out of
deep admiration for the composer. One such club, in Brooklyn,
was founded in 1898 and played host to the composer one evening during her stay in New York. In April 1923 it sent Chaminade a copy of its silver-anniversary program. Prominently
displayed, the anagram-motto underscored the group's inspira-
tional link with the composer:

"Chaminade"

C = Concentrated & Concerted Effort
H = Harmony of Spirit & Work
A = Artistic Ideals
M = Musical Merit Maintained
I = Inspiration
N = Notes (every kind except Promissory)
A = Ardor & Aspiration
D = Devotion to Duty
E = Earnest Endeavor

Amelia Gray-Clarke[57]

Uncertainty surrounds the exact number and locations of
the Chaminade clubs in these early years. For example, an article of 1904 in *L'Echo Musical* listed 100 clubs, but Chaminade crossed out that figure in her copy, replacing it with
"200." In any case, the clubs were numerous, widespread, and
fast forming. Even as late as 1940 clubs were being organized.[58] Most Chaminade clubs performed music by various composers. The repertoire was not restricted to Chaminade works,
and was fashioned by the taste, abilities, and goals of the
particular group. Nonetheless, the clubs served as formal
recognition of Chaminade's popularity as well as impetus to
further renown.

The time was ripe for a personal appearance. Ever since
the mid 1890s Chaminade had been invited to concertize in
America. In 1898, for example, a newspaper in Le Mans reported that "very recently, she was offered a fortune to cross
the Atlantic."[59] Repeatedly she would attribute her refusal
to her mother's advanced age and her own unwillingness to
leave her alone for such an extended period.[60] She also drea-
ded the long and dangerous journey. But sometime in the
spring of 1908 she changed her mind--perhaps, as she later
put it, "to forget; to find new impressions inspiring me in
my work."[61] This rings true considering the recent death of
her husband and the dearth in creativity.

The tour was sponsored by the John Church Company, American agent for her music, and managed by one Metzer.[62] In the months leading up to her arrival in mid October a report was published stating that

> only a favored few will be able to hear her play, because she has refused to appear in public. Her performances will all be given at the musical recitals of multi-millionaires who can afford to sign their names to four figures for a night's entertainment. Mlle. Chaminade's excuse is that physically she is not strong enough to endure the fatigue of a concert season.[63]

This turned out to be false: Chaminade performed for the public. Extant correspondence reveals that several details were not finalized as late as September.[64]

Chaminade arrived in New York aboard the "Savoie" on 17 October. The tour began and ended with concerts in New York and took her to eleven other cities over the next two months:[65]

24 October	New York	Carnegie Hall
29 October	Brooklyn	Academy of Music
6-7 November	Philadelphia	Academy of Music
9 November	Louisville	Macauley's
12 November	Cincinnati	Grand Opera House
16 November	Milwaukee	Pabst Theater
17 November	Minneapolis	Auditorium
22 November	Chicago	Orchestra Hall
24 November	St. Louis	Odeon
3 December	Indianapolis	English Opera House
8 December	Washington	New National Theater
9 December	Philadelphia	Academy of Music
12 December	Boston	Symphony Hall
15 December	New York	Carnegie Hall

Except for the first series in Philadelphia, which featured *Concertstück* with orchestra, and the last event in New York, which included the *Trio No. 2*, all the recitals were a mixture of piano pieces and songs. Almost all were devoted exclusively to her compositions. Two vocalists, the mezzo-soprano Yvonne de St.-André and the English baritone Ernest Groom, traveled with Chaminade and interpreted the *mélodies*. Typical of such an ambitious tour in such a limited amount of time, the repertoire varied little from city to city. There seem to have been two standard programs, with minor modifications, made up mostly of new pieces (e.g. *Thème Varié, Contes Bleus, Deuxième Gavotte, Amour Invisible, La Reine de Mon Coeur*); some old favorites (e.g. *L'Anneau D'Argent, Ritournelle*); and other older works (e.g. *Troisième Valse, Viatique*). Two of her most popular piano works in America, *Pas Des Echarpes* and *Sérénade*, were often given as encores. Chaminade said that had she known the enormous popularity of these pieces in this country she would have scheduled them on the programs.

As anticipated, the tour was a tremendous financial success. The halls were generally filled to capacity and then some, and people were regularly turned away. *Musical Courier* reported the figure of $5,000 grossed at the first Carnegie Hall recital. "Not in a dozen years has there been such a profitable concert event in New York."[66] Only the second Philadelphia concert, under the auspices of the local Chaminade Club, had a sizeable number of empty seats.

As suggested by the large number of bibliographical entries from October to December 1908 (B299-395), Chaminade's visit was treated as a major musical event. Critical reception was mixed. The most negative evaluations issued from the larger cities--New York, Philadelphia, Boston, and Chicago. In some other locations her recital was significant as much for its society-page value as its musical interest. For example, an item in the "Social and Personal" column of 8 December in *The Washington Post* told of Chaminade's luncheon at the French Embassy and her being taken to the White House to meet President and Mrs. Roosevelt. The next day, the *Post* included two items on Chaminade: a favorable review of her recital of the 8th, and a discussion in the "Social and Personal" section concerning who attended and what they wore.[67] As for Chaminade's view of America, she was impressed with the people and the quality of musical institutions. Special praise was reserved for the Philadelphia Orchestra.[68] On Christmas Eve a tired Chaminade set sail for home.

The decade of the nineteen-teens was one of transition. Her lifelong companion, her mother, died in 1912, well into her upper eighties.[69] The war erupted two years later. In 1915 Chaminade moved to her seaside villa at Tamaris, near Toulon, which had been procured in 1903 by Carbonel. Creative activity ceased almost entirely. It was replaced by daily ministration to soldiers in a convalescent home in nearby Les Sablettes. The continual physical labor and generalized weakness due to an extreme vegetarian diet would take their toll later.

Meanwhile, in 1913 the French Government accorded her its highest honor: Chevalier of the Legion of Honor. The list of winners was announced in the summer, and Chaminade opted to have the official presentation ceremony at an orphanage in Paris in which she had taken an active interest. Lorel narrates the event thus:

> The children sang some of Cécile's songs and choruses, and Monsieur Poilpot [an artist friend] made a charming speech in which he traced the story of the new legionnaire's gifted and virtuous career. . . The whole proceedings were filmed and shown as a news item in the cinemas. . . . [But], as the cinema of that time was not very far advanced, the film itself was extremely poor.[70]

Although the Legion of Honor had been conferred numerous times on women, Chaminade was the first female composer to be so honored. But this was not her first award. Previous French decorations included Officier de L'Académie (1886 or 1887) and Officier de L'Instruction Publique (1892). In addition she had been recognized in several foreign countries: the Jubilee Medal from Queen Victoria (1897), the Chefekat from the Sultan of Constantinople (1901), The Order of St. John the Lateran from the Pope (date unknown), and honorary membership in the Philharmonic Society of Barcelona (before 1903). No doubt there were more of the last type.

In 1913 and 1914 Chaminade went to London to record a series of piano rolls for the Aeolian Company. *Musical America* of 1 March 1913 reported her adoption of the mechanical piano player as her substitute in concerts. In early July, in Aeolian Hall, she rendered duets and *mélodies* with rolls she recorded. Such concert use of rolls, however, had taken place previously--at a Paris recital in May 1910 in which she performed duets of *Callirhoë* and *Valse Carnavalesque*.[71] Chaminade had been recording piano rolls for the Aeolian Company at least as early as 1908. In November of that year it was reported that "Mme. Chaminade has defined for the Pianola no less than 36 pieces of her own composition."[72] The recording of rolls for Aeolian resumed after the War, although the technology shifted away from the Pianola in favor of the Duo-Art mechanism, hailed as a more faithful rendering of the subtleties of the original performance. Even though rolls were on the decline in the mid 1920s, Aeolian wrote to Chaminade on 19 November 1928 asking her to make a "rouleau autobiographique" (autobiographical roll). It would contain excerpts of several of her pieces and end with a complete composition. Written commentary on structure, background, literary connections, and biography would accompany the release. Aeolian pointed out that other composers, such as Stravinsky, had recorded such rolls, and that Ravel was currently making one. Aware of her precarious health and eager to do the project, the firm offered to send someone to Tamaris to do the recording.[73] It is not clear whether the project was ever realized. Meanwhile, however, other artists were active in recording her music on 78 disks (see "Discography").

On 2 November 1917 Chaminade signed a contract with her principal publishing firm, Enoch, effective 1 January 1920. She would provide 12 pieces for publication per year, Enoch would be her sole publisher, and she would participate in two concerts per year sponsored by the firm (expenses paid, but no fee). Although Chaminade had already enjoyed a long relationship with Enoch, this is the earliest extant contract among the family's papers. A Jewish concern, Enoch was liquidated during the Nazi occupation and documents were probably lost or destroyed. Lorel believes Chaminade was naive to accept what the family later considered unfavorable terms from Enoch.[74] There had been other firms as well in the early years, such as Léon Grus, J. Maho, Heugel, Durand, and Hachette. Unfortunately we do not have contractual documents from these firms. In addition, typical of 19th-century practice, a few pieces had appeared in magazines, such as *L'Art Musical*, *L'Illustration* (musical supplement), and *The Ladies Home Journal*.

In 1925 Chaminade decided to sell her property in Le Vésinet and take up year-round residence in her villa near Toulon. Meanwhile her health was continuing to deteriorate. In 1926 she was diagnosed with decalcification of the left foot, a consequence of her stringent vegetarian diet. She suffered considerable pain and, as she indicated in letters of 1930, was immobile for several years.[75] In 1936 she moved to Monte Carlo. Approximately two years later the foot had to be amputated. Lorel describes how Chaminade refused to use a wheelchair and thus became an invalid. Although Chaminade's last published composition, *La Nef Sacrée*, was issued in 1928, the composer created a few works in later years, largely through the urging of her niece. Unpublished works with nostalgic titles like *Légende Du Vieux Manoir* and *Comme Autrefois--Le Bon Vieux Temps* probably date from this period.

At the time of the amputation Chaminade was approximately 80 years old. For at least ten years she had already felt obsolete. Disability and advancing age intensified the sense of isolation. A letter of 1942 to her American friend Irving Schwerké is revealing:

> I just received your exquisite letter, which was for me a great joy and a great comfort. I see that you haven't been forgetting your musical friends and they're deeply grateful. Not to be forgotten, to live in the heart and memory of those who understand you--that is the supreme consolation for an artist. Thanks to all who remember . . .[76]

Chaminade also shared thoughts on being forgotten with the American composer Amy Beach, roughly her contemporary.[77] One can appreciate her joy in receiving several thousand birthday greetings in 1939 from all over the world, as a result of an invitation extended by *The Etude* to its readers. Almost five years later, on 13 April 1944, toward the end of the occupation, Chaminade died in Monte Carlo.

*   *   *

Given the presence of so few reliable documents penned by Chaminade herself it is not easy to form a picture of her personality. She seems to have been a proud, independent woman. Until her largely self-inflicted bone illness she had considerable stamina and energy. Her prolific output and demanding concert schedule attest to a capacity for hard work. A tinge of mysticism colors her persona. Even well before the séances she attended after her mother's death in 1912, we have, for example, her published account of seeing a flame after her return home from a visit to Beethoven's house in Bonn, and feeling that in the flame she experienced the soul of Beethoven.[78]   Although she had friends she does not appear to have mingled extensively in the musical mainstream. She did, however, consider Emmanuel Chabrier a close friend. By temperament, by upbringing, or both she stayed close to home and seemed to prefer the company of her mother and the family's circle of friends. Perhaps this unadventurous attitude kept her from breaking into leading artistic circles whose penetration, even in the best of circumstances, would require an iconoclastic type of woman. Despite her choice of a career path that *ipso facto* branded her a nonconformist, all evidence indicates that Chaminade was traditional in her deportment and social relationships.

This traditionalism contrasts sharply with the more individualistic behavior of two of her contemporaries: Augusta Holmès and Ethel Smyth. Holmès, who died in 1903, composed predominantly in the larger forms and was quite successful in securing performances and gaining acceptance by the Parisian critical establishment. She and Chaminade were considered the leading women composers of France.[79] But their temperament differed as much as their music. Holmès's quick wit and wide-ranging artistic interests rendered her a focal point of the progressive *salons*. She mingled regularly with the leading lights of the Parisian musical world. This social and intellectual intercourse assisted her immensely in entering the professional mainstream and obtaining performances of her symphonies. Ethel Smyth, of course, contrasts with Chaminade in her activist political feminism.

The many published accounts of Chaminade between 1900 and 1911 shed light on her methods of composing. She preferred to work at night. Her villa at Tamaris allowed her to be near the sea, a favored locale for creative inspiration. She claims that she would think through a piece in her head, and when it was completely worked out notate it rather quickly. But at that point, she said,

> I am reluctant to have it published immediately, preferring to keep it hidden in a drawer for some considerable time until I come across it again and find I have confidence in it . . . If I find that it continues to please me, I send it to the publisher, but I have a horror of being pressed for time and of working quickly or under compulsion.[80]

One article claims that she "often sends her first proof to the publishers without any corrections."[81] This is borne out by an examination of the musical manuscripts: they are remarkably free of erasures or crossouts yet are not fair copies. Changes, often in blue pencil, appear to be editorial additions at the time of publication.

Chaminade's output of approximately 400 compositions is dominated by solo piano works and songs--the small genres. But regardless of the medium one can identify certain style characteristics as typically Chaminadian. Appealing, tuneful melody qualifies as the most striking feature. It unfolds in a regular phrase structure, which aids its memorability. Homophony throws it into high relief. Formal schemes are most often ternary, although other regular plans appear occasionally. Functional tonality and its supporting syntactical apparatus are clearly in place. Many compositions betray a generalized Spanish influence in their surface vocabulary. This was a commonplace of late 19th-century French music, as in Bizet's *Carmen*, Chabrier's *España*, or Debussy's *Iberia*. In

Chaminade some examples are *La Sévillane*, *La Lisonjera*, and *Sérénade Espagnole*. She may have been partially influenced by the proximity of the family's home in Périgord to Spain. Aesthetically, Chaminade's music typifies French music in its avoidance of overt or covert philosophical associations. The composer sums up her style by claiming "I am essentially of the romantic school, as all my work shows."[82]

The piano music embraces a host of styles. Some pieces, like the *Sérénade* Op. 29 or the *Romances Sans Paroles* Op. 76, continue the "song without words" tradition of Felix Mendelssohn and Fanny Hensel. Others, like those of Chaminade's French contemporaries at the end of the century, show the legacy of Chopin in their emphasis on mood and elegant melody, and even in their title (eg *Nocturne* or *Barcarolle*). Also akin to her French colleagues, Chaminade likes to exploit Renaissance or Baroque idioms on occasion. This retrospective stance governs such pieces as the 5 *Gavottes*, *Trois Danses Anciennes* Op. 95, *Gigue* Op. 43, and *Pièce Dans Le Style Ancien* Op. 74. Technically the piano works span a wide range. Some pieces, such as the challenging *Six Etudes De Concert* Op. 35 or the *Toccata* Op. 39, demand a seasoned player and are clearly meant for the concert professional. Paderewski is reputed to have programmed the *Toccata* frequently.[83] At the other extreme stand compositions written expressly for children, such as the two *Albums Des Enfants* Opp. 123 and 126 or *Pastorale Enfantine* Op. 12. Most pieces lie somewhere in between and are targeted to a mixed group, including professionals, adult amateurs, and students at various levels of expertise. Chaminade offered guidance on difficulty and interpretation in a few articles she authored for *The Etude* and *The Ladies Home Journal* (see B287, B299, and B368).

One noteworthy composition is the *Sonata* Op. 21. Chaminade's only piano sonata, the work emphasizes formal and developmental processes, typical for the genre. Published as late as 1895 yet bearing the early opus number of 21, its date of composition is uncertain. It probably was at least begun much earlier, perhaps with the encouragement of Moszkowski, a strong champion, to whom it is dedicated. Stylistically it is arguably Chaminade's most Germanic piano piece: do we see the shadow of Moszkowski here? It was not written primarily for touring as it was rarely programmed on her concerts. Although no statistics are available, it probably boasted modest sales at best. One can reasonably conclude that she wrote it for herself--a sort of "composer's music"-- rather than for the consuming public.

Although *Pas Des Echarpes* was perhaps the most popular Chaminade work in the United States, *Automne*, Op. 35 No. 2, probably carried that distinction internationally. Its style was likened to that of Chabrier.[84] Chaminade performed it often, even well after its initial appearance in print (see W42a-W42f). *Madame* claims it was Chaminade's playing of this piece that prompted her being awarded the Jubilee Medal.[85] The relatively large number of recordings attests to its popularity (see D48-63, D205, D213, D226, and D248). A letter to the composer of 21 December 1931 confirms the great success of a particular recording of the work--sales in the British

Empire of 21,000 in a three-year period.[86] Even as late as 1950 *Automne* is the leading seller in Great Britain among Chaminade's works.[87]

As Chaminade's only work for orchestra and piano, the *Concertstück* holds a special place in her *oeuvre*. The choice of a German title by a French composer, with the availability of a title such as *Pièce de Concert*, is curious and significant. As in the *Sonata*, the German-trained Moszkowski may have exerted considerable influence. Many critics rightly pointed to the Wagnerian qualities of the work. Particularly striking is the opening, which bears a strong resemblance to the start of the Overture to *The Flying Dutchman*. Even the initial interval of the principal theme, the ascending perfect fourth, is identical to its counterpart in Wagner. What is therefore surprising about the many reviews of the *Concertstück* is how *few* writers note the likeness. The piece also features thematic transformation and thematic recall, and in places brings to mind the evocative Grieg *Piano Concerto* (1868).

Among the *mélodies*, *L'Anneau D'Argent* ranks as the most popular. Composed in 1891, it was a frequent member of Chaminade programs. The poem is by Rosemonde Gérard, friend and wife of Edmond Rostand.[88] Chaminade set several of her texts, including "Vieux Portrait" and "Ma Première Lettre." *L'Anneau* was almost a signature piece for Chaminade. For example, a substantial article of 1907 is entitled "The Composer of The Little Silver Ring"; the homage on Radio Monte Carlo the day after her death broadcasts the song in her memory. In 1904 it is considered one of her most popular songs in France.[89] *The Musical Leader* of 22 August 1929 reports that it has been included on programs of John McCormack since 1927. Among the numerous recordings of this piece (see D6-D43) there are several by the famous tenor (see D18-19, D23, D36, and D43). And finally, its reputation can be gauged by its selection for use in the French movie *Florence est Folle* (c. 1945).[90]

Concerning recordings, the overwhelming majority are of piano works or songs. These, of course, being of short length, suited the 78 or the roll format very well. But they serve as another barometer of the basis of Chaminade's popularity and acceptance as a composer. Except for the *Concertino* recordings that include orchestra, Chaminade is barely represented orchestrally. The first recording of the *Concertstück*, for example--a work that was prominent through c. 1910--may be as recent as 1979.

During Chaminade's American tour of 1908 reporters were eager to discover her opinions on other musicians. Chaminade reserves her highest praise for Saint-Saëns and has warm words for Charpentier. She also thinks well of Massenet, for whom "sentiment is everything."[91] Her comments on Debussy merit quotation:

> Debussy, of course, depends very heavily upon his orchestra for his effects, and his music is to my ears, well, gray--a bit gray, don't you think so?[92]

> You do not grasp Debussy's music because it
> is wanting in significant ideas. . . . I do
> not like the personality his music reveals,
> because it is to me insincere.[93]

She goes on to lament Chausson's untimely death as well as
the contemporary disparagement of Saint-Saëns. Ravel she
finds "more eccentric than Debussy." And of other contemporaries,

> The modern Italian composers are, I believe,
> the most wholesome of the present. Puccini
> knows how to write beautiful melodies. Mas-
> cagni writes well for the theater. But he is
> too coarse for the concert hall, whereas Puc-
> cini is beautiful in any environment. [Rich-
> ard] Strauss is a little coarse, too, is he
> not?[94]

Rupert Hughes asks her about American composers. She knows of
MacDowell and is impressed with the music of Amy Beach, which
she heard in London.[95]   As a whole these opinions underscore
Chaminade's conservatism: her roots in the aesthetic of her
formative years and her firm belief in traditional syntax and
vocabulary.

How did the critical establishment assess Chaminade's
music? Often with an overlay of sexual aesthetics--a late-
19th, early-20th century standard that divided musical pheno-
mena into masculine and feminine traits and devised a gender-
linked vocabulary to describe them. Charm and grace are two
qualities categorized as feminine, and these were often applied to Chaminade's style, as in the following assessments
of 1908:

> There are . . . distinctly feminine traits
> about Chaminade's music, which are decidedly
> to its advantage. There is one word which
> sums it all up . . . *charmante!* There is a
> feminine charm, if you will, about Chamin-
> ade's music that makes it individual--I know
> of no other woman's music which has just that
> quality, and, of course, no mere man *could*
> possess that identical quality to which I
> refer.[96]

> It is her unequalled grace in expressing as a
> woman musical ideas in a woman's way that has
> lifted Mme. Chaminade from the mob of women
> composers who are trying to disguise their
> femininity under a bearded mask and who con-
> fuse racket with virility.[97]

The second excerpt embodies another component of sexual aesthetics: a woman can be criticized for overstepping the boun-
dary between her own territory and that prescribed for men.
For example, the *Concertstück* is deemed

> a work that is strong and virile, too virile
> perhaps, and that is the reproach I would be
> tempted to address to it. For me, I almost
> regretted not having found further those qua-
> lities of grace and gentleness that reside in
> the nature of women, the secrets of which she
> possesses to such a degree.[98]

Yet for many reviewers feminine traits meant creative defi-
ciency. Chaminade was often ensnared in this net, as in the
following review of her Carnegie Hall recital of 24 October:

> [Her music] has a certain feminine daintiness
> and grace, but it is amazingly superficial
> and wanting in variety. . . . But on the
> whole this concert confirmed the conviction
> held by many that while women may some day
> vote, they will never learn to compose any-
> thing worth while. All of them seem superfi-
> cial when they write music . . .[99]

Sometimes sexual aesthetics manifested itself when reviewers
expressed surprise at Chaminade's success in some activity
considered masculine, such as orchestrating *Callirhoë* or wri-
ting in the "difficult" genre of chamber music (*Trio No. 2*).
Perhaps the fairest statement is that attributed to Ambroise
Thomas after he heard Chaminade's music in the early 1880s:
"This is not a woman who composes but a composer who is a
woman."

Chaminade was well aware of the gender issue and recognized societal restrictions placed on women:

> I do not believe that the few women who have
> achieved greatness in creative work are the
> exception, but I think that life has been
> hard on women; it has not given them oppor-
> tunity; it has not made them convincing. . .
> . Woman has not been considered a working
> force in the world and the work that her sex
> and conditions impose upon her has not been
> so adjusted as to give her a little fuller
> scope for the development of her best self.
> She has been handicapped, and only the few,
> through force of circumstances or inherent
> strength, have been able to get the better of
> that handicap.
>   There is no sex in art. Genius is an in-
> dependent quality. The woman of the future,
> with her broader outlook, her greater oppor-
> tunities, will go far, I believe, in creative
> work of every description.[100]

The concept of "salon music" has also figured prominently in the critical reception of Chaminade. In the 19th century a neutral description of music of an intimate setting
and scope, in the 20th it assumes a derogatory tone. In part
the change is attributable to the new function of the salon:
a parlor for bourgeois relaxation rather than a meeting

ground for the intellectual elite. Amateurism replaces pro-
fessionalism. The association with a supposedly undiscrimi-
nating clientele, composed mostly of women, is considered a
negative. The term, therefore, acts to lessen the worth of
Chaminade's compositions--to trivialize them. It was applied
mostly to her piano pieces and songs. Her orchestral works,
in comparison, were taken much more seriously and frequently
compared to those of the leading composers, including Massenet, Delibes, and even Wagner.

In France, the provinces accorded Chaminade much more
critical attention and acclaim than Paris. Furthermore,
Paris press coverage declined markedly from her heyday in
large forms in the 1880s to her immersion in small forms in
the 1890s and after. The capital was never very interested in
instrumental recitals--opera was always central. In addition,
newer currents, notably Wagner and Debussy, were wafting
through the city and displacing the old Gallic guard.

*   *   *

As mentioned at the start of the chapter and as we have
seen in the ensuing discussion, Chaminade enjoyed great success around 1900 but gradually fell into oblivion. The reasons are many. Her reputation rested on her piano pieces and
songs, which were relegated to the category of salon music
and thereby trivialized. After World War I and its great
social upheavals Chaminade's music was considered part of the
outmoded parlor tradition. Its intrinsic worth was devalued
by sheer force of its categorization. Because of her immersion in the small forms after 1890 the orchestral works of
the 1880s were completely forgotten.

Another factor is Chaminade's era. Born in 1857, she
reached her pinnacle at about age 40 and found herself out of
step with new currents. She was nurtured in the aesthetic of
the 1860s and 1870s, whose principal exponent was Saint-
Saëns. The piano style of Benjamin Godard, a mentor, also
served as an important model. By the time of the Great War of
1914 her style was considered passé. The progressivism of
Debussy and Ravel, which replaced it, she found abhorrent.
Innate conservatism prevented her from being able to modify
her style beyond what it had been some twenty years earlier.
In this regard there is no early or late Chaminade style. Her
neglect is also symptomatic of a more general condition: dis-
affection toward French music written in the thirty years or
so before Debussy's ascent. Composers like Godard, Massenet,
and Delibes have also been victims of this attitude, although
American musicological circles have in the last few years
stirred a revival of interest in this music.

Also critical is Chaminade's isolation from the centers
of musical power. This began early. She was not permitted to
attend the Conservatoire but only to take private lessons
from its professors. She was educated but at the same time
denied personal interaction with other students and musicians, and thus potential contacts for the future. This experience was to serve as a metaphor for the course of her
life: Chaminade going it alone, on the periphery. How much is

directly attributable to her being a woman is impossible to establish. But certainly it was extremely difficult for a woman to break into the Parisian musical world--to be performed, to be taken seriously by the critical establishment. Her conservatism, an outgrowth of class expectation, gender socialization, and innate temperament, rendered the possibilities of official success that much more remote.

Since her death there have been several attempts to revivify Chaminade's music and reputation. The earliest came from her niece. Lorel wrote a biography c. 1948, entitled "Viatique," that was submitted to and then rejected by the British publisher Bodley House.[101] A few years later she hired one Elza Schallert to devise a scenario for a projected Hollywood film on Chaminade.[102] In 1957 Lorel organized a piano competition, in Monte Carlo, in honor of the Chaminade centenary (see B463-64, B466). Some twenty years later commenced the next phase of activity. In 1978-79 Wilfrid Maggiar, French pianist and passionate admirer of Chaminade's music, presented a recital of her works in Aix-en-Provence and Paris (see B470).[103] Danielle Laval recorded a disk of Chaminade's piano works (see D205) and also gave at least one recital, in Nice in 1982 (see B477). Gérard Condé's commentary for the sleeve of Laval's recording was the first account to be based on the family's large collection of documents (see B471).

With the confluence of three recent trends--heightened respect for French music, serious exploration of women composers, and renewed interest in her music--the time is ripe for a new look at Cécile Chaminade. She is, after all, not merely the composer of *Scarf Dance* and *Concertino*, but of a host of other works that deserve re-examination and performance. It is hoped that this volume will function as a catalyst to further research on this most interesting composer. Now, at least, we can provide a more informed response to that basic question, "Who was Cécile Chaminade?"

NOTES

[1]Alain-Marie Foy, "Qui Etait Cécile Chaminade?" *Revue Municipale du Vésinet* No. 58 (March 1982): 73.

[2]"Mme. Chaminade, Greatest Woman Composer, Who is Now Visiting America, Tells of Her Dreams," *The Washington Post*, 1 November 1908, "Magazine" section, p. 4. Antoinette Lorel, "Viatique," unpublished biography of Chaminade, in typescript (c. 1948), p. 8; the information on Bizet's visit appears on page 11. "Echos Du Passé: Cécile Chaminade," *Revue Municipale Du Vésinet* No. 38 (April 1977): 43.

[3]In a later interview, published in *Musical America*, Chaminade is quoted as saying, "I was once Godard's pupil" (8 No. 24 [24 October 1908]: 1].

[4]Lorel, pp. 13-14.

[5]"Georges Bizet," *The Century Library of Music*, 20 Vols., ed. Paderewski (New York: The Century Co., 1900): VI 165-80.

[6]A copy of the recital program is located in the Fonds Montpensier of the Département de la Musique of the Bibliothèque Nationale.

[7]The author wishes to express her deep gratitude to the family for their generosity in permitting her to view these invaluable documents.

[8]This diary is corroborated by the composer herself, in a letter to an unspecified woman ("Chère Mademoiselle") of 22 November [1913]. Autograph letter signed, in Library of Congress; No. 87 of "Letters from Musical Celebrities."

[9]Charles Darcours, "Notes de Musique," *Le Figaro*, 22 March 1882.

[10]E.-Mathieu D'Auriac. *Le Monde Artiste* 22 (23 December 1882).

[11]Autograph letter signed, in the Mary Flagler Cary (Bennett) collection at the Pierpont Morgan Library, New York. The curator, J. Rigbie Turner, has kindly provided the information that the letter also appears in Joseph Bennett's *Dramatic and Musical Correspondence*, second series, p. 61.

[12]Statistics published in *Le Ménestrel* in May 1886 concerning the 1884-85 season of Les Concerts Modernes disclose that Chaminade works were performed three times (Vol. 52 No. 9 [9 May 1886]: 186).

[13]Germany was actually his adopted country; he was born in Poland.

[14]Lorel, p. 30, provides merely the year. The highly romanticized, undocumented biography by Laura Kerr is more specific, stating that he died on 27 July 1887 (*Scarf Dance; The Story of Cecile Chaminade* [New York: Abelard Press, 1953], 103).

[15]A biography of Chaminade written c. 1930, by "an Englishwoman and M. Ferti," unpublished and still in typescript in the family's possession, states that the hardship also occasioned the selling of their home in Angoulême, Château de La Farge (p. 32). But this source must be viewed with some skepticism. It states, for example, that Hippolyte died in 1897 (same page), and also bears a handwritten comment on the title page, probably penned by Antoinette Lorel, that "Cécile didn't like [this biography] at all."

[16]Cécile Chaminade, "Recollections of My Musical Childhood," *The Etude* 29 (December 1911): 806.

[17]Percy Mitchell, "The Composer of the Little Silver Ring," *New Idea Woman's Magazine* (New York) (May 1907): 30. Also Philip, "Mlle. Chaminade," *Le Petit Marseillais*, 18

March 1888, 2. The local account is particularly trustworthy as it is based on an interview with Chaminade.

[18]Lorel, p. 31.

[19]Jules Pradelle, "Chronique Musicale: Grand-Théâtre," *Le Sémaphore de Marseille*, [18] March 1888.

[20]Mitchell, p. 30, lists 17 successive performances.

[21]See especially Silvio, "Chronique Musicale: Un Mot Sur La Couleur Locale et La Convention du Coloris Antique Dans La Musique Moderne," *Le Petit Provençal*, [30] March 1888.

[22]P. Lassalvy, "Deuxième Correspondance--Grand Théâtre," *Le Progrès Artistique* 11 (c. early April 1888).

[23]She also composed *Egmont*, a work never published or performed, which might qualify as a symphony. It is dubbed "Scène Dramatique, d'après Goethe," and is for orchestra, chorus, and vocal soloists. See WU13.

[24]"This winter we shall probably hear a marvelous symphonic poem--'La Reine des Amazones,' by Cécile Chaminade." From an article in *La France*, in 1884, as quoted in Lorel, p. 24.

[25]J. H., "Le Concert 'C. Chaminade' au 'Cercle Catholique'," *L'Escart* (Anvers), [19] April 1888.

[26]"Autographe de Mlle. Cécile Chaminade," *L'Art Musical* 27 ([July] 1888): 226.

[27]*L'Escart*, [19] April 1888. The report in *Le Guide Musical* 34 No. 17 (26 April 1888): 133, echoes the judgments of the earlier review.

[28]Amédée Boutarel, "Concerts et Soirées--Concerts Lamoureux," *Le Ménestrel* 55 (27 January 1889): 31; and "Les Grands Concerts," *La Semaine Artistique et Musicale*, [c. 27 January 1889].

[29]One of the eight or so autograph letters of Chaminade in the Bibliothèque Nationale concerns the *Concertstück*. Dated 3 September 1889, it is addressed to an unidentified copyist from whom Chaminade would like to have information regarding fees. This person has been recommended by Chabrier ("mon ami"). She requests his prices for copying an orchestral score, parts, and piano music, and asks for a quick reply because she has an orchestral score of 100 pages with a separate piano part ready to be copied. No doubt this refers to the *Concertstück*. The letter is in the collection of Charles Malherbe, in the possession of the Conservatoire, housed in the Département de la Musique.

[30]L. Ménard, "Causerie Musicale," 26 February 1892, 2.

[31]According to Lorel, p. 91, Chaminade was to conduct on two later occasions, in Neuchâtel and in Belgium.

[32]Lorel, p. 66, claims that it was 1889. But I have not found any reviews for this program.

[33]Rachel Challice, "Madame C. Carbonel Chaminade," *Madame* (England) (24 January 1903): 175.

[34]In addition Chaminade declares they will have a great deal to talk about, including her projected trip to America. Autograph letter signed, 20 May [1908], in Mary Flagler Cary Collection of the Pierpont Morgan Library, New York.

[35]Lorel, pp. 137 and 144; and a loose clipping, dated but without title, in the "Chaminade Clippings" file in the Music Research Division of the New York Public Library.

[36]Lorel, p. 148.

[37]For the bibliographic particulars, see B209, B230, B244, B251, and B267.

[38]Lorel, pp. 69-71.

[39]In a review of Louise Steiger's rendition of *Concertstück* in Angers, Chaminade responds to a question of the writer by declaring that she will be in Germany "this year" ("Chronique Musicale: 18ème Concert Populaire," *Le Patriote de L'Ouest* [late February 1889]).

[40]Lorel, p. 92.

[41]"Nouvelles Diverses: Etranger" 64 (5 June 1898): 182. That it occurred in 1898 is confirmed by a review: Ae. Sd., "Komponistin Cécile Chaminade," *Neues Frauenblatt* No. 12 (1898): 233.

[42]Edward Baxter Perry, "Sophie Menter and Cécile Chaminade," *The Etude* 17 (November 1899): 348-49.

[43]The date appears in George Kehler, *The Piano in Concert*, 2 Vols. (Metuchen: Scarecrow Press, 1982), I 238. It is verified by the announcement in the *Neue Freie Presse* (Vienna), No. 12400, 28 February 1899, 13. Unfortunately the concert is not reviewed.

[44]Lorel, pp. 94-95; and typescript biography of c. 1930, p. 37.

[45]As documented in a French-language review of [3] December 1895 in an unidentified newspaper, presumably issued in Brussels, as found in the Fonds Montpensier collection at the Département de la Musique in the Bibliothèque Nationale.

[46]J. Martin, *Nos Auteurs et Compositeurs Dramatiques* (Paris: Flammarion, 1897).

[47]Challice, p. 175.

[48]Mitchell, p. 30.

[49]*The Washington Post*, p. 4. Also in *The Minneapolis Journal* (see B349).

[50]Lorel, p. 88.

[51]Lorel, pp. 95, 108-09.

[52]Lorel, p. 90; and "Mme. Chaminade in New York," *The Sun* (New York), Sunday 18 October 1908, sec. 1, p. 4 cols. 1-2.

[53]Rupert Hughes, "Mme. Chaminade and John Philip Sousa Talk About Music," *The New York Herald*, Sunday 15 November 1908, "Magazine" section, part II, p. 9.

[54]*The Washington Post*, p. 4.

[55]Lorel, p. 42.

[56]Lorel, pp. 42-49.

[57]In possession of family.

[58]For example, the Chaminade Club of Middletown, New York, as related in a letter to Chaminade of 10 January 1940.

[59]Léon Hiaulmé, "Mlle Cécile Chaminade," *La Sarthe*, 3 July 1898.

[60]See, for instance, Emma Bullett, "A Talk With Cecile Chaminade," *The Brooklyn Daily Eagle*, 14 July 1907, "News Special Section," p. 4 col. 1.

[61]"Philadelphia Orchestra Program," *Philadelphia Inquirer*, 1 November 1908, 8.

[62]Lorel, p. 131.

[63]"A Parisian Idol," article probably from summer 1908, found in the "Clippings File," without source, at the New York Public Library. The family also has a copy of the clipping.

[64]Letter of 24 September, presumably 1908, in possession of the family, from Mary Ayller, concert manager for Chaminade's prospective recital in Washington.

[65]She seems to have been as far west as Seattle, on vacation, probably during the gap between 24 November and 3 December. The family possesses a photograph of Chaminade standing next to a body of water, with the caption on reverse, "A part of the Olympic mountain range, and Puget Sound."

[66]"Cecile Chaminade's Debut" (28 October 1908): 35.

[67]See B377 and B379-80.

[68]Lorel, p. 126.

69Lorel, p. 136.

70Lorel, p. 143.

71"La Musique: Le Récital Chaminade," *Figaro Illustré*, [April] 1910.

72"Chaminade's Autograph," *Philadelphia Times*, [6] November 1908.

73Letter in possession of the family.

74Lorel, pp. 85 and 171. Enoch is the copyright holder of almost all Chaminade compositions, although it has no protective rights in the United States.

75Letter to Irving Schwerké of c. 1930, in Library of Congress. Also letter to an American fan, David James, of 12 June 1920, in the David James Collection of the Sibley Music Library, Eastman School of Music.

76Letter of 23 April 1942, in the Library of Congress.

77Beach was born ten years later, in 1867. The information on Chaminade's letters comes verbally from Adrienne Fried Block, who is researching Amy Beach and has copies of a fair amount of correspondence from Chaminade in this period.

78Published frequently, as in, for example, "An Interview With Cecile Chaminade," *The Musical Age* 62 No. 13 (25 July 1908): 293.

79See especially Paula Barillon-Bauché, *Augusta Holmès et La Femme Compositeur* (Paris: Librairie Fischbacher, 1912).

80Chaminade, "Recollections of My Musical Childhood," *The Etude* 29 (December 1911): 806.

81Shippen, p. 5.

82*The Washington Post*, p. 4.

83Lorel, p. 26. In addition, the virtuosic *Etude Symphonique*, Op. 28, is dedicated to Paderewski.

84Eduard Reuss, "Klavierstücke von Cécile Chaminade," [source unknown], [1890].

85Challice, p. 175.

86Letter from Société Générale Internationale de L'Edition Phonographique et Cinématographique, in family possession, regarding recording Piccadilly 137 (the performer is not given). I did not come across this recording elsewhere and thus did not list it in the "Discography." Perhaps, however, it is listed under an alternate label.

[87]Letter to Lorel from the firm of Enoch, 30 March 1951, in which the publisher relays information it received from its London affiliate, Edwin Ashdown.

[88]Wilfrid Maggiar, pianist and ardent enthusiast of Chaminade's music, kindly informed me that Gérard had told him that she had given up her rights to the song to Enoch for 60 francs.

[89]Philippe D'Ohsson, "Les Femmes du XXe Siècle: Madame Cécile Chaminade," *L'Echo Musical* 2 (1904).

[90]Letter from Enoch to Lorel, 10 September 1945, in family possession. Permission had been granted during the occupation by the Administration handling the firm's affairs.

[91]Agnes Gordon Hogan, "Woman's View of French Music," *Philadelphia Record*, 8 November 1908, 5.

[92]*The Sun*, p. 4.

[93]"Chaminade's Tolerance," *The Musical Leader And Concert Goer* 14 (17 December 1908): 5.

[94]*The Musical Leader and Concert Goer*, p. 5.

[95]Hughes, p. 10.

[96]William Henry Humiston, "Chaminade," *Independent* 65 (29 October 1908): 977.

[97]Hughes, p. 9.

[98]"Quatorzième Concert Populaire," *Angers Revue* [late February 1889].

[99]"Music and Drama: Mme. Chaminade's Concert," *New York Evening Post*, 26 October 1908, p. 7.

[100]*The Washington Post*, p. 4.

[101]Letter of rejection dated 12 July 1949, in possession of family.

[102]Prose scenario of 106 typed pages, undated, in possession of family. This was a revised version. Schallert details the weaknesses in the earlier outline and also points out some historical implausibilities that might still have to remain. "The previous outline was largely built around a situation, Cecile Chaminade's disappointment in love. I think we have a better approach along an entirely different line. . . ." That approach is crystallized in the ideal, "*To create one must be wedded to what is eternal.*"

[103]Maggiar is very enthusiastic about recording all her piano works and compiling a complete edition.

Works and Performances

Cross-references with a "B" pertain to the "Bibliography" chapter, with a "D" to the "Discography," and with "WC" or "WU" to later sections in this chapter.

PUBLISHED WORKS WITH OPUS NUMBERS

W1-2   Deux Mazurkas, [Op. 1]. Piano. Marcel Colombier, 1869. PPN C.M. (C.C. No. 1), (C.C. No. 2). No. 1, 5 pages, dedicated to her mother; No. 2, three pages, dedicated to Madame Edmond de Guerle.

       Chaminade later claimed these were her earliest pieces.

W3   Etude in A-flat, [Op. 1]. Piano. J. Maho, 1876. PPN G.P. 3164. 5 pages. Dedicated "à mon maître M. F. Le Couppey." AUTOGRAPH: Family. See also WC2, with title Etude Printanière.

       See B4.

       Premiere

       W3a   1878 (25 April); Paris; home of Le Couppey; Chaminade, piano. See B8.

W4   Presto (2me Etude), Op. 2. Piano. J. Hamelle, [n.d.]. PPN J. 1402 H. 9 pages. Dedicated to Augustin Savard. See also WC2.

       Premiere

       W4a   1878 (25 April); Paris; home of Le Couppey; Chaminade, piano.

W5   Scherzo-Etude, Op. 3. Piano. Hamelle, [n. d.]. PPN 1403. 4 pages. Dedicated to Joseph Marsick. See also WC2.

Selected performance

W5a 1880 (8 February); Paris; Salle Erard; Chaminade,
    piano. See B14.

W6   Caprice-Etude, Op. 4. Piano. Hamelle, [n. d.]. PPN
      1404. 8 pages. Dedicated to Marmontel. See also WC2.

Premiere

W6a   1878 (25 April); Paris; home of Le Couppey; Cha-
       minade, piano. See B8.

W6b   1882 (22 January); Paris; home of Le Couppey;
       Chaminade, piano. See B24.

W7   Menuet, Op. 5. Piano. Hamelle, [n.d.]. PPN 1405. 11
      pages. Dedicated to Ambroise Thomas. See WU20 for an
      unpublished orchestral version.

Premiere

W7a   1878 (25 April); Paris; home of Le Couppey; Cha-
       minade, piano. See B5, B8-9.

Selected performances

W7b   1881 (early April); Paris; series of M. and Mme.
       Charles Lebouc; Chaminade, piano. See B21.

W7c   1882 (6 May); Paris; Salle Pleyel; Société Na-
       tionale de Musique; orchestral version. See
       B58-61.

W7d   1884 (25 February); Paris; Salle Erard; Chami-
       nade, piano. See B71.

W7e   1888 (11 March); Marseille; at home of the Liv-
       ons; Chaminade, piano. See B99.

W8   Berceuse, Op. 6. Piano. Hamelle, [n.d.]. PPN 1406. 7
      pages. Dedicated to Madame Emile Biottot. AUTOGRAPH:
      Family.

Premiere

W8a   1878 (25 April); Paris; home of Le Couppey; Cha-
       minade, piano.

Selected performance

W8b   1882 (22 January); Paris; home of Le Couppey;
       Chaminade, piano. See B24.

W9   Barcarolle, Op. 7. Piano. Hamelle, [n. d.]. PPN 1557.
      7 pages. Dedicated to Jeanne Halbronn.

In collection Album des Enfants, Op. 123; See W179.

Selected performances

W9a   1880 (8 February); Paris; Salle Erard; Chami-
        nade, piano. See B15.

W9b   1880 (27 March); Paris; Salle Pleyel; Société
        Nationale de Musique; Chaminade, piano. See
        B16.

W9c   1884 (25 February); Paris; Salle Erard; Chami-
        nade, piano. See B71.

W10   Chaconne, Op. 8. Piano. Hamelle, [n.d.]. PPN 1558. 5
      pages. Dedicated to "Madame Chéné, Professeur au
      Conservatoire." See also WC2, WC3.

Selected performance

W10a   1880 (27 March); Paris; Salle Pleyel; Société
        Nationale de Musique; Chaminade, piano. See
        B16.

W11-12 Pièce Romantique et Gavotte, Op. 9. Piano. Durand,
      Schoenewerk & Cie, 1880. PPN D.S. & Cie 2818. 6
      pages. Dedicated to F. Le Couppey.

      No. 1 published later in L'Illustration. Supplément
      Musicale, 1897, pp. 121-23.

      No. 2 in collection Album des Enfants, Op. 123; see
      W176.

Selected performances

W11a   1880 (8 February); Paris; Salle Erard; Chami-
        nade, piano. See B15.

W12a   1882 (22 January); Paris; home of Le Couppey;
        Chaminade, piano. See B24.

W13   Scherzando, Op. 10. Piano. Durand, 1880. PPN 2819. 7
      pages. Dedicated to Madame Wable.

W14   Trio, Op. 11. Violin, cello, and piano. Durand, 1881.
      PPN 2828. 45 pages. Dedicated to Joseph Marsick.

      See B22.

Premiere

W14a 1880 (8 February); Paris; Salle Erard; Joseph
      Marsick, violin; Hekking, cello; Chaminade,
      piano. See B10-12, B14-15.

Selected performances

W14b   1880 (27 March); Paris; Salle Pleyel; Sociéte
        Nationale de Musique; Joseph Marsick, vio-

lin; Hekking, cello; Chaminade, piano. See B16-17.

W14c   1881 (early April); Paris; series organized by M. and Mme. Charles Lebouc; Joseph Marsick, violin; Charles Lebouc, cello; Chaminade, piano. See B21.

W14d   1882 (early March); Paris; Mlle. Godard, violin; Mariotti, cello; Chaminade, piano. See B40.

W14e   1884 (25 February); Paris; Salle Erard; Joseph Marsick, violin; Brandoukoff, cello; Chaminade, piano. See B71, B74-76.

W14f   1885 (late December); Paris; Société de Musique Française; Edouard Nadaud, violin; Gros-Saint-Ange, cello; Louise Steiger, piano.

W14g   1888 (last half); Lyon; at music publisher E. Clot; two movements; Merlen, violin; Perronet, cello; Chaminade, piano. See B137.

W15   Les Noces d'Argent, Op. 12. Fantaisie très facile pour un seul piano à 8 mains. Enoch frères & Costallat, 1892. PPN 2049. 9 pages. Dedicated "à mes petits amis du Vésinet: Jeanne, Marcel, Suzanne, Marcel."

Version for piano solo: Hachette, 1907. PPN H. 1578. 4 pages.

W16   Pastorale Enfantine, Op. 12. Piano. Enoch & Cie, 1897. PPN E. & Cie 5006. 4 pages. Dedicated "à ma nièce Antoinette Chaminade."

Version for piano duet: in Le Receuil des Enfants, ed. F. Le Couppey. Hamelle, 1885. PPN F.L.C. 32.

[Opp. 13 to 17 are empty]

W17   Capriccio, Op. 18. Violin and piano. Enoch & Costallat, [n.d.] PPN 1769. Dedicated to Joseph Marsick. AUTOGRAPH: Family.

Version for piano: Enoch, 1912. PPN 7398. 8 pages. No dedication.

W17a   1899 (late May); St.-Quentin; [Alberto] Bachmann, violin; Chaminade, piano. See B266.

W18   La Sévillane [Overture], Op. 19. From her one-act opéra comique; libretto by Edouard Guinand. Orchestral version unpublished (see WU26). Piano. La Semaine Artistique et Musicale, 1889. PPN A.S. 7.

Version for two pianos: Enoch & Costallat, 1891. PPN 1898. Dedicated to M. et Mme. A. Bosquet.

Premiere (of opera)

W18a   1882 (23 February); private performance, un-
        staged, with piano; overture and 10 vocal
        numbers; at family home in Paris; vocalists:
        Messieurs Hermann-Léon and Sujol, Mlles.
        Thuiller and Jeanne Perrouze; Chaminade,
        piano. See B25-39.

Selected performances (of overture or excerpts)

W18b   1884 (25 February); Paris; Salle Erard; over-
        ture and excerpts, with piano accompaniment;
        vocalists: Mlle. Lépine, Mme. Castillon, and
        M. Lauwers; Chaminade, piano. See B68-73,
        B75-76.

W18c   1886 (4 February); Paris; Salle Erard; Sérén-
        ade; Mazalbert, tenor; Chaminade, piano.

W18d   1888 (15 March); Marseille; Association Ar-
        tistique; overture. See B102-03.

W18e   1888 (18 April); Anvers, Belgium; Cercle
        Catholique; Société de Musique; orchestra
        conducted by Joseph Moreel. See B129.

W18f   1889 (4 April); Paris; Société Chorale d'Ama-
        teurs (Société Guillot de Sainbris). See
        B154.

See also B56.

W19-22 Suite d'Orchestre, Op. 20. Flutes, oboes, clarinets,
        [bassoons], horns, timpani, bass drum, violins I and
        II, violas, cellos, and double basses. L. Grus,
        1881. PPN L.G. 3644. Movements are Marche, Inter-
        mezzo, Scherzo, and Choral.

        Version for piano duet: Grus, 1881. PPN 3639-42.
        Dedicated to Benjamin Godard.

        Version for piano: Intermezzo. Grus, 1892. PPN 4612.
        7 pages. AUTOGRAPH: Family; Scherzo. Grus, 1892. PPN
        4611. 11 pages; Choral. Marseille: Carbonel, 1902.
        PPN M.C. 328. 4 pages.

        Later versions for piano, and piano duet, with new
        titles and ordering of the movements, issued by Ha-
        chette: Columbine (Scherzo); Les Noces d'Or, Fan-
        taisie; Marche-Impromptu; Pas des Sylphes (Intermez-
        zo). Piano version: 1908 (H. 1572), 11 pages; 1907
        (H. 1578), 4 pages; 1908 (H. 1563), 5 pages; 1907
        (H. 1588), 7 pages.

Premiere

W19-22a 1881 (4 April); Paris; Salle Erard; Société
         Nationale de Musique; orchestra. See B18-
         20.

Selected performances

W19-22b 1882 (19 March); Paris; Cirque d'Eté; Orches-
         tre de la Société des Grands-Concerts, con-
         ducted by Broustet. See B41-53.

W19-22c 1882 (17 December); Paris; Cirque d'Hiver;
         Pasdeloup concerts, conducted by Jules Pas-
         deloup. See B62-65.

W19-22d 1885 (29 March); Paris; Concerts Modernes; at
         concert of Benjamin Godard. See B81-82.

W20e   1884 (25 February); Paris; Salle Erard. See
         B71.

W20f   1886 (4 February); Paris; Salle Erard; two-
         piano version; Camille Chevillard and Cha-
         minade, piano. See B86.

W20g   1888 (11 March); Marseille; at home of the
         Livons; Chaminade, piano. See B99.

W21e   1888 (c. 18 March); Marseille. See B114.

W22e   1888 (c. 18 March); Marseille. See B114.

W23   Sonata, Op. 21. Piano. Enoch, 1895. PPN 2610. 25
      pages. Dedicated to Maurice Moszkowski. Three move-
      ments. Last movement same as Appassionato, Op. 35
      No. 4; see W44. See also WC5.

      Selected performance

      W23a   1893 (1 June); London; St. James's Hall; first
               movement; Chaminade, piano.

W24   Orientale, Op. 22. Piano. Hamelle, [n.d.]. PPN 2169.
      10 pages. Dedicated to Gabrielle Turpin. See WU23
      for an unpublished orchestral version.

W25   Minuetto, Op. 23. Piano. Enoch & Costallat, [1883].
      PPN 731. 7 pages. Dedicated to Hortense Parent.

W26   Libellules, Op. 24. Piano. Enoch, 1881. PPN 730. Ded-
      icated to Mary Moll. See also WC1.

      See B168.

      Premiere

      W26a   1882 (22 January); Paris; home of Le Couppey;
               Chaminade, piano. See B24.

Selected performances

W26b   1884 (25 February); Paris; Salle Erard; Cha-
        minade, piano. See B71.

W26c   1908 (22 November); Chicago; Orchestra Hall;
        Chaminade, piano. Performed as an encore.

W27-28 Deux Morceaux, Op. 25. Piano. Berlin & Leipzig: A-
        dolphe Fürstner, [c. 1885]. No. 1: Mélancholie. PPN
        2516. 3 pages. Dedicated to Henriette Chaminade.
        AUTOGRAPH: University of Michigan; No. 2: Humores-
        que. PPN 2517. 9 pages. Dedicated to Mme. Roger-Mi-
        clos. AUTOGRAPH: University of Michigan.

W29   Les Amazones, Symphonie Dramatique, Op. 26. Orchestra,
        chorus, and soloists. Orchestral version un-
        published; see WU1. Text by Charles Grandmougin.
        Piano/vocal score: Enoch & Costallat, [1884]. PPN
        1043. 133 pages.

        See B136, B364, B456, B461, B474.

        Premiere (orchestral version)

W29a   1888 (18 April); Anvers, Belgium; Cercle
        Catholique; Société de Musique; orchestra
        conducted by Joseph Moreel; vocal soloists:
        Mme. De Give, Mlle. Hasselmans, Léon Van
        Hoof, tenor. See B128-29, B132, B134.

W30-31 Deux Morceaux, Op. 27. Piano. Breslau: Jules Hainauer,
        [n.d.]. No. 1: Duetto. PPN J. 2730 H. 10 pages. Ded-
        icated to Magdeleine Godard. AUTOGRAPH: Family;   No.
        2: Zingara. PPN J. 2731 H. 11 pages. Dedicated to
        Louise Steiger. See WU30 for an unpublished orches-
        tral version.

        See B368.

        Selected performances

W31a   1885 (22 February); Paris; Concerts Modernes;
        orchestral version. See B77-79.

W31b   1888 (11 March); Marseille; at home of the
        Livons; piano version; Chaminade, piano. See
        B99.

W31c   1888 (15 March); Marseille; Association Ar-
        tistique; orchestral version. See B102-03.

W32   Etude Symphonique, Op. 28. Piano. Enoch & Costallat,
        1890. PPN 1776. 11 pages. Dedicated to J. J. Pader-
        ewski. See also WC2, WC3, and WC5.

        Appeared earlier, in an anthology: F. Le Couppey,
        ed. Le Décameron. 10 Etudes Difficiles Prises dans
        les Oeuvres de divers Auteurs. Hamelle, 1884. PPN

(anthology): F.L.C. 31. The following appears before the piece:

"We owe this Etude--or rather this Capriccio--to the kindness of a composer whose works, stamped with an originality that never touches on the bizarre, are skillfully written and always interesting. Although the nuances are carefully marked, it's nonetheless necessary to rely a little on the musical intelligence of the performer to render them exactly with the desired feeling."

Selected performance

W32a   1978 (9 December); Aix-en-Provence; Le Rex; Wilfrid Maggiar, piano. See B470.

W33   Sérénade, Op. 29. Piano. Enoch & Costallat, 1884. PPN 1055. 5 pages. Dedicated to F. Lévy. See also WC1. See WU24 for an unpublished orchestral version.

See B288.

Selected performances

W33a   1885 (22 February); Paris; Concerts Modernes; orchestral version. See B77-79.

W33b   1888 (last half); Lyon; at music publisher E. Clot; Chaminade, piano. See B137.

W33c   1892 (23 June); London; St. James's Hall; Chaminade, piano. See B198.

W33d   [1894] (June); Manchester; Free-Trade Hall; Chaminade, piano. See B232.

W33e   1978 (9 December); Aix-en-Provence; Le Rex; Wilfrid Maggiar, piano. See B470.

W34   Air de Ballet, No. 1, Op. 30. Piano. Enoch & Costallat, 1884. PPN 1056. 9 pages. Dedicated to Madame G. Costallat.

See B368.

Selected performances

W34a   1886 (4 February); Paris; Salle Erard; Chaminade, piano.

W34b   1886 (December); Paris; Salle Pleyel; Chaminade, piano. See B94.

W34c   1888 (last half); Lyon; at home of music publisher E. Clot; Chaminade, piano. See B137.

W34d   1893 (November); Lille; Concert Populaire; Chaminade, piano. See B212.

W34e   1908 (9 December); Philadelphia; American Academy of Music; Chaminade, piano.

W35-37 Trois Morceaux, Op. 31. Violin & piano. Breslau: Hainauer, [c. 1885]. No. 1: Andantino; No. 2: Romanza [Appassionata]; No. 3: Bohémienne. AUTOGRAPH: Family, but pieces have different titles: Révérie, Sérénade (dedicated to Le Cointe), and Menuet (dedicated to Joseph Marsick).

Version for cello & piano of No. 2: AUTOGRAPH: Family.

Premiere

W36-37a 1886 (4 February); Paris; Salle Erard; Joseph Marsick, violin; Chaminade, piano. See B85.

Selected performances

W37b   1890 (14 March); Paris; Salle de la rue de Grenelle; Marcel Herwegh, violin; Chaminade, piano. See B165.

W37c   1890 (5 May); Paris; Salle de Géographie; Société des Concerts du Conservatoire; Marie Saintel, violin; Frémaux, piano. See B167.

W38   Guitare (Caprice), Op. 32. Piano. Enoch & Costallat, 1885. PPN 1128. 7 pages. Dedicated to Albert Lavignac. See also WC1.

See B427.

Selected performances

W38a   1886 (4 February); Paris; Salle Erard; Chaminade, piano.

W38b   1886 (December); Paris; Salle Pleyel; Chaminade, piano. See B94.

W39   Valse Caprice, Op. 33. Piano. Enoch & Costallat, 1885. PPN 1129. 9 pages. Dedicated to Octavie Ratisbonne. See also WC1.

See B288, B368.

Selected performances

W39a   1892 (23 June); London; St. James's Hall; Chaminade, piano.

W39b   1894 (2 June); London; St. James's Hall; Chaminade, piano. See B230.

W40   Trio [Deuxième], Op. 34. Violin, cello, & piano. Enoch & Costallat, 1887. PPN 1319. 64 pages. Dedicated to "M. J. Delsart, Professeur au Conservatoire."

Premiere

W40a   1886 (4 February); Paris; Salle Erard; Joseph Marsick, violin; Gros-Saint-Ange, cello; Chaminade, piano. See B85.

Selected performances

W40b   1889 (2 April); Paris; Concerts Herwegh; Salle de la Société d'Horticulture; Marcel Herwegh, violin; Chaminade, piano. See B151-53.

W40c   1892 (23 June); London; St. James's Hall; Johannes Wolff, violin; Joseph Hollman, cello; Chaminade, piano. See B188, B193, B196-97, B200.

W40d   1893 (c. 20 February); Paris; White chamber music ensemble; Chaminade, piano. See B204.

W40e   [1896]; Lausanne; Adolphe Rehberg, cello; Chaminade, piano. See B245.

W40f   1898; Berlin; Bechsteinsaal; Herr Zajic, violin; Heinrich Grünfeld, cello; Chaminade, piano. See B254.

W40g   [1899]; Epinal; Le Théâtre; Anton Hekking, violin; Pollain, cello; Chaminade, piano. See B263.

W40h   1899 (c. October); Berlin; Chaminade, piano. See B268.

W40i   1904 (April); Paris; Salle Aeolian; [José] White, violin; Choinet, cello; Chaminade, piano. See B284.

W40j   1908 (15 December); New York; Carnegie Hall; Edouard Déthier, violin; Darbyshire Jones, cello; Chaminade, piano. See B390.

See also B399, B412-15, B433.

W41-46 Six Etudes de Concert, Op. 35. Piano. Enoch & Costallat, 1886. See also WC5. No. 1: Scherzo. PPN 1311. 8 pages. Dedicated to G. Lewita; No. 2: Automne. PPN 1312. 7 pages. Dedicated to Hélène Kryzanowska; No. 3: Fileuse. PPN 1313. 12 pages. Dedicated to Louis Livon. AUTOGRAPH: Family; No. 4: Appassionato. PPN 1314. 7 pages. Dedicated to Madame de Serres-Montigny. Same as last movement of Op. 21; See W23. No. 5: Impromptu. PPN 1315. 7 pages. Dedicated to Marguerite Lamoureux; No. 6: Tarentelle. PPN 1316. 9 pages. Dedicated to Marie Jaëll. AUTOGRAPH:

Family. See WU29 for an unpublished orchestral version.

See B168, B288, B403, B416.

Selected performances

W41a   1886 (December); Paris; Salle Pleyel; Chaminade, piano. See B94.

W42a   1886 (December); Paris; Salle Pleyel; Chaminade, piano. See B94.

W42b   1888 (11 March); Marseille; at home of the Livons; Chaminade, piano. See B99.

W42c   1892 (23 June); London; St. James's Hall; Chaminade, piano. See B198.

W42d   1908 (6-7 November); Philadelphia; American Academy of Music; Chaminade, piano. See B332.

W42e   1908 (9 December); Philadelphia; American Academy of Music; Chaminade, piano. See B381-82.

W42f   1978 (9 December); Aix-en-Provence; Le Rex; Wilfrid Maggiar, piano. See B470.

W43a   1886 (December); Paris; Salle Pleyel; Chaminade, piano. See B94.

W43b   1890 (30 January); Paris; Salle Erard; Chaminade, piano. See B162.

W43c   1892 (23 June); London; St. James's Hall; Chaminade, piano. See B195, B198.

W46a   1886 (31 October); Paris; Cirque d'Hiver; Concerts Populaires; orchestral version, conducted by Jules Pasdeloup. See B90-93.

W46b   1978 (9 December); Aix-en-Provence; Le Rex; Wilfrid Maggiar, piano. See B470.

W47   Intermède, Op. 36 No. 1. Piano duet. Enoch & Costallat, 1887. PPN 1344. 15 pages. Dedicated to Lydie & Jenny Pirodon.

Version for two pianos: Enoch & Costallat, 1887. PPN 1346. Same dedicatees.

Selected performances

W47a   1886 (4 February); Paris; Salle Erard; two-piano version; Camille Chevillard and Chaminade, piano.

W47b   1888 (11 March); Marseille; at home of the Livons; Louis Livon and Chaminade, piano.

W47c   1908 (15 December); New York; Carnegie Hall; two-piano version; Charles Gilbert Spross and Chaminade, piano.

W48   Pas des Cymbales, Op. 36 No. 2. Piano duet. Enoch & Costallat, 1887. PPN 1345. Dedicated to Madame Jacquard. See also W50.

Premiere

W48a   1886 (4 February); Paris; Salle Erard; two-piano version; Camille Chevillard and Chaminade, piano. See B86.

Selected performances

W48b   1888 (11 March); Marseille; at home of the Livons; Louis Livon and Chaminade, piano. See B99.

W48c   1889 (15 December); Paris; Lamoureux concerts; Cirque des Champs-Elysées; orchestral version, conducted by Charles Lamoureux. See B156-60.

W48d   1892 (23 June); London; St. James's Hall; Chaminade, piano. See B186.

W48e   1898; Berlin; Bechsteinsaal; two-piano version; Fräulein Siebold and Chaminade, piano. See B254.

W48f   1908 (15 December); New York; Carnegie Hall; two-piano version; Charles Gilbert Spross and Chaminade, piano.

W49   Callirhoë, Ballet Symphonique, Op. 37. Orchestral score not found, probably unpublished; see WU6. Scenario by Elzéar Rougier. Piano score: Enoch & Costallat, [1888]. PPN 1505. 99 pages. Dedicated to Edouard Brunel. Instrumentation listed in piano score: 2 flutes, 1 piccolo, 2 oboes, 2 clarinets, 2 bassoons, 4 horns, 2 natural trumpets, 2 valve trumpets, 3 trombones, tuba, 3 timpani, bass drum, cymbals, [2] harps, violins I & II, violas, cellos, double basses.

See B253.

Premiere

W49a   1888 (16 March); Marseille; Grand-Théâtre; conducted by Brunel; choreographed by Victor Natta; dansed by Natta (Alcméon), Comolli (Callirhoë), Mlles. Bercé, Gautier, and the

corps de ballet. See B104-09, B111-13, B115-
18, B120-27, B131, B134.

Selected performances

W49b   1891 (12 February); Lyon; Grand-Théâtre; con-
        ducted by Luigini; dansed by G. Monge (Cal-
        lirhoë), V. Natta (Alcméon), Mlles. Coronna,
        Amalia, and Boggio. See B177-79.

W49c   [1892] (mid November); Toulouse; Théâtre du
        Capitole; conducted by Tartanac; dansed by
        Natta (Alcméon); Mlle. Colombo (Callirhoë),
        and Mlle. Sacchi (Venus-Aphrodite). See
        B202.

W49d   [1895]; Toulon; Le Casino; conducted by Péle-
        grin; dansed by Victor Natta ballet troupe.
        See B238.

See also B279.

W50   Callirhoë, Suite d'Orchestre, [Op. 37]. 4 movements.
       Enoch & Costallat, [1890]. PPN 1733. 83 pages. Same
       dedicatee. No. 1: Prélude. 21 pages; No. 2: Pas Du
       Voile (= Pas Des Echarpes; see W52). 12 pages; No.
       3: Scherzettino. 10 pages (see also W82); No. 4: Pas
       Des Cymbales. 40 pages (see also W48). See W49 for
       the instrumentation.

       Premiere

W50a   1890 (23 and 30 November); Paris; Châtelet;
        Concerts Colonne. See B169-73, B176.

       Selected performances

W50b   1893 (November); Lille; Concerts Populaires;
        orchestra conducted by Ratez. See B212.

W50c   1894 (19 February); Geneva; orchestra conduc-
        ted by Chaminade. See B214-15.

W50d   [1895]; Marseille; Concerts Classiques; or-
        chestra conducted by Chaminade. See B237.

W50e   1928 (5 February); Rouen; Mustel's; festival
        organized by Marie Capoy. See B429.

See also B174, B216.

       [The following 6 entries are from Callirhoë. They
       are listed separately because they become very
       important as independent piano pieces.]

W51   Pas des Amphores, Deuxième Air de Ballet, from Op. 37.
       Piano. Enoch & Costallat, 1888. PPN 1513. 5 pages.
       Dedicated to Madame Charles Canivet. See also WC1.

See B288, B368.

W52 Pas des Echarpes [= Scarf Dance], Troisième Air de
     Ballet, from Op. 37. Piano version of Pas Du Voile
     (see W50). Piano. Enoch & Costallat, 1888. PPN 1512.
     7 pages. Dedicated to Marguerite Balutet. See also
     WC1.

     See B168, B288, B368, B455-56.

     Selected performances

     W52a 1888 (last half); Lyon; at music publisher E.
           Clot; Chaminade, piano. See B137.

     W52b 1891 (early May); Paris; home of Léon Dela-
           fosse; Léon Delafosse, piano. See B180.

     W52c 1892 (23 June); London; St. James's Hall; Cha-
           minade, piano. See B192.

     W52d 1908 (9 December); Philadelphia; American Aca-
           demy of Music; Chaminade, piano. See B381.

     W52e 1908 (15 December); New York; Carnegie Hall;
           Chaminade, piano; performed as an encore.
           See B392.

     W52f 1939 (c. 8 August); Lowell, Mass.; on a radio
           broadcast, in honor of her birthday; Louis
           Guilbault, piano. See B443.

W53 Callirhoë, Quatrième Air de Ballet, from Op. 37.
     Piano. Enoch & Costallat, 1888. PPN 1514. 5 pages.
     Dedicated to Eugénie Hunger. See also WC1.

     See B288.

     Selected performance

     W53a 1910 (20 May); Paris; two-piano version; Cham-
           inade, piano, and Pianola roll of herself.
           See B402.

W54 Danse Pastorale, Cinquième Air de Ballet, from Op. 37.
     Piano. Enoch & Costallat, 1888. PPN 1515. [2 pages.]
     Dedicated to Madame Henry Marchand. In Le Figaro (20
     June 1888), 8; see B135.

W55 Danse Orientale, from Op. 37. Piano. Published with
     W54 by Enoch, 1913. PPN 7639. 11 pages.

     Andante et Scherzettino, from Op. 37. Published as
     Opus 59; see W82.

W56 Marine, Op. 38. Piano. Enoch & Costallat, [1887]. PPN
     1333. 5 pages. Dedicated to Madame Jean Richepin.
     AUTOGRAPH: Family. In Anthology of French Piano

Music, ed. Isidor Philipp. Boston: Ditson, 1906.
Reprint: Dover, 1977.

Selected performances

W56a   1886 (December); Paris; Salle Pleyel; Chami-
        nade, piano. See B94.

W56b   1888 (11 March); Marseille; at home of the
        Livons; Chaminade, piano. See B99-100.

W56c   1888 (last half); Lyon; at music publisher E.
        Clot; Chaminade, piano.

W56d   1890 (30 January); Paris; Salle Erard; Chami-
        nade, piano. See B162.

W56e   1893 (1 June); London; St. James's Hall; Cha-
        minade, piano.

W57   Toccata, Op. 39. Piano. Enoch & Costallat, [1887]. PPN
       1334. 7 pages. Dedicated to Galliano. AUTOGRAPH:
       Family.

       See B403.

Selected performances

W57a   1887 (December); Marseille; Association Ar-
        tistique; Louis Livon, piano. See B98.

W57b   1888 (last half); Lyon; at music publisher E.
        Clot; Chaminade, piano.

W57c   1898; Berlin; Bechsteinsaal; Chaminade, piano.
        See B254.

W57d   1978 (9 December); Aix-en-Provence; Le Rex;
        Wilfrid Maggiar, piano. See B470.

W58   Concertstück, Op. 40. Piano & orchestra: 2 flutes,
       piccolo, 2 oboes, English horn, 2 clarinets, 2 bas-
       soons, 4 horns, 4 trumpets, 3 trombones, tuba, tri-
       angle, 3 timpani, cymbals, bass drum, violins I &
       II, violas, cellos, double basses. Enoch & Costal-
       lat, [c. 1893]. PPN 2276. 67 pages. Dedicated to
       Louise Steiger.

       Version for 2 pianos: Enoch & Costallat, 1888. PPN
       1526.

       See B404.

Premiere

W58a   1888 (18 April); Anvers, Belgium; Cercle
        Catholique; Société de Musique; orchestra
        conducted by Joseph Moreel; Chaminade,
        piano. See B128-30, B132, B134.

Selected performances

W58b   1889 (20 January); Paris; Cirque d'Eté; Lam-
        oureux concerts, conducted by Charles Lam-
        oureux; Chaminade, piano. See B138-43.

W58c   1889 (late February); Angers; 14th Concert
        Populaire; Louise Steiger, piano. See B146-
        48.

W58d   1889 (4 March); Paris; Salle Pleyel; orchestra
        conducted by Edouard Colonne; Louise Stei-
        ger, piano. See B149.

W58e   1890 (30 January); Paris; Salle Erard; Chami-
        nade, piano. See B164.

W58f   1892 (c. 25 February); Marseille; Association
        Artistique; Louis Livon, piano. See B183-
        84.

W58g   1892 (23 June); London; St. James's Hall; two-
        piano version; Amina Goodwin and Chaminade,
        piano. See B193.

W58h   1894 (19 February); Geneva; orchestra conduc-
        ted by Chaminade; Willy Rehberg, piano. See
        B214-16, B218, B234.

W58i   1894 (16 March); Reims; Grand Théâtre; Société
        Philharmonique; Chaminade, piano. See B223-
        25.

W58j   1896 (December); Chicago; Auditorium; Theodore
        Thomas Orchestra, conducted by Theodore Tho-
        mas; Hans von Schiller, piano.

W58k   1908 (6-7 November); Philadelphia; American
        Academy of Music; Philadelphia Orchestra,
        conducted by Carl Pohlig; Chaminade, piano.
        See B327-29, B332-34.

W58L   1919 (7 December); Philadelphia; American Aca-
        demy of Music; Philadelphia Orchestra; Is-
        rael Vichnin, piano. See B421-23.

W58m   1928 (c. 25 March); Toulon; Le Théâtre; Con-
        certs du Conservatoire; festival of Cham-
        inade works; orchestra conducted by Gré-
        goire; Excoffier, piano. See B431-32.

See also B133-34, B236, B252, B255, B446.

W59   Pierrette, Air de Ballet, Op. 41. Piano. Enoch & Cost-
       allat, 1889. PPN 1641. 5 pages. Dedicated to André
       Gresse. AUTOGRAPH: Family. See also WC1.

       See B288, B368.

Selected performances

W59a   1890 (30 January); Paris; Salle Erard; Chami-
       nade, piano. See B162.

W59b   1892 (23 June); London; St. James's Hall; Cha-
       minade, piano. See B192.

W59c   [1894] (June); Manchester; Free-Trade Hall;
       Chaminade, piano. See B232.

W59d   1908 (9 December); Philadelphia; American Aca-
       demy of Music; Chaminade, piano.

W59e   1978 (9 December); Aix-en-Provence; Le Rex;
       Wilfrid Maggiar, piano. See B470.

W60   Les Willis, Caprice, Op. 42. Piano. Enoch & Costallat,
      1889. PPN 1632. Dedicated to Clotilde Kleeberg. AU-
      TOGRAPH: Family.

W61   Gigue, Op. 43. Piano. Enoch & Costallat, 1889. PPN
      1663. 9 pages. Dedicated to Camille Chevillard.

      Choeurs, Opp. 44-49 [W62-67]. Women's voices, with
      soloists, & piano. Texts by Armand Silvestre. Opp.
      44-48: three equal parts; Op. 49: two equal parts.

W62   Les Feux de St. Jean, Op. 44. Enoch & Costallat, [c.
      1890]. PPN 1755. 11 pages. Dedicated to Duteil d'O-
      zanne.

W63   Sous L'Aile Blanche des Voiles (Barcarolle-Nocturne),
      Op. 45. Enoch & Costallat, [c. 1890]. PPN 1754. 9
      pages. Dedicated to Edouard Guinand. AUTOGRAPH: Fam-
      ily.

Selected performances

W63a   1894 (c. early April); Paris; Mme. Molé Truf-
       fier and Clément, vocalists; Chaminade,
       piano. See B227.

W63b   [1894]; Manchester; Free-Trade Hall; Mlle.
       Landi and Andrew Black, vocalists; Chamin-
       ade, piano.

W63c   [1901]; Le Havre; chorus of 24 women and young
       amateurs, conducted by Mazalbert. See B274.

W64   Pardon Breton, Op. 46. Enoch & Costallat, [c. 1890].
      PPN 1752. 11 pages. Dedicated to Madame Edouard Col-
      onne.

Selected performances

W64a   1893 (12 March); Paris; Vocalists: Mlles. Gen-
       oud and Boyer; Chaminade, piano.

W64b   1894 (c. early April); Paris; Mme. Molé Truf-
fier and Clément, vocalists; Chaminade,
piano. See B227.

W64c   [1901]; Le Havre; chorus of 24 women and young
amateurs, conducted by Mazalbert. See B274.

W65   Noce Hongroise, Op. 47. Enoch & Costallat, [c. 1890].
PPN 1753. 7 pages. Dedicated to Madame Moreau-Sainti. AUTOGRAPH: Family.

Selected performance

W65a   1894 (16 March); Reims; Grand Théâtre; chorus
of the Société Philharmonique; Chaminade,
piano. See B224-25.

W66   Noël des Marins, Op. 48. Enoch & Costallat, [c.
1890]. PPN 1756. 9 pages. Dedicated to Jules Griset.

Selected performances

W66a   1891 (March); Paris; Salle Erard; Société Chorale d'Amateurs. See B179.

W66b   1894 (16 March); Reims; Grand Théâtre; chorus
of the Société Philharmonique; Chaminade,
piano. See B223-25.

W67   Les Filles d'Arles, Op. 49. Enoch & Costallat, [c.
1890]. PPN 1757. 11 pages. Dedicated to Madame
Roger. AUTOGRAPH: Family.

W68   La Lisonjera [= L'Enjoleuse, or The Flatterer], Op.
50. Piano. Milan: G. Ricordi, [c. 1890]. PPN C 94163
C. 8 pages. Dedicated to Madame La Marquise de St.
Paul. See also WC1.

See B288, B368, B428.

Selected performances

W68a   1908 (22 November); Chicago; Orchestra Hall;
Chaminade, piano. Performed as an encore.

W68b   1908 (9 December); Philadelphia; American Academy of Music; Chaminade, piano. See B381.

W68c   1939 (c. 8 August); Lowell, Mass.; on a radio
broadcast, in honor of her birthday; Louis
Guilbault, piano. See B443.

W68d   1978 (9 December); Aix-en-Provence; Le Rex;
Wilfrid Maggiar, piano. See B470.

W69   La Livry, Air de Ballet, Op. 51. Piano. Ricordi, [c.
1890]. PPN 94164. 10 pages. Dedicated to Léon Dela-
fosse.

Selected performance

W69a   1891 (early May); Paris; at home of Léon De-
        lafosse; Léon Delafosse, piano. See B180.

W70   Capriccio Appassionato, Op. 52. Piano. Ricordi, [c.
       1890]. PPN 94356. 8 pages. Dedicated to Madame A.
       Larvor.

W71   Arlequine, Op. 53. Piano. Ricordi, [c. 1890]. PPN
       94357. 8 pages. Dedicated to Henriette Thuillier.

W72   Lolita, Caprice Espagnole, Op. 54. Piano. Enoch & Cos-
       tallat, 1890. PPN 1768. 7 pages. Dedicated to Cécile
       Boutet de Monvel.

W73-78 Six Pièces Romantiques, Op. 55. Piano duet. Enoch &
       Costallat, [c. 1890]. No. 1: Primavera. PPN 1781.
       Dedicated to Madame Breton-Halmagrand. AUTOGRAPH:
       Family; No. 2: La Chaise à Porteurs. PPN 1782. Ded-
       icated to Adolphe Rehberg. Version for violin &
       piano: PPN 2825. Version for cello & piano: Enoch &
       Costallat, 1896. AUTOGRAPH: Family. See WU8 for an
       unpublished orchestral version; No. 3: Idylle Arabe.
       PPN 1783. Dedicated to Madame Fabre. AUTOGRAPH: Fam-
       ily. Version for piano: Enoch & Cie, 1923. PPN 8254.
       See WU10 for an unpublished orchestral version; No.
       4: Sérénade d'Automne. PPN 1784. Dedicated to Madame
       Th. Dubois. AUTOGRAPH: Family. See WU25 for an un-
       published orchestral version; No. 5: Danse Hindoue.
       PPN 1785. Dedicated to Madame Ducatez-Lévy. Version
       for piano: Enoch & Cie, 1923. PPN Enoch 8255; No. 6:
       Rigaudon. PPN 1786. Dedicated to Madame Lyon. Ver-
       sion for piano: Enoch & Cie, 1923. PPN 8256.

Selected performances

W74a   1893 (12 March); Paris; Madame Ratisbonne and
        Chaminade, piano duet.

W74b   [1895]; Marseille; orchestral version. See
        B237.

W74c   1928 (5 February); Rouen; Concerts Dubruille;
        E. Dubruille, cello; Mlle. Grégoire, piano.
        See B430.

W76a   1893 (12 March); Paris; Madame Ratisbonne and
        Chaminade, piano duet.

W76b   [1895]; Marseille; orchestral version. See
        B237.

W78a   1893 (12 March); Paris; Madame Ratisbonne and
        Chaminade, piano duet.

W79   Scaramouche, Op. 56. Piano. Enoch & Costallat, 1890.
       PPN 1787. 7 pages. Dedicated to Paul Braud. See
       also WC1.

W80   Havanaise, Op. 57. Piano. Enoch & Costallat, 1891.
       PPN 1905. 7 pages. AUTOGRAPH: Family.

       Capriccio, Op. 57. Violin & piano. Reissue of Op. 18.
       See W17.

W81   Mazurk' Suédoise, Op. 58. Piano. Enoch & Costallat,
       1891. PPN 1906. 7 pages. Dedicated to Madame Pon-
       tet. AUTOGRAPH: Family.

W82   Andante et Scherzettino, Op. 59. From Callirhoë, Op.
       37 (see W49-55). Two pianos. Enoch & Costallat,
       1891. PPN 1903. 7 pages. Dedicated "à mon amie Mar-
       guerite Enoch."

       Selected performances

       W82a   1889 (15 December); Paris; Cirque des Champs-
               Elysées; Lamoureux concerts; Scherzettino
               only; orchestral version. See B156-60.

       W82b   1892 (23 June); London; St. James's Hall;
               Amina Goodwin and Chaminade, piano. See
               B186.

       W82c   1908 (24 October); New York; Carnegie Hall;
               Chaminade, piano.

W83   Les Sylvains, Op. 60. Piano. Enoch & Costallat, 1892.
       PPN 2044. 7 pages. Dedicated to Gabrielle Turpin.
       See also WC1.

       See B288.

       Selected performances

       W83a   1894 (19 February); Geneva; Chaminade, piano.
               See B214.

       W83b   1908 (9 December); Philadelphia; American
               Academy of Music; Chaminade, piano.

       W83c   1978 (9 December); Aix-en-Provence; Le Rex;
               Wilfrid Maggiar, piano. See B470.

W84   Arabesque, Op. 61. Piano. Enoch & Costallat, 1892.
       PPN 2047. 7 pages. Dedicated to Marthe Plançon. See
       also WC1.

       Selected performances

       W84a   1893 (1 June); London; St. James's Hall; Cha-
               minade, piano.

       W84b   1893 (November); Lille; Concert Populaire;
               Chaminade, piano. See B212.

       W84c   1898; Berlin; Bechsteinsaal; Chaminade,
               piano. See B254.

Duos avec Accompagnement de Piano, Opp. 62-65, Opp.
68-71 (W85-88, W91-94). Two vocal parts & piano.
Enoch & Costallat.

W85   Barcarolle, Op. 62. Duos No. 1. Mezzo-soprano, baritone, & piano. Text by Edouard Guinand. 1892. PPN
2041. 8 pages. "Oui, mon âme est charmée." Dedicated to M. et Mme. Oudin. AUTOGRAPH: Family.

   Selected performances

   W85a   1894 (4 June); London; St. James's Hall;
           Mlle. Landi and Liza Lehmann, vocalists;
           Chaminade, piano. See B230.

   W85b   [1894]; Manchester; Free-Trade Hall; Mlle.
           Landi and Andrew Black, vocalists; Chamin-
           ade, piano.

   W85c   1908 (18 October); New York; German Theatre;
           Jeanne Jomelli and David Bispham, vocal-
           ists. See B305.

W86   A Travers Bois, Op. 63. Duos No. 6. Soprano, tenor
[baritone], & piano. Text by Edouard Guinand. 1892.
PPN 2042. 8 pages. "Que la forêt est calme." Dedicated to Madame Payen-Paulin. AUTOGRAPH: Family.

   Selected performance

   W86a   1899 (May); St.-Quentin; Mme. Danner, voca-
           list, and Georges Mauguière, tenor; Chami-
           nade, piano. See B266.

W87   Marthe et Marie, Op. 64. Duos No. 4. Soprano, contralto, & piano. [Text by Edouard Guinand.] [1893.]
PPN 2043. 8 pages. "Ma soeur rappelons nous." Dedicated to Ad. Maton. AUTOGRAPH: Family.

W88   Nocturne Pyrénéen, Op. 65. Duos No. 8. Contralto,
bass, & piano. [Text by Edouard Guinand.] 1892. PPN
2048. 8 pages. "Sur le soleil." Dedicated to Edmond
Duvernoy. AUTOGRAPH: Family.

   Selected performance

   W88a   1895 (7 June); London; St. James's Hall;
           Mlle. Landi, contralto; Pol Plançon, bass;
           Chaminade, piano.

W89   Studio, Op. 66. Piano. Enoch & Costallat, 1892. PPN
2054. 7 pages. Dedicated to Amina Goodwin.

   Composed April 1878 or earlier.

   Premiere

   W89a   1878 (25 April); Paris; home of Le Couppey;
           Chaminade, piano.

W90   Caprice Espagnole (La Morena), Op. 67. Piano. Enoch &
       Costallat, 1892. PPN 2055. 7 pages. Dedicated to
       Victor Staub.

W91   Les Fiancés, Op. 68. Duos No. 2. Mezzo-soprano, bari-
       tone, & piano. Text by Armand Silvestre. [1892.]
       PPN 2070. 8 pages. "Depuis que le grand jour ap-
       proche." Dedicated to M. & Mme. Ciampi. AUTOGRAPH:
       Family.

W92   L'Angélus, Op. 69. Duos No. 3. Mezzo-soprano, bari-
       tone, & piano. Text by Armand Silvestre. [1893.]
       PPN 2081. 7 pages. "Penchés sur le sillon." Dedi-
       cated to Laure Taconet. AUTOGRAPH: Family.

       Selected performance

       W92a   [1894]; Manchester; Free-Trade Hall; Mlle.
               Landi and Andrew Black, vocalists; Chamin-
               ade, piano.

W93   Le Pêcheur et l'Ondine, Op. 70. Duos No. 7. Soprano,
       tenor, & piano. Text by Armand Silvestre. 1893. PPN
       2248. 8 pages. "O voix qui n'es qu'une caresse."
       Dedicated to M. & Mme. Delaquerrière. AUTOGRAPH:
       Family.

       Selected performance

       W93a   [1896]; Lausanne; M. and Mme. Troyon, vocal-
               ists; Chaminade, piano.

W94   Duo d'Etoiles, Op. 71. Duos No. 5. Soprano, mezzo-
       soprano, & piano. Text by Armand Silvestre. 1892.
       PPN 2098. 8 pages. "Etoile, ma soeur aimée." Dedi-
       cated to Elisabeth & Noëmie Fuchs. AUTOGRAPH: Fami-
       ly.

       Selected performance

       W94a   1894 (4 June); London; St. James's Hall;
               Mlle. Landi and Liza Lehmann, vocalists;
               Chaminade, piano. See B230.

       [Opus 72 is empty.]

W95   Valse Carnavalesque, Op. 73. Two Pianos. Enoch & Cos-
       tallat, 1894. PPN 2275. Dedicated to Willy Rehberg.

       Selected performances

       W95a   1894 (c. early April); Paris; Chaminade and
               an unnamed pianist. See B227.

       W95b   1910 (20 May); Paris; Chaminade, piano, and
               Pianola roll of herself. See B402.

W96   <u>Pièce dans le Style Ancien</u>, Op. 74. Piano. Enoch & Costallat, 1893. PPN 2201. 7 pages. Dedicated to Madeleine Ten Have.

           Version for violin & piano: Enoch, 1925. PPN 8297.

           <u>See</u> B403.

           Selected performance

       W96a   1894 (4 June); London; St. James's Hall; Chaminade, piano. <u>See</u> B230.

W97   <u>Danse Ancienne</u>, Op. 75. Piano. Enoch & Costallat, 1893. PPN 2202. 7 pages. Dedicated to Marguerite Weyler.

W98-103   <u>Romances Sans Paroles</u>, Op. 76. Piano. Enoch & Costallat, 1893. PPN 2221-26. 27 pages. No. 1: <u>Souvenance</u>. Dedicated to J.A. Wiernsberger; No. 2: <u>Elévation</u>. Dedicated to Docteur Paul Landowski. AUTOGRAPH: Family; No. 3: <u>Idylle</u>. Dedicated to Henri Kaiser. AUTOGRAPH: Family; No. 4: <u>Eglogue</u>. Dedicated to Georges Falkenberg. AUTOGRAPH: Family; No. 5: <u>Chanson Bretonne</u>. Dedicated "à M. Wouters (Professeur Au Conservatoire Royal de Musique de Bruxelles)." AUTOGRAPH: Family; No. 6: <u>Méditation</u>. Dedicated to Charles René. AUTOGRAPH: Family.

           <u>See</u> B466.

           Selected performances

       W99a   1893 (November); Lille; Concert Populaire; Chaminade, piano. <u>See</u> B212.

       W99b   1894 (19 February); Geneva; Chaminade, piano. <u>See</u> B214.

       W98-103c   [1898]; Le Havre; Chaminade, piano. <u>See</u> B255.

       W99d   1908 (9 December); Philadelphia; American Academy of Music; Chaminade, piano. <u>See</u> B381.

       W99e   1978 (9 December); Aix-en-Provence; Le Rex; Wilfrid Maggiar, piano. <u>See</u> B470.

W104   <u>Deuxième Valse</u>, Op. 77. Piano. Enoch, 1895. PPN 2411. 11 pages. Dedicated to Madame Billa-Manotte.

W105   <u>Prélude</u>, Op. 78. Piano or organ. Enoch, 1895. Dedicated to Théodore Dubois. 7 pages. Piano version: PPN 2397. Organ version: PPN 2465. AUTOGRAPH (organ): Family.

See B428.

Selected performance

W105a   [1928] [29 March]; Toulon; Concerts du Con-
         servatoire; organ version; Lacaze, organ.
         See B432.

W106-07 Deux Pièces, Op. 79. Orchestra, but probably un-
         published (see WU12). Version for two pianos:
         Enoch, 1895. No. 1: Le Matin. PPN 2414; No. 2: Le
         Soir. PPN 2415.

Selected performances

W106a   [1896]; Lausanne; Rudolph Ganz and Chami-
         nade, piano. See B245.

W106b   1904 (April); Paris; Salle Aeolian; Gabri-
         elle Turpin and Chaminade, piano.

W106c   1928 (5 February); Rouen; Mustel's; fes-
         tival of Chaminade music, organized by
         Marie Capoy; orchestral version. See
         B429.

W107a   [1896]; Lausanne; Rudolph Ganz and Chami-
         nade, piano. See B245.

W107b   1904 (April); Paris; Salle Aeolian; Gabri-
         elle Turpin and Chaminade, piano.

W108   Troisième Valse Brillante, Op. 80. Piano. Enoch,
         1898. PPN 3744. 11 pages. Dedicated to Ella Pan-
         cera.

Selected performances

W108a   1908 (16 November); Milwaukee; Pabst Thea-
         ter; Chaminade, piano. See B352.

W108b   1908 (8 December); Washington, D. C.; Na-
         tional Theater; Chaminade, piano. See
         B379.

W108c   1978 (9 December); Aix-en-Provence; Le Rex;
         Wilfrid Maggiar, piano. See B470.

W109   Terpsichore, 6me Air de Ballet, Op. 81. Piano.
         Enoch, 1896. PPN 2793. 7 pages. Dedicated to Mad-
         ame Emile S. Enoch.

W110   Chanson Napolitaine, Op. 82. Piano. Enoch, 1896.
         PPN 2794. 5 pages. Dedicated to Eschmann Dumur.

W111   Ritournelle, Op. 83. Piano. Transcription of the
         song; see W265. Enoch, 1896. PPN 2795.

W112-14   Trois Préludes Mélodiques, Op. 84. Piano. Enoch,
           1896. Dedicated to Berthe Marx-Goldschmidt. AUTO-
           GRAPH: Family. No. 1: a minor. PPN 2796; No. 2: F
           major. PPN 2797; No. 3: d minor. PPN 2798.

           See B438.

           Selected performances

           W114a   1928 (5 February); Rouen; Mustel's; fes-
                    tival of Chaminade works, organized by
                    Marie Capoy; Mlle. Grégoire, piano.

           W112-14b 1978 (9 December); Aix-en-Provence; Le
                     Rex; Wilfrid Maggiar, piano. See B470.

W115   Vert-Galant, Op. 85. Piano. Enoch, 1896. PPN 3092.
           7 pages. AUTOGRAPH: Family.

           Selected performances

           W115a   [1897]; Berlin; Bechsteinsaal; Chaminade,
                    piano.

           W115b   1978 (9 December); Aix-en-Provence; Le Rex;
                    Wilfrid Maggiar, piano. See B470.

W116   Ballade [Impromptu], Op. 86. Piano. Enoch, [1896].
           PPN 3101. 9 pages. Dedicated to Francis Planté.

W117-22   Six Pièces Humoristiques, Op. 87. Piano. Enoch,
           1897. PPN 3117-22. No. 1: Réveil. 5 pages. Dedi-
           cated to Marie Gabry. AUTOGRAPH: Family; No. 2:
           Sous Bois. 6 pages. Dedicated to Gustave Dionis.
           AUTOGRAPH: Family; No. 3: Inquiétude. 7 pages.
           Dedicated to Rudolphe Ganz. AUTOGRAPH: Family;
           No. 4: Autrefois. [7 pages.] Dedicated to Stefan-
           ski. AUTOGRAPH: Family; No. 5: Consolation. 8
           pages. Dedicated to Aimée Gabry; No. 6: Norwégi-
           enne. 7 pages. Dedicated to Lucien Wurmser.

           Selected performances

           W120a   1898 (10 June); London; St. James's Hall;
                    Chaminade, piano. See B251.

           W117-22a [1898]; Le Havre; Chaminade, piano. See
                     B255.

           W121b   1908 (24 October); New York; Carnegie Hall;
                    Chaminade, piano. See B316, B319.

           W121c   1908 (9 November); Louisville; Macauley's
                    Theater; Chaminade, piano.

           W121d   1908 (8 December); Washington, D. C.; Na-
                    tional Theater; Chaminade, piano. See
                    B378.

W121e   1979 (16 May); Paris; Salle Cortot; Wilfrid
Maggiar, piano.

W123   Rimembranza, Op. 88. Piano. Enoch, 1898. PPN 3558.
7 pages. Dedicated to L. Carembat. AUTOGRAPH:
Family.

W124   Thème varié, Op. 89. Piano. Enoch, 1898. PPN 3559.
9 pages. Dedicated to Rose Dépecker. AUTOGRAPH:
Family.

See B437.

Selected performances

W124a   1908 (24 October); New York; Carnegie Hall;
Chaminade, piano. See B312.

W124b   1908 (17 November); Minneapolis; Auditorium; Chaminade, piano.

W124c   1908 (22 November); Chicago; Orchestra
Hall; Chaminade, piano. See B362-63.

W124d   1908 (8 December); Washington, D. C.; National Theater; Chaminade, piano. See
B378.

W125   Légende, Op. 90. Piano. Enoch, 1898. PPN 3637. 9
pages. Dedicated to Gabriel Pierné.

W126   Quatrième Valse, Op. 91. Piano. Enoch, 1901. PPN
4849. 11 pages. Dedicated to Lucien Wurmser. AU-
TOGRAPH: Family.

Selected performances

W126a   1908 (6-7 November); Philadelphia; American
Academy of Music; Chaminade, piano. See
B332, B334.

W126b   1908 (9 December); Philadelphia; American
Academy of Music; Chaminade, piano. See
B381.

W127   Deuxième Arabesque, Op. 92. Piano. Enoch, 1898. PPN
3709. 8 pages. Dedicated to Santiago Rièra. AUTO-
GRAPH: Family.

W128   Valse Humoristique, Op. 93. Piano. Enoch, 1906. PPN
6428. 8 pages. Dedicated to Madame Charbonnet-
Kellermann.

W129   Danse Créole (Deuxième Havanaise), Op. 94. Piano.
Enoch, 1898. PPN 3896. 5 pages. Dedicated "à ma
nièce Antoinette Chaminade." AUTOGRAPH: Family.

See B288.

Selected Performance

W129a   1979 (16 May); Paris; Salle Cortot; Wilfrid
         Maggiar, piano.

W130-32 Trois Danses Anciennes, Op. 95. Piano. Enoch, 1899.
         PPN 4028-30. AUTOGRAPH: Family. No. 1: Passepied.
         4 pages. Dedicated to Alice Garnier; No. 2: Pa-
         vane. 5 pages. Dedicated to Edmond de Laheudrie;
         No. 3: Courante. 4 pages. Dedicated to Gustave
         Baume.

         See B403.

         Selected performances

W131a   1928 (5 February); Rouen; Mustel's; fes-
         tival of music by Chaminade, organized by
         Marie Capoy; Mlle Grégoire, piano. See
         B429.

W132a   1908 (6-7 November); Philadelphia; American
         Academy of Music; Chaminade, piano. See
         B332, B334.

W132b   1928 (5 February); Rouen; Mustel's; fes-
         tival of music by Chaminade, organized by
         Marie Capoy; Mlle. Grégoire, piano. See
         B429.

W133   Chant du Nord, Op. 96. Piano. Enoch, 1899. PPN 40-
         26. 7 pages. Dedicated to Edouard Naduad.

         Selected performance

W133a   1928 (5 February); Rouen; Mustel's; fes-
         tival of Chaminade works, organized by
         Marie Capoy; G. Tessier, violin; Mlle.
         Grégoire, piano.

W134   Rondeau, Op. 97. Violin & piano. Enoch, 1899. PPN
         4027. Dedicated to Paul Viardot.

W135-40 Six Feuillets d'Album, Op. 90. Piano. Enoch, 1900.
         PPN 4339-44. No. 1: Promenade. 7 pages. Dedicated
         to L. L. Jouve; No. 2: Scherzetto. 6 pages. Dedi-
         cated to Clotilde Kleeberg; No. 3: Elégie. 5
         pages. Dedicated to Alice Sauvrezis; No. 4: Valse
         Arabesque. 8 pages. Dedicated to Madame Roger-
         Miclos; No. 5: Chanson Russe. 5 pages. Dedicated
         to Auzende. See WC4; No. 6: Rondo Allègre. 8
         pages. Dedicated to Madame Riss-Arbeau.

W141-46 Poèmes Evangéliques, Op. 99. Female choir & piano.
         Text by Edouard Guinand. Enoch, 1903. Dedicated
         "à Madame Ryckebusch, Supérintendante des Maisons
         Nationales d'Education de la Légion d'Honneur."
         No. 1: L'Etoile. PPN 5229. 8 pages. "L'étoile a
         dirigé la route;" No. 2: Les Humbles. PPN 5231. 7

pages. "Humbles;" No. 3: <u>Les Pêcheurs</u>. PPN 52-
33. 11 pages. "Sur la marque;" No. 4: <u>La Jeune</u>
<u>Fille</u>. PPN 5235. 7 pages. "Devant la maison;" No.
5: <u>Les Petits Enfants</u>. PPN 5237. 7 pages. "Au
delà;" No. 6: <u>Sainte-Magdeleine</u>. PPN 5239. 8
pages. "Magdeleine."

See B272.

W147   <u>Aux Dieux Sylvains</u>, Op. 100. Female choir (sopranos
& contraltos) & piano. Text by Paul Collin.
Enoch, 1900. PPN 4499. 11 pages. Dedicated to
Mademoiselle Jumel. "Aux dieux familiers." AUTO-
GRAPH: Family.

W148   <u>L'Ondine</u>, Op. 101. Piano. Enoch, 1900. PPN 4566. 7
pages. Dedicated to Madame J. Schidenhelm.

<u>Selected performances</u>

W148a   1908 (24 October); New York; Carnegie Hall;
Chaminade, piano. <u>See</u> B316.

W148b   1908 (22 November); Chicago; Orchestra
Hall; Chaminade, piano. <u>See</u> B358, B362.

W148c   1908 (8 December); Washington, D. C.; National Theater; Chaminade, piano. <u>See</u>
B378.

W148d   1978 (9 December); Aix-en-Provence; Le Rex;
Wilfrid Maggiar, piano. <u>See</u> B470.

W149   <u>Joie d'Aimer</u>, Op. 102. Mezzo-soprano, baritone, &
piano. Text by Edouard Guinand. Enoch, 1900. PPN
4567. 8 pages. Dedicated to Fernand Raquez. "Eb-
louissons nos yeux."

<u>Selected performances</u>

W149a   1908 (24 October); New York; Carnegie Hall;
Yvonne de St. André, mezzo soprano; Ernest Groom, baritone; Chaminade, piano.

W149b   1908 (9 October); Philadelphia; American
Academy of Music; Yvonne de St. André,
mezzo soprano; Ernest Groom, baritone;
Chaminade, piano.

W150   <u>Moment Musical</u>, Op. 103. Piano. Enoch, 1900. PPN
4569. 7 pages. Dedicated to Mademoiselle Barbier-
Jussy.

<u>Selected performance</u>

W150a   1979 (16 May); Paris; Salle Cortot; Wilfrid
Maggiar, piano.

W151   Tristesse, Op. 104. Piano. Enoch, 1901. PPN 4848. 7
        pages. Dedicated to Alice Beaufils.

        Selected performance

        W151a   1978 (9 December); Aix-en-Provence; Le Rex;
                 Wilfrid Maggiar, piano. See B470.

W152   Divertissement, Op. 105. Piano. Enoch, 1901. PPN
        4847. 9 pages. Dedicated to Mademoiselle Rivet.

W153   Expansion, Op. 106. Piano. Enoch, 1901. PPN 4861. 7
        pages. Dedicated to Madame Lacroix-Lamoureux.

W154   Concertino, Op. 107. Flute & orchestra: flute, 2
        oboes, 2 clarinets, 2 bassoons, 4 horns, 3 trom-
        bones, tuba, 3 timpani, harp, violins I & II,
        violas, cellos, double basses. Enoch, [1902]. PPN
        6683. 46 pages.

        Composed as an official contest piece for the
        1902 competition at the Paris Conservatoire.

        Version for flute & piano: Enoch, 1902. PPN 5161.

        See B474.

        Selected performances

        W154a   1904 (April); Paris; Hall of Musica magaz-
                 ine; version with piano; Lafleurance,
                 flute; Gabrielle Turpin, piano. See B284.

        W154b   1907 (21 October); London; Aeolian Hall;
                 Frederic Griffith, flute; Chaminade,
                 piano. See B293.

        W154c   [1909] (November); Bordeaux; Grande Salle
                 Franklin; Hennebains, flute; Chaminade,
                 piano. See B399.

        W154d   1922 (30 September); London; Central Hall;
                 Louis Fleury, flute; Chaminade, piano.
                 See B425.

        W154e   [1928] (6 July); Rouen; part of lecture and
                 performance of works of Chaminade organ-
                 ized by Marie Capoy; Louis Martin, flute;
                 Thérèse Mauger, piano. See B433.

        W154f   1937 (2-3 January); New York; Carnegie
                 Hall; Philharmonic-Symphony Society of
                 New York, conducted by John Barbirolli;
                 John Amans, flute. See B439-40.

W155   Agitato, Op. 108. Piano. Enoch, 1902. PPN 5215. 7
        pages. Dedicated to Yvonne Péan.

W156   Cinquième Valse (Valse Militaire), Op. 109. Piano.
            Enoch, 1902. PPN 5216.

W157   Novelette, Op. 110. piano. Enoch, 1903. PPN 5632. 7
            pages. Dedicated to Ricardo Castro.

            Selected performance

            W157a   1979 (16 May); Paris; Salle Cortot; Wilfrid
                     Maggiar, piano.

W158   Souvenirs Lointains, Op. 111. Piano. Enoch, 1903.
            PPN 5633. 7 pages. Dedicated to Madame Charles
            Ganivet.

W159   Valse-Ballet (Sixième Valse), Op. 112. Piano.
            Enoch, 1904. PPN 5674. 8 pages. Dedicated to Clé-
            mentine Koch.

W160   Caprice Humoristique, Op. 113. Piano. Enoch, 1904.
            PPN 5762. 11 pages. Dedicated to Théodore Thur-
            ner.

            Selected performances

            W160a   1907 (29 May); London; Aeolian Hall; Chami-
                     nade, piano. See B291.

            W160b   1908 (12 November); Cincinnati; Grand Opera
                     House; Chaminade, piano.

            W160c   1908 (8 December); Washington, D. C.; Na-
                     tional Theater; Chaminade, piano. See
                     B378.

W161   Pastorale, Op. 114. Piano. PPN 5913. 7 pages. Dedi-
            cated to Gabrielle Steiger.

            Selected performances

            W161a   1908 (24 October); New York; Carnegie Hall;
                     Chaminade, piano. See B312, B316, B319.

            W161b   1908 (22 November); Chicago; Orchestra
                     Hall; Chaminade, piano. See B358.

            W161c   1908 (8 December); Washington, D. C.; Na-
                     tional Theater; Chaminade, piano. See
                     B378-80.

W162   Valse Romantique (Septième Valse), Op. 115. Piano.
            Enoch, 1905. PPN 5949. 11 pages. Dedicated to
            Marie Panthès.

            Selected performances

            W162a   1907 (29 May); London; Aeolian Hall; Chami-
                     nade, piano. See B290.

W162b   1908 (24 October); New York; Carnegie Hall; Chaminade, piano. See B312, B319.

W162c   1908 (16 November); Milwaukee; Pabst Theater; Chaminade, piano. See B352.

W162d   1908 (8 December); Washington, D. C.; National Theater; Chaminade, piano. See B378-79.

W163   Sous Le Masque, Op. 116. Piano. Enoch, 1905. PPN 6025. 7 pages. Dedicated to Madame Saillard-Dietz.

W164   Duo Symphonique, Op. 117. Two pianos. Enoch, 1905. PPN 6194. Dedicated to Joseph Baume.

W165   Etude Mélodique, Op. 118. Piano. Enoch, 1906. PPN 6235. 8 pages. Dedicated to Jeanne Dionis. See WC3.

See B403.

Selected Performance

W165a   1907 (29 May); London; Aeolian Hall; Chaminade, piano. See B291.

W166   Valse Tendre, Op. 119. Piano. Enoch, 1906. PPN 6260. 8 pages. Also published by Enoch (same year, same plates) with title Débutante-Waltz. Under the latter it was probably published also in The Ladies Home Journal, sometime in 1906. No dedicatee.

W167   Variations sur un Thème Original, Op. 120. Piano. Enoch, 1906. PPN 6308. 12 pages. Dedicated to André Turcat.

Selected Performance

W167a   1978 (9 December); Aix-en-Provence; Le Rex; Wilfrid Maggiar, piano. See B470.

W168   Deuxième Gavotte, Op. 121. Piano. Enoch, 1906. PPN 6309. 7 pages. Dedicated to Madame A. Thurner.

Selected performances

W168a   1908 (24 October); New York; Carnegie Hall; Chaminade, piano.

W168b   1978 (9 December); Aix-en-Provence; Le Rex; Wilfrid Maggiar, piano. See B470.

W169-71   Contes Bleus, Op. 122. Piano. Enoch, 1906. PPN 6321-23. No. 1: 5 pages. Dedicated "à ma nièce Antoinette Lorel"; No. 2: 5 pages. Dedicated to

Marguerite Livon; No. 3: [5] pages. Dedicated to
Louise Perny.

See B368.

Selected performances

W169-71a   1908 (22 November); Chicago; Orchestra
            Hall; two of the three are performed
            (titles unspecified); Chaminade, piano.
            See B358, B362-63.

W169-71b   1908 (8 December); Washington, D. C.;
            National Theater; Chaminade, piano. See
            B378-79.

W172-83   Album des Enfants, 1re Série, Op. 123. "Douze mor-
           ceaux très-faciles pour piano." Enoch, 1906. PPN
           6402-13. Most, if not all, are simpler versions
           of other compositions. No. 1: Prélude; No. 2:
           Intermezzo; No. 3: Canzonetta; No. 4: Rondeau;
           No. 5: Gavotte; No. 6: Gigue; No. 7: Romance; No.
           8: Barcarolle; No. 9: Orientale; No. 10: Taren-
           telle; No. 11: Air de Ballet; No. 12: Marche
           Russe.

W184   Etude Pathétique, Op. 124. Piano. Enoch, 1906. PPN
           6429. 8 pages. Dedicated "à Vicente Espinosa y
           Cuevas, Comte del Peñasco." See WC3.

W185-96   Album des Enfants, 2me Série, Op. 126. "Douze mor-
           ceaux très-faciles pour piano." Enoch, 1907. PPN
           6648-59. Like Op. 123, most, if not all, are sim-
           pler versions of other compositions. No. 1: I-
           dylle; No. 2: Aubade; No. 3: Rigaudon; No. 4:
           Eglogue; No. 5: Ballade; No. 6: Scherzo-Valse;
           No. 7: Elégie; No. 8: Novelette; No. 9: Patrouil-
           le; No. 10: Villanelle; No. 11: Conte de Fées;
           No. 12: Valse Mignonne. Dedicated to Rolande
           Beaudouin.

See B466.

Selected performances

W190a   1939 (c. 8 August); Lowell, Mass.; on a
         radio broadcast, in honor of Chaminade's
         birthday; Louis Guilbault, piano. See
         B443.

W192a   1939 (c. 8 August); same radio broadcast.
         See B443.

W197-200 Poème Provençal, Op. 127. Piano. Enoch, 1908. PPN
         6765-68. 4 volumes in one. No dedicatee. Vol. 1:
         Dans la Lande. 4 pages; Vol. 2: Solitude. 5
         pages; Vol. 3: Le Passé. 5 pages; Vol. 4: Les
         Pêcheurs de Nuit. 9 pages.

See B368.

W201   Pastel (Rosemary), Op. 128. Piano. Enoch, 1908. PPN
         6804. 8 pages. Dedicated to Mrs. Harry B. Hirsch.
         It may have appeared first in The Ladies Home
         Journal, in its issue of November 1908 (vol. 25,
         page 53); the sub-title reads, "Written Expressly
         for the Ladies Home Journal in Celebration of
         Mme. Chaminade's Present American Visit."

W202   Menuet Galant, Op. 129. Piano. Enoch, 1909. PPN
         6966. 7 pages. Dedicated to Frédéric Rowley.

W203   Pasacaille, Op. 130. Piano. Enoch, 1909. PPN 6967.
         7 pages. Dedicated to Désiré Walter.

W204   Marche Américaine, Op. 131. Piano. Enoch, 1909. PPN
         6968. 7 pages. Dedicated to John Philip Sousa.

W205   Etude Romantique, Op. 132. Piano. Enoch, 1909. PPN
         6973. 12 pages. Dedicated to Ossip Gabrilowitsch.
         See WC3.

         Selected Performance

W205a   1978 (9 December); Aix-en-Provence; Le Rex;
         Wilfrid Maggiar, piano. See B470.

W206   Ronde du Crépuscule, Op. 133. Female choir & solo-
         ist. Text by L. Fortolis. Enoch, 1909. PPN 6969.
         12 pages. "A l'heure." Dedicated to Léopold Ket-
         ten.

         Selected performance

W206a   [1928] (6 July); Rouen; Salle de la Société
         Industrielle; festival of Chaminade works
         organized by Marie Capoy; 6 voice stu-
         dents of Marie Capoy.

W207   Le Retour, Op. 134. Piano. Enoch, 1909. PPN 6972. 7
         pages. Dedicated to Madame Bloomfield-Zeisler.

         Selected performance

W207a   [1928] (6 July); Rouen; Salle de la Société
         Industrielle; festival of Chaminade works
         organized by Marie Capoy; Marie Capoy,
         piano. See B433.

W208   La Barque d'Amour, Op. 135. Piano. Enoch, 1910. PPN
         7173. 5 pages. Dedicated to Marguerite Labori.

W209   Capricietto, Op. 136. Piano. Enoch, 1910. PPN 7174.
         7 pages. Dedicated to Madame Moulinas.

W210   Romance en Ré, Op. 137. Piano. Enoch, 1910. PPN
         7175. 5 pages. Dedicated to Madame Reichard.

Selected performance

W210a   1978 (9 December); Aix-en-Provence; Le Rex;
         Wilfrid Maggiar, piano. See B470.

W211   Etude Humoristique, Op. 138. Piano. Enoch, 1910.
        PPN 7194. 11 pages. Dedicated to Francis Coye.
        See WC3.

W212   Etude Scolastique, Op. 139. Piano. Enoch, 1910. PPN
        7195. Dedicated to Alice Kellermann. See WC3.

Selected performance

W212a   1978 (9 December); Aix-en-Provence; Le Rex;
         Wilfrid Maggiar, piano. See B470.

W213   Aubade, Op. 140. Piano. Based on Op. 126 No. 2; see
        W186. Enoch, 1911. PPN 7305. 4 pages.

W214   Suédoise, Op. 141. Piano. Enoch, 1911. PPN 7350. 7
        pages. Dedicated to Charles Gilbert Spross.

W215   Sérénade aux Etoiles, Op. 142. Flute & piano.
        Enoch, 1911. PPN 7352. 8 pages. Dedicated "à M.
        Hennebains, Professeur au Conservatoire."

W216   Cortège, Op. 143. Piano. Enoch, [1911]. PPN 7360. 8
        pages.

W217   Troisième Gavotte, Op. 144. Piano. Based on Op. 126
        No. 3; see W187. Enoch, 1911. PPN 7365. 8 pages.
        Dedicated to Madame Barrey-Allard.

W218   Scherzo-Caprice, Op. 145. Piano. Enoch, 1912. PPN
        7482. 11 pages. Dedicated to Will G. Cliff.

W219   Feuilles d'Automne, Op. 146. Piano. Enoch, 1912.
        PPN 7486. 7 pages. Dedicated to Madeleine Pin-
        cherle.

Selected performance

W219a   1978 (9 December); Aix-en-Provence; Le Rex;
         Wilfrid Maggiar, piano. See B470.

W220   Les Bohémiens, Scènes de Ballet, Op. 147. Piano.
        Enoch, 1913. PPN 7531. 11 pages. Dedicated to
        Elise Merlin.

W221   Scherzo-Valse, Op. 148. Piano. Based on Op. 126 No.
        6; see W190. Enoch, 1913. PPN 7542. 7 pages. Ded-
        icated to Marie-Anne Sallentin.

Selected performance

W221a   1978 (9 December); Aix-en-Provence; Le Rex;
         Wilfrid Maggiar, piano. See B470.

W222   Quatrième Gavotte, Op. 149. Piano. Enoch, 1913. PPN
        7573. 8 pages. Dedicated to Madame Hiard-Kuehn.

W223   Chanson (Sérénade) Espagnole, Op. 150. Transcrip-
        tion, for various media, of the song; see W315.
        Dedicated to Mesdemoiselles Rondanelli.

        Version for piano: Enoch, 1895. 5 pages. See also
        WC4.

        Version for piano duet: Enoch, [c. 1913].

        Version for violin & piano: transcribed by Leder-
        er. Enoch, 1903. PPN 5593. Also transcribed by
        Fritz Kreisler. Enoch, 1925. PPN 8397. AUTOGRAPH:
        Library of Congress. The Kreisler transcription
        is the version most often recorded.

        Selected performances

        W223a   1928 (5 February); Rouen; Mustel's; fes-
                 tival of Chaminade works, organized by
                 Marie Capoy; for violin and piano; G.
                 Tessier, violin; Mlle. Grégoire, piano.
                 See B430.

        W223b   [1928] (6 July); Rouen; Salle de la Société
                 Industrielle; lecture and demonstration
                 of works by Chaminade, organized by Marie
                 Capoy; Mlle. Mahé-Boislandelle, violin;
                 Thérèse Mauger, piano. See B433.

        W223c   1979 (16 May); Paris; Salle Cortot; Wilfrid
                 Maggiar, piano.

W224   Ecossaise, Op. 151. Piano. Enoch, 1914. PPN 7731. 8
        pages. Dedicated to Madame M. T. Amirian.

W225   Interlude, Op. 152. Piano. Enoch, 1914. PPN 7732. 7
        pages. Dedicated to Madame Luis Alonso.

W226   Caprice-Impromptu, Op. 153. Piano. Enoch, 1914. PPN
        7745. 8 pages. Dedicated to Yvonne Hédoux.

W227   Sérénade Vénitienne, Op. 154. Piano. Enoch, 1914.
        PPN 7767. 7 pages.

W228   Au Pays Dévasté, Op. 155. Piano. Enoch, 1919. PPN
        7837. 5 pages. Dedicated to Joseph Baume.

W229   Berceuse du Petit Soldat Blessé, Op. 156. Piano.
        Enoch, 1919. PPN 7838. Dedicated to Germaine
        Lack.

        Selected performance

        W229a   1922 (30 September); London; Central Hall;
                 Chaminade, piano. See B425.

W230   Chanson d'Orient, Op. 157. Piano. Enoch, 1919. PPN
        7839. 4 pages. Dedicated "à la signorina Giovanna
        Bruna Balducci."

W231   Danse Paienne, Op. 158. Piano. Enoch, 1919. PPN
        7840. 9 pages. Dedicated to Renée Gardon.

W232   Les Elfes des Bois, Op. 159. Female choir, soloist,
        & piano. Text by L. Fortolis. Enoch, 1920. PPN
        7890.

W233   Les Sirènes, Op. 160. Mixed chorus, soloists, &
        piano. Enoch, 1920. PPN 7892. 12 pages. "Il a
        neigé plus d'un hiver." Dedicated "à Maxime Tho-
        mas et à sa chorale."

W234   Chanson Nègre, Op. 161. Piano. Enoch, 1921. PPN
        7969. 8 pages. Dedicated to C. Budden-Morris.

        Selected performance

        W234a   1922 (30 September); London; Central Hall;
                 Chaminade, piano. See B425.

W235   Cinquième Gavotte, Op. 162. Piano. Enoch, 1921. PPN
        7970. 7 pages. Dedicated to Blanche David.

W236   Romanesca, Op. 163. Piano. Enoch, 1923. PPN 8106. 5
        pages.

W237   Air à Danser, Op. 164. Piano. Enoch, 1923. PPN
        8107. 5 pages. No dedicatee.

W238   Nocturne, Op. 165. Piano. Enoch, 1925. PPN 8381. 7
        pages. Dedicated to Reginald Reynolds.

        Selected performance

        W238a   1928 (5 February); Rouen; Mustel's; fes-
                 tival of Chaminade works, organized by
                 Marie Capoy; Mlle. Grégoire, piano.

W239   Berceuse Arabe, Op. 166. Piano. Enoch, 1925. PPN
        8382. 4 pages. Dedicated to Jeanne Pinkerle.

W240-44 Messe, Op. 167. Two equal voice parts & organ or
        harmonium. Enoch, 1927. PPN 8611-15. Dedicated
        "au Révérand Père J. B. Charbonnier." Kyrie, Glo-
        ria, Sanctus & Benedictus, O Salutaris, Agnus
        Dei. AUTOGRAPH (entire): Family.

        Selected performances

        W241a   1928 (5 February); Rouen; Mustel's; fes-
                 tival of music by Chaminade, organized by
                 Marie Capoy; chorus of students of Marie
                 Capoy. See B429.

W243a   1928 (5 February); Rouen; Mustel's; fes-
         tival of music by Chaminade, organized by
         Marie Capoy; chorus of students of Marie
         Capoy. See B429.

W245   Dans l'Arène, Op. 168. Piano. Enoch, 1928. PPN 86-
        37.

W246   Valse d'Automne, Op. 169. Piano. Enoch, 1928. PPN
        8638. 7 pages. Dedicated to Madame Pellenc.

W247   Air Italien (Au Pays Bleu), Op. 170. Enoch, [1928].
        PPN 8665. See also WC4.

W248-56   La Nef Sacrée. Receuil de Pièces pour Orgue ou Har-
           monium, Op. 171. Enoch, 1928. PPN 8711. Contains
           9 pieces: Offertoire (Au Christ-Roi); Offertoire
           (ou Communion); Offertoire (La Madone); Offer-
           toire (Le 2 Novembre); Offertoire (pour une Messe
           de Mariage); Offertoire (pour la Toussaint); Qua-
           tre Pastorales (pour la Messe de Minuit); Marche
           Funèbre; Cortège Nuptial.

PUBLISHED WORKS WITHOUT OPUS NUMBERS
Mélodies: Voice and Piano

W257   L'Heure du Mystère. Text by Pierre Barbier. J.
        Maho, [c. 1878]. Published later in collection
        Mélodies pour Chant et Piano. J. Hamelle, [c.
        1898].

        See B9.

        W257a   1880 (8 February); Paris; Salle Erard; Mad-
                 ame Brunet-Lafleur, soprano; Chaminade,
                 piano.

W258   Ninette. Text by M. de Fos. J. Maho, [c. 1878].
        Published in Hamelle collection of c. 1898.

        See B9.

W259   Les Papillons. Text by Théophile Gautier. J. Maho,
        [c. 1878]. Published in Hamelle collection of c.
        1898. Dedicated to Pauline de Potocka. AUTOGRAPH:
        Bibliothèque Nationale.

        See B9.

        Premiere

        W259a   1878 (25 April); Paris; home of Le Couppey;
                 Henriette Fuchs, soprano; Chaminade,
                 piano. See B7-8.

W260   Sous Ta Fenêtre. Text by M. de Fos. J. Maho, [c.
       1878]. Published in Hamelle collection of c.
       1898.

       See B9.

       Premiere

       W260a   1878 (25 April); Paris; home of Le Couppey;
               Vergnet, male vocalist; Chaminade, piano.

W261   Te Souviens-Tu. J. Maho, [c. 1878]. Probably pub-
       lished in Hamelle collection of c. 1898.

       See B9.

       Premiere

       W261a   1878 (25 April); Paris; home of Le Couppey;
               Vergnet, male vocalist; Chaminade, piano.
               See B7.

       Selected performances

       W261b   1880 (8 February); Paris; Salle Erard; Mon-
               sieur Bosquin, vocalist; Chaminade,
               piano. See B14-15.

       W261c   1882 (15 April); Paris; Salle Herz; Mazal-
               bert, tenor; Chaminade, piano. See B54.

W262   Chanson Slave. Text by Paul Ginisty. Published in
       Album du Gaulois, 15 December 1885, pp. 162-65.
       Later published by Enoch & Costallat, 1887. PPN
       1362. 5 pages. "Dans mon beau pays." Dedicated to
       Madame Brunet-Lafleur. See also WC6.

       Selected performances

       W262a   1880 (8 February); Paris; Salle Erard; Mme.
               Brunet-Lafleur, soprano; Chaminade,
               piano. See B14-15.

       W262b   1886 (4 February); Paris; Salle Erard; Maz-
               albert, tenor; Chaminade, piano.

       W262c   1888 (11 March); Marseille; home of the
               Livons; Pauline Costes, vocalist; Chami-
               nade, piano. See B101.

       W262d   1888 (18 April); Anvers, Belgium; Cercle
               Catholique; Mme. De Give, vocalist; Cha-
               minade, piano. See B128b.

       W262e   1888 (last half); Lyon; home of music pub-
               lisher E. Clot; Mme. Mauvernay, vocalist;
               Chaminade, piano. See B137.

W262f   1891 (20-21 February); New York; Carnegie
         Hall; Philharmonic-Symphony Society; Mrs.
         W. C. Wyman, vocalist.

W262g   1897 (10 June); London; St. James's Hall;
         Clara Butt, vocalist; Chaminade, piano.
         See B251.

W262h   1908 (9 December); Philadelphia; American
         Academy of Music; Yvonne de St. André,
         mezzo soprano; Chaminade, piano.

W263   Madeleine. Text by Edouard Guinand. Enoch & Costal-
        lat, 1886. PPN 1133. 7 pages. "Nous allions
        boire." Dedicated to Mademoiselle E. Bonnefin.

        Selected performances

        W263a   1880 (8 February); Paris; Salle Erard; Mad-
                 ame Brunet-Lafleur, soprano; Chaminade,
                 piano.

        W263b   1888 (11 March); Marseille; home of the
                 Livons; Pauline Costes, vocalist; Chami-
                 nade, piano. See B101.

W264   Souhait. Text by Georges van Ormelingen. Enoch &
        Costallat, 1886. PPN 1134. 5 pages. "Si quelque
        bonne fée." Dedicated to Marie Tayau. See also
        WC6.

W265   Ritournelle. Text by François Coppée. Enoch & Cos-
        tallat, 1886. PPN 1136. 5 pages. "Dans la plaine
        blonde." Dedicated to Lauwers. AUTOGRAPH: Biblio-
        thèque Nationale; see also WC6. See also the
        piano version, W111 (Op. 83).

        Selected performances

        W265a   1886 (4 February); Paris; Salle Erard; Maz-
                 albert, tenor; Chaminade, piano.

        W265b   1888 (11 March); Marseille; home of the
                 Livons; Mlle. Rastit, vocalist; Chami-
                 nade, piano. See B101.

        W265c   1888 (last half); Lyon; home of music pub-
                 lisher E. Clot; Mme. Mauvernay, vocalist;
                 Chaminade, piano. See B137.

        W265d   1899 (late May); St.-Quentin; Mme. Danner,
                 vocalist; Chaminade, piano. See B266.

        W265e   1908 (24 October); New York; Carnegie Hall;
                 Ernest Groom, baritone; Chaminade, piano.

W266   Madrigal. Text by Georges van Ormelingen. Enoch &
        Costallat, 1886. PPN 1138. 5 pages. "Tes doux

baisers." Dedicated to Madame W. Enoch. AUTO-
GRAPH: Library of Congress. See also WC6.

Selected performances

W266a   1886 (4 February); Paris; Salle Erard; Maz-
         albert, tenor; Chaminade, piano.

W266b   1888 (11 March); Marseille; home of the
         Livons; Mlle. Rastit, vocalist; Chami-
         nade, piano. See B101.

W266c   1888 (18 April); Anvers, Belgium; Cercle
         Catholique; Mlle. Hasselmans, vocalist;
         Chaminade, piano. See B128.

W266d   1888 (last half); Lyon; home of music pub-
         lisher E. Clot; Mme. Mauvernay, vocalist;
         Chaminade, piano. See B137.

W266e   1891 (early May); Paris; home of Léon Dela-
         fosse; Marie Veyssier, female vocalist;
         Delafosse, piano. See B180.

W266f   1894 (early June); London; St. James's
         Hall; Liza Lehmann, vocalist; Chaminade,
         piano. See B230.

W266g   1897 (10 June); London; St. James's Hall;
         Blanche Marchesi, vocalist; Chaminade,
         piano. See B251.

W266h   [1899]; Epinal; Le Théâtre; Mme. Nadier de
         Montjau, vocalist; Chaminade, piano. See
         B263.

W267   La Fiancée du Soldat. Text by Charles Grandmougin.
        Enoch & Costallat, 1887. PPN 1363. 5 pages. "Mon
        bien aimé." Dedicated to Madame Maurice Lecointe.
        See also WC6.

        Version for piano: Enoch, [1912]. No. 31 of ser-
        ies, Les Pianistes de Demain.

        Selected performances

        W267a   1888 (last half); Lyon; home of music pub-
                 lisher E. Clot; Mme. Mauvernay, vocalist;
                 Chaminade, piano. See B137.

        W267b   [1899]; Epinal; Le Théâtre; Mme. Nadier de
                 Montjau, vocalist; Chaminade, piano. See
                 B263.

W268   Auprès de Ma Vie. Text by Octave Pradels. Enoch &
        Costallat, [1888]. PPN 1466. 5 pages. "Si j'étais
        l'oiseau léger." Dedicated to Madame E. de Laval-
        lée. See also WC6.

Selected performance

W268a   1894 (early June); London; St. James's
         Hall; Mlle. Landi, vocalist; Chaminade,
         piano. See B230.

W269   L'Idéal. Text by Sully Prudhomme. Enoch & Costal-
        lat, 1888. PPN 1468. 3 pages. "La lune est gran-
        de." Dedicated to Léon van Hoof. See also WC6.

W270   Voisinage. Text by Henry Maigrot. Enoch & Costal-
        lat, 1888. PPN 1470. 5 pages. "Je n'avais pas
        encore vingt ans." Dedicated to Camille Périer.

Selected performance

W270a   1892 (23 June); London; St. James's Hall;
         Eugène Oudin, vocalist; Chaminade, piano.

W271   L'Absente. Text by Edouard Guinand. Enoch & Costal-
        lat, 1888. PPN 1471. 7 pages. "Vois le vent chas-
        sant la nue." Dedicated to Fanny Lépine. AUTO-
        GRAPH: Library of Congress. See also WC6.

Selected performance

W271a   1886 (4 February); Paris; Salle Erard; Maz-
         albert, tenor; Chaminade, piano.

W272   Serenata. Text by Edouard Guinand. Enoch & Costal-
        lat, 1888. PPN 1473. 5 pages. "La nuit est ser-
        eine et douce." Dedicated "à M. Delaquerrière de
        l'Opéra-Comique."

W273   Nice La Belle. Text by Auguste Marin. Enoch & Cos-
        tallat, 1889. PPN 1633. 7 pages. "Quand ton ciel
        se dore." Dedicated to Rose Delaunay.

Selected performance

W273a   1893 (12 March); Paris; Georges Mauguière,
         tenor; Chaminade, piano.

W274   Fragilité. Text by L. Hameau. Enoch & Costallat,
        1889. PPN 1635. 5 pages. "A travers la prairie."
        Dedicated to Madame Castillon.

W275   Fleur Jetée. Text by Armand Silvestre. Enoch & Cos-
        tallat, 1889. PPN 1636. 3 pages. "Emporte ma
        folie." Dedicated "à M. Giraudet Professeur au
        Conservatoire." See also WC6.

W276   Amour d'Automne. Text by Armand Silvestre. Enoch &
        Costallat, 1889. PPN 1638. 5 pages. "L'âpre hiver
        a passé." Dedicated to Madame M. Gallet. AUTO-
        GRAPH: Family. See also WC6.

W277   Les Deux Ménétriers. Scène pour baritone. Text by
        Jean Richepin. Enoch & Costallat, 1890. PPN 1715.

11 pages. "Sur des noirs chevaux." Dedicated "à M. Plançon de l'Opéra." AUTOGRAPH: Family. See WU11 for an unpublished orchestral version.

Selected performance

W277a   1894 (19 February); Geneva; Sylvain, bass; Chaminade, piano. See B214-15.

W278   Rêve d'Un Soir. Text by Eugène Adenis. Enoch & Costallat, 1890. PPN 1777. 3 pages. "Rêve d'un soir." Dedicated to Boudouresque, Jr. See also WC6.

Selected performance

W278a   1894 (19 February); Geneva; Sylvain, bass; Chaminade, piano. See B214-15.

W279   Vieux Portrait. Text by Rosemonde Gérard. Enoch & Costallat, 1890. PPN 1778. 5 pages. "Dans le vieux salon." Dedicated to Madame Edouard Colonne.

W280   Les Rêves. Text by Louis Guays. Enoch & Costallat, 1891. PPN 1876. 5 pages. "Les rêves se posent sur nous." Dedicated to Madame Paul Hillemacher. See also WC6.

Selected performance

W280a   1893 (12 March); Paris; Georges Mauguière, tenor; Chaminade, piano.

W281   Plaintes d'Amour. Text by Eugène Adenis. Enoch & Costallat, 1891. PPN 1876. 5 pages. "L'amour, l'amour, fleur que Dieu bénit." Dedicated to Suzanne Lacombe. See also WC6.

Selected performances

W281a   1893 (12 March); Paris; Lucy Lammers, soprano; Chaminade, piano.

W281b   1907 (29 May); London; Aeolian Hall; Lydia Obree, vocalist; Chaminade, piano. See B291.

W282   Tu Me Dirais. Text by Rosemonde Gérard. Enoch & Costallat, 1891. PPN 1880. 4 pages. "Tu me dirais." Dedicated to Marie Veyssier. In Modern French Songs, ed. Philip Hale. Boston: Ditson, 1904. Reprint: Dover, 1978. See also WC6.

Selected performances

W282a   1892 (23 June); London; St. James's Hall; Eugène Oudin, vocalist; Chaminade, piano.

W282b   1894 (16 March); Reims; Grand Théâtre; Soc-
         iété Philharmonique; Mme. Essiani, vocal-
         ist; Chaminade, piano. See B223.

W282c   1897 (10 June); London; St. James's Hall;
         Blanche Marchesi, vocalist; Chaminade,
         piano. See B251.

W283   Amoroso. Text by Armand Silvestre. Enoch & Costal-
        lat, 1891. PPN 1882. 5 pages. "Du printemps, son-
        nant le baptème." Dedicated to Mademoiselle E.
        Manière. AUTOGRAPH: Family. See also WC6.

        Selected performance

W283a   1893 (1 June); London; St. James's Hall;
         Eugène Oudin, vocalist; Chaminade, piano.
         See B209.

W284   L'Anneau d'Argent. Text by Rosemonde Gérard. Enoch
        & Costallat, 1891. PPN 1895. 3 pages. "Le cher
        anneau d'argent." Dedicated to Madame Conneau.
        AUTOGRAPH: Family. See also WC6.

        See B294, B435, B447, B451, B454.

        Selected performances

W284a   1893 (12 March); Paris; P. Seguy, male vo-
         calist; Chaminade, piano.

W284b   1894 (early April); Paris; Mme. José Maya,
         vocalist; Chaminade, piano. See B227.

W284c   1894 (c. 4 June); London; St. James's Hall;
         Mlle. Landi, vocalist; Chaminade, piano.
         See B230.

W284d   1908 (24 October); New York; Carnegie Hall;
         Yvonne de St. André, mezzo soprano; Cham-
         inade, piano.

W284e   1908 (17 November); Minneapolis; Auditori-
         um; Yvonne de St. André, mezzo soprano;
         Chaminade, piano. See B353.

W284f   1908 (22 November); Chicago; Orchestra
         Hall; Yvonne de St. André, mezzo soprano;
         Chaminade, piano. See B363.

W284g   1928 (6 July); Rouen; Salle de la Société
         Industrielle; festival of Chaminade works
         organized by Marie Capoy; Marie Capoy,
         vocalist; Thérèse Mauger, piano.

W284h   1944 (14 April); broadcast on Radio Monte-
         Carlo the day after her death, as part of
         a tribute. See B446.

W285   Colette. Text by Pierre Barbier. Enoch & Costallat,
        1891. PPN 1911. 5 pages. "Avril a parlé." Dedi-
        cated to Félix Lévy. See also WC6.

W286   Sur la Plage. Text by Edouard Guinand. Enoch & Cos-
        tallat, [1892]. PPN 1972. 4 pages. "La vague
        vient sans cesse." Dedicated to Madame Deschamps-
        Jéhin. AUTOGRAPH: Family. See also WC6.

        Selected performance

        W286a   1895 (early June); London; St. James's
                 Hall; Mlle. Landi, vocalist; Chaminade,
                 piano. See B244.

W287   Berceuse. Text by Edouard Guinand. Enoch & Costal-
        lat, [1892]. PPN 2035. 3 pages. "Viens près de
        moi." Dedicated to Rosa Leo. AUTOGRAPH: Family.

W288   A L'Inconnue. Text by Charles Grandmougin. Enoch &
        Costallat, 1892. PPN 2037. 5 pages. "Toi que j'ai
        rencontré." Dedicated to Georges Mauguière. AUTO-
        GRAPH: Family.

        Selected performance

        W288a   1893 (12 March); Paris; Georges Mauguière,
                 tenor; Chaminade, piano.

W289   Le Rendez-Vous. Text by Charles Cros. Enoch & Cos-
        tallat, 1892. PPN 2039. 4 pages. "Ma belle amie
        est morte." Dedicated to Engel.

W290   Viens, Mon Bien-Aimé. Text by Armand La Prique.
        Enoch & Costallat, 1892. PPN 2051. 3 pages. "Les
        beaux jours." Dedicated to Madame Watto. AUTO-
        GRAPH: Family.

        See B447, B451, B454.

        Selected performances

        W290a   1893 (12 March); Paris; Bouyer, female voc-
                 alist; Chaminade, piano.

        W290b   1893 (1 June); London; St. James's Hall;
                 Mme. Oudin, vocalist; Chaminade, piano.
                 See B209.

        W290c   [1899]; Epinal; Le Théâtre; Mme. Nadier de
                 Montjau, vocalist; Chaminade, piano. See
                 B263.

W291   Invocation. Text by Victor Hugo. Enoch & Costallat,
        [1893]. PPN 2102. 5 pages. "O terre!" Dedicated
        "à Pol Plançon de l'Opéra." AUTOGRAPH: Family.

W292   L'Amour Captif. Text by Thérèse Maquet. Enoch &
        Costallat, [1893]. 4 pages. "Mignonne, à l'am-

our." Dedicated "à Pol Plançon de l'Opéra." AUTO-
GRAPH: Library of Congress.

Selected performances

W292a   1893 (12 March); Paris; P. Seguy, male vo-
         calist; Chaminade, piano.

W292b   1893 (1 June); London; St. James's Hall;
         Eugène Oudin, vocalist; Chaminade, piano.
         See B209.

W293   Ma Première Lettre. Text by Rosemonde Gérard. Enoch
        & Costallat, 1893. 4 pages. "Hélas! que nous oub-
        lions vite." Dedicated to Mademoiselle Landi.
        AUTOGRAPH: Family.

Selected performance

W293a   1928 (5 February); Rouen; Mustel's; fes-
         tival of Chaminade works, organized by
         Marie Capoy; Georges Mauguière, tenor;
         Mlle. Grégoire, piano. See B429.

W294   Malgré Nous. Text by Rosemonde Gérard. Enoch & Cos-
        tallat, 1893. PPN 2210. 5 pages. "Ce n'est pas la
        faute." Dedicated to Liza Lehmann. AUTOGRAPH:
        Family.

W295   Les Deux Coeurs (Chanson Bretonne). Text by Hippo-
        lyte Lucas. Enoch & Costallat, 1893. PPN 2227. 4
        pages. "Le coeur que tu m'avais donné." Dedicated
        to Madame de Saint-Armand Bowes.

W296   Si J'Etais Jardinier. Text by Roger Milès. Enoch &
        Costallat, 1893. PPN 2228. 5 pages. "Si j'étais
        jardinier." Dedicated "à M. Clément de l'Opéra
        Comique." AUTOGRAPH: Family. In Modern French
        Songs, ed. Philip Hale. Boston: Ditson, 1904.
        Reprint: Dover, 1978.

        See B447, B451, B454.

Selected performances

W296a   1895 (late May); Paris; Hôtel Continental;
         benefit concert organized by H. Logé;
         Marie Roze, vocalist. See B243.

W296b   1897 (10 June); London; St. James's Hall;
         Blanche Marchesi, vocalist; Chaminade,
         piano.

W296c   1908 (9 December); Philadelphia; American
         Academy of Music; Yvonne de St. André,
         mezzo soprano; Chaminade, piano.

W297   Le Noël des Oiseaux. Text by Armand Silvestre.
        Enoch & Costallat, 1893. PPN 2230. 5 pages.

"Petit Jésus." Dedicated "à Mme. Molé-Truffier, de l'Opéra Comique."

Selected performances

W297a   1895 (early June); London; St. James's Hall; Mlle. Landi, vocalist; Chaminade, piano. See B244.

W297b   1908 (9 December); Philadelphia; American Academy of Music; Yvonne de St. André, mezzo soprano; Chaminade, piano.

W298   Rosemonde. Text by Marc Constantin. Henri Tellier, [1894]. PPN 1130. 4 pages. "Pourquoi tarde-t-il à venir." Dedicated to Marie Hasselmans. See also WC6.

Composed April 1878 or earlier.

Premiere

W298a   1878 (25 April); Paris; home of Le Couppey; Henriette Fuchs, soprano; Chaminade, piano. See B7.

W299   Sérénade Sévillane. Text by Edouard Guinand. Henri Tellier, [1894]. PPN 1131. 6 pages. "Sur les bords." Dedicated to Mazalbert.

W300   Chanson Groënlandaise. Text by Jules Verne. Henri Tellier, [1894]. PPN 1132. 5 pages. "Le ciel est noir." Dedicated to Madame Edouard Lalo.

W301   Sombrero. Text by Edouard Guinand. Henri Tellier, [1894]. PPN 1133. 6 pages. "Qu'elle était mutine." Dedicated to Soulacroix.

W302   Mignonne. Text by Pierre de Ronsard. Henri Tellier, [1894]. PPN 1134. 4 pages. "Mignonne allons voir si la rose." Dedicated to Madame Brousse.

W303   L'Eté. Text by Edouard Guinand. Henri Tellier, [1894]. PPN 1135. 12 pages. "Ah! chantez." Dedicated to Mademoiselle Kiréevsky. See also WC6. See WU14 for an unpublished orchestral version.

W304   Ballade à La Lune. Text by Alfred de Musset. Henri Tellier, [1894]. PPN 1136. 7 pages. "C'était dans la nuit brune." Dedicated to Madame Edouard Colonne. AUTOGRAPH: Boston Public Library.

W305   Chant d'Amour. Text by Edouard Guinand. Henri Tellier, [1894]. PPN 1137. 4 pages. "Veux tu des diamants." Dedicated to Marcella Pregi.

W306   Villanelle. Text by Edouard Guinand. Henri Tellier, [1894]. PPN 1138. 8 pages. "Le blé superbe." Ded-

icated to Madame Jules Gouin. Also in Supplement
to L'Illustration, No. 2737, 1895.

Selected performance

W306a   [1899]; Epinal; Le Théâtre; Mme. Nadier de
          Montjau, vocalist; Chaminade, piano. See
          B263.

W307   Vieille Chanson. Text by Edouard Guinand. Henri
          Tellier, [1894]. PPN 1139. 4 pages. "Chaque prin-
          temps les hirondelles." Dedicated to Madame La-
          borde.

W308   Trahison. Text by Edouard Guinand. Henri Tellier,
          [1894]. PPN 1140. 7 pages. "Tu m'as trahie."
          Dedicated to Madame Mauvernay.

Selected performance

W308a   1899 (late May); St.-Quentin; Mme. Danner,
          vocalist; Chaminade, piano. See B266.

W309   Aubade. Text by Edouard Guinand. Henri Tellier,
          [1894]. PPN 1141. 5 pages. "Viens! la terre à
          peine éveillée." Dedicated to Madame de Lancha-
          tres.

          Piano version: see W186.

W310   Ressemblance. Text by Jean Rameau. Enoch, 1895. PPN
          2387. 4 pages. "J'eus un frère." Dedicated to
          Gabrielle Krauss.

W311   Ronde d'Amour. Text by Charles Fuster. Enoch, 1895.
          PPN 2389. 7 pages. "Ah! si l'amour." Dedicated to
          Madame Colombel. AUTOGRAPH: Family. Later pub-
          lished in Chansons Fin de Siècle et 1900, P. D'-
          Anjou, editor. La Lyre Chansonnière, 1943.

Selected performance

W311a   1928 (6 July); Rouen; Salle de la Société
          Industrielle; festival of Chaminade works
          organized by Marie Capoy; Marie Capoy,
          vocalist; Thérèse Mauger, piano.

W312   Râvana (Ballade Aryenne). Text by Chabrol. Enoch,
          1895. PPN 2398. 7 pages. "Il est une forêt loin-
          taine." AUTOGRAPH: Family.

W313   Viatique. Text by Eugène Manuel. Enoch, 1895. PPN
          2399. 4 pages. "Si vous voulez chanter." Dedi-
          cated to Jean de Reszké. AUTOGRAPH: Family.

Selected performances

W313a   1895 (early June); London; St. James's
         Hall; Ben Davies, vocalist; Chaminade,
         piano. See B244.

W313b   1898; Berlin; Bechsteinsaal; Georges Mau-
         guière, tenor; Chaminade, piano. See
         B254.

W313c   1899 (late May); St.-Quentin; Georges Mau-
         guière, tenor; Chaminade, piano. See
         B266.

W313d   1908 (24 October); New York; Carnegie Hall;
         Ernest Groom, baritone; Chaminade, piano.

W313e   1928 (5 February); Rouen; Mustel's; fes-
         tival of Chaminade works organized by
         Marie Capoy; Georges Mauguière, tenor;
         Mlle. Grégoire, piano. See B429.

W314   Toi. Text by Madame J. Thénard. Enoch, 1895. PPN
        2401. 3 pages. "Toi, rien que toi." Dedicated to
        Gabrielle Krauss.

W315   Chanson Espagnole. Text by Armand Lafrique. Enoch,
        1895. PPN 2403. 5 pages. "Brille encore." Dedi-
        cated to Emma Calvé. AUTOGRAPH: Family.

        Other versions: see W223.

W316   Partout. Text by Charles Fuster. Enoch, 1895. PPN
        2412. 7 pages. "Partout où l'amour a passé." Ded-
        icated to Madame Melba.

        Selected performance

        W316a   1895 (early June); London; St. James's
                 Hall; Esther Palliser, vocalist; Chami-
                 nade, piano. See B244.

W317   Espoir. Text by Charles Fuster. Enoch, 1895. PPN
        2675. 5 pages. "Ne dis pas que l'espoir." Dedi-
        cated to Mario Ancona. AUTOGRAPH: Family.

W318   Sans Amour. Text by Charles Fuster. Enoch, 1895.
        PPN 2677. 5 pages. "Oh! comme je les plains pour-
        tant." Dedicated to Madame Léopold Ketten. AUTO-
        GRAPH: Family.

        Selected performance

        W318a   1897 (10 June); London; St. James's Hall;
                 Blanche Marchesi, vocalist; Chaminade,
                 piano. See B251.

W319   Mandoline. Text by Charles Foley. Enoch, 1895. PPN
          2680. 7 pages. "Sous la balcon." Dedicated to
          Alfred Cottin. AUTOGRAPH: Family.

W320   Le Ciel est Bleu. Text by Charles Foley. Enoch,
          1895. PPN 2681. 4 pages. "Comment peut-on dire."
          Dedicated to F. Paolo Tosti.

W321   Mon Coeur Chante. Text by Charles Fuster. Enoch,
          1896. PPN 3093. 4 pages. "Mon coeur chante." Ded-
          icated to Madame Albani. AUTOGRAPH: Family.

          Selected performances

          W321a   1908 (24 October); New York; Carnegie Hall;
                   Yvonne de St. André, mezzo soprano; Cha-
                   minade, piano.

          W321b   1908 (17 November); Minneapolis; Chaminade,
                   piano. See B353.

W322   Fleur du Matin. Text by Charles Fuster. Enoch, -
          1896. PPN 3096. 4 pages. "Si tu pouvais venir."
          Dedicated to Henriette Moszkowski. Album leaf of
          the first four measures, in the composer's hand,
          signed, in the Pierpont Morgan Library, New York.

          Selected performance

          W322a   1908 (24 October); New York; Carnegie Hall;
                   Yvonne de St. André, mezzo soprano; Cha-
                   minade, piano.

W323   Avril S'Eveille. Text by Robert Myriel. Enoch, 18-
          96. PPN 3099. 4 pages. "Le printemps fond." Dedi-
          cated to Hardy-Thé. AUTOGRAPH: Family.

W324   Veux-Tu? Text by Paul Collin. Enoch, 1896. PPN 31-
          02. 4 pages. "Aux jours envolés." Dedicated to
          Blanche Marchesi. AUTOGRAPH: Family.

          Selected performance

          W324a   1897 (10 June); London; St. James's Hall;
                   Blanche Marchesi, vocalist; Chaminade,
                   piano. See B251.

W325   Couplets Bachiques. Text by H. Jacquet. Enoch, 18-
          96. PPN 3109. 5 pages. "Verse, verse." Dedicated
          to Mario Ancona.

W326   Nuit d'Eté. Text by Charles Fuster. Enoch, 1896.
          PPN 3114. 7 pages. "O nuit clémenté." Dedicated
          to Carlotta Desvignes.

Selected performances

W326a   1899 (9 June); London; St. James's Hall;
         Cécile Ketten, mezzo soprano; Chaminade,
         piano. See B267.

W326b   1908 (24 October); New York; Carnegie Hall;
         Yvonne de St. André, mezzo soprano; Cha-
         minade, piano.

W326c   1908 (22 November); Chicago; Orchestra
         Hall; Yvonne de St. André, mezzo soprano;
         Chaminade, piano. See B358, B363.

W326d   1928 (5 February); Rouen; Salle de la Soci-
         été Industrielle; festival of Chaminade
         works organized by Marie Capoy; Marie
         Capoy, vocalist; Thérèse Mauger, piano.

W327   Pièce Romantique. Text by Stéphan Bordide. A. Dur-
        and & Fils, 1897. PPN 5313. 3 pages. "Je rêvais,
        la douce folie." Transcription of Op. 9 No. 1;
        see W11.

W328   Bleus. Text by Charles Fuster. Enoch, 1898. PPN
        3497. 4 pages. "Le bleu des fleurs." Dedicated to
        Raymond Chanoine Davranches. AUTOGRAPH: Family.

W329   Chanson Triste. Text by Comtesse Joseph Rochaid.
        Enoch, 1898. PPN 3500. 5 pages. "Dans les pro-
        fondes mers." Dedicated to Charlotte Wyns. AUTO-
        GRAPH: Family.

W330   Les Présents. Text by Charles Fuster. Enoch, 1898.
        PPN 3503. 4 pages. "Bien aimé, tu m'as mis." Ded-
        icated to Madame Melba.

W331   Mots d'Amour. Text by Charles Fuster. Enoch, 1898.
        PPN 3543. 4 pages. "Quand je te dis." Dedicated
        to Paul Pecquery.

W332   Au Pays Bleu. Text by Charles Fuster. Enoch, 1898.
        PPN 3555. 5 pages. "C'était là-bas." Dedicated to
        Pol Plançon. AUTOGRAPH: Family. See W170, and
        also Petite Suite (WC4).

Selected performances

W332a   1899 (9 June); London; St. James's Hall;
         Pol Plançon, bass; Chaminade, piano. See
         B267.

W332b   1908 (24 October); New York; Carnegie Hall;
         Ernest Groom, baritone; Chaminade, piano.

W332c   1908 (24 November); St. Louis; Odeon; Er-
         nest Groom, baritone; Chaminade, piano.

W333   Amertume. Text by D. Enoch. Enoch, 1898. PPN 3617.
        5 pages. "Mon pauvre coeur." Dedicated to the
        Countess Mniszech.

W334   Vous Souvient-Il? Text by Marguerite Dreyfus. Ham-
        elle, 1898. PPN 4240. 5 pages. "Vous souvient-
        il." Dedicated to Maurice Lecointe.

W335   La Chanson du Fou. Hamelle, 1898.

        Premiere

        W335a   1878 (25 April); Paris; home of Le Couppey;
                 Vergnet, male vocalist; Chaminade, piano.
                 See B7-8.

W336   Immortalité. Text by Charles Fuster. Enoch, 1899.
        PPN 3890. 4 pages. "Nous ne gravons pas." Dedi-
        cated to Ed. Wancermez.

        Selected performances

        W336a   1899 (9 June); London; St. James's Hall;
                 Pol Plançon, bass; Chaminade, piano. See
                 B267.

        W336b   1908 (24 October); New York; Carnegie Hall;
                 Ernest Groom, baritone; Chaminade, piano.

W337   Jadis. Text by Edouard Guinand. Enoch, 1899. PPN
        3893. 5 pages. "Elle est vieille." Dedicated to
        Paul Seguy.

W338   Reste. Text by Robert Myriel. Enoch, 1899. PPN 39-
        73. 4 pages. "Reste près de moi." "Respectueuse-
        ment dédié à son Altesse Royalle la Princesse
        Henry de Battenberg."

        Selected performances

        W338a   1899 (9 June); London; St. James's Hall;
                 Pol Plançon, bass; Chaminade, piano. See
                 B267.

        W338b   1908 (24 October); New York; Carnegie Hall;
                 Ernest Groom, baritone; Chaminade, piano.

        W338c   1908 (22 November); Chicago; Orchestra
                 Hall; Ernest Groom, baritone; Chaminade,
                 piano. See B358.

W339   Les Trois Baisers. Text by Stéphan Bordèse. Enoch,
        1899. PPN 3976. 4 pages. "Sur ton col." Dedicated
        to Claire Cabanne. In collection Chansons de
        Page, with settings of Bordèse by twelve compo-
        sers.

W340   Rêves Défunts. Text by D. Enoch. Enoch, 1899. PPN
        3999. 4 pages. "Je songe encore." Dedicated to
        Georges Mauguière.

W341   Nuit Etoilée. Text by Camille Roy. Enoch, 1899. PPN
        4023. 5 pages. "La nuit t'apporte." Dedicated to
        Cécile Ketten.

W342   Le Beau Chanteur. Text by Robert Myriel. Enoch,
        1900. PPN 4345. 4 pages. "Mon ami." Dedicated to
        Madame Georges Marty.

W343   L'Extase. Text by Paul Robiquet. Enoch, 1900. PPN
        4348. 7 pages. "C'est l'heure." Dedicated to Mad-
        ame Georges Marty.

W344   Nous Nous Aimions. Text by Charles Fuster. Enoch,
        1900. PPN 4351. 4 pages. "Nous nous aimions."
        Dedicated to Rosa Verriest.

W345   C'Etait En Avril. Text by Edouard Pailleron. Enoch,
        1900. PPN 4354. 4 pages. "C'était en avril." Ded-
        icated to Louise Genicoud.

W346   L'Allée D'Eméraude et D'Or. Text by Robert Myriel.
        Enoch, 1900. PPN 4357. 4 pages. "Seul je m'avan-
        ce." Dedicated to Jane Bathori.

W347   Petits Coeurs. Text by Paul Robiquet. Enoch, 1900.
        PPN 4360. 4 pages. "Petits coeurs." Dedicated to
        Lucien Fugère.

W348   Console-Moi. Text by Charles Fuster. Enoch, 1900.
        PPN 4517. 5 pages. "Toute ma vie." Dedicated to
        Jeanne Perrouze.

W349   Conte de Fées. Text by Charles Fuster. Enoch, 1900.
        PPN 4520. 5 pages. "Je suis venu vers vous." Ded-
        icated "à M. Vaguet, de l'Opéra."

W350   La Damoiselle. Text by Robert Myriel. Enoch, 1900.
        PPN 4523. 4 pages. "Si notre nid d'aigle." Dedi-
        cated to Mademoiselle Ducasse.

W351   Le Charme D'Amour. Text by Robert Myriel. Enoch,
        1900. PPN 4581. 7 pages. "Chacun montre au
        doigt." Dedicated "à Mme. Renée Richard (de l'O-
        péra)."

W352   Au Firmament. Text by Paul Mariéton. Enoch, 1901.
        PPN 4651. 4 pages. "Montez au ciel." Dedicated to
        Mademoiselle de Mentque.

W353   Ton Sourire. Text by René Niverd. Enoch, 1901. PPN
        4664. 5 pages. "Ton sourire est léger." Dedicated
        to Maurice Bagès.

W354   La Plus Jolie. Text by Robert Myriel. Enoch, 1901.
        PPN 4839. 5 pages. "Sous le soleil." Dedicated to
        Le Lubez.

W355   L'Orgue. Text by Charles Cros. Enoch, 1901. PPN
        4842. 5 pages. "Sous un roi d'Allemagne." Dedi-
        cated to Lucien Fugère.

W356   Pourquoi. Text by J. Thénard. Enoch, 1901. PPN
        4844. 5 pages. "Pourquoi faut-il." Dedicated to
        Esther Palliser.

        Selected performance

        W356a   1908 (9 December); Philadelphia; American
                 Academy of Music; Yvonne de St. André,
                 mezzo soprano; Chaminade, piano.

W357   Alleluia. Text by Paul Mariéton. Enoch, 1901. PPN
        4862. 4 pages. "J'avais douté." Dedicated to Mar-
        cella Pregi. AUTOGRAPH: Bibliothèque Nationale.

W358   Mirage. Text by Edouard Guinand. Enoch, 1902. PPN
        5196. 5 pages. "J'ai vu, dans l'ombre." Dedicated
        to Madame O. Hériot.

W359   Ecrin. Text by René Niverd. Enoch, 1902. PPN 5217.
        5 pages. "Tes yeux malicieux." Dedicated "à Mlle.
        Jeanne Leclerc de l'Opéra Comique. Mélodie spé-
        cialement composée pour Musica. . . . Le Vésinet,
        5 juillet 1902." Appeared in Album-Musica, No. 1.
        Pierre Lafitte & Cie, 1902. Page 16 of the jour-
        nal contains tips on the performance of this
        piece, as well as the others in this supplement;
        see B279.

        Selected performances

        W359a   1904 (April); Paris; Salle Aeolian; Jeanne
                 Leclerc, vocalist; Chaminade, piano.

        W359b   1922 (30 September); London; Central Hall;
                 Dorothy Robson, vocalist; Chaminade,
                 piano. See B425.

W360   Infini. Text by Charles Fuster. Enoch, 1902. PPN
        5220. 4 pages. "Poursuivis par le même rêve."
        Dedicated to Yvonne de Saint-André.

W361   Roulis Des Grèves. Text by Baroness d'Ottenfels.
        Enoch, 1902. PPN 5223. 5 pages. "Roulis des grè-
        ves." Dedicated to Henriette Fuchs.

W362   Sommeil D'Enfant. Text by Amélie de Wailly. Enoch,
        1903. 5 pages. "Mon enfant s'est endormi." Dedi-
        cated to Madame Poilpot.

Selected performance

W362a   1928 (5 February); Rouen; Mustel's; fes-
         tival of Chaminade works organized by
         Marie Capoy; E. Dubruille, cello; Mlle.
         Grégoire, piano. See B430.

W363   Bonne Humeur. Text by Amélie de Wailly. Enoch, 19-
        03. PPN 5419. 4 pages. "Nous marchions." Dedi-
        cated to Madame Constans.

        Selected performances

W363a   1908 (24 October); New York; Carnegie Hall;
         Yvonne de St. André, mezzo soprano; Cha-
         minade, piano.

W363b   1908 (22 November); Chicago; Orchestra
         Hall; Yvonne de St. André, mezzo soprano;
         Chaminade, piano. See B358, B363.

W363c   1908 (3 December); Indianapolis; English's;
         Yvonne de St. André, mezzo soprano; Cha-
         minade, piano.

W364   Refrain De Novembre. Text by Paul Gravollet. Enoch,
        1903. PPN 5662. 4 pages. "Lonlaire lonla, voici
        la froidure." Dedicated to Ida Ekman. Also in Les
        Frissons. Poésies de Paul Gravollet. Hamelle,
        1905.

W365   Exil (Chanson Ancienne). Text by René Niverd.
        Enoch, 1904. PPN 5675. 4 pages. "Sans toi." Dedi-
        cated to Louis Dervis.

W366   Portrait (Valse Chantée). Text by Pierre Reyniel.
        Enoch, 1904. PPN 5678. 7 pages. "Son nom m'est
        doux." Dedicated to Madame Albani. See W386-87
        for other versions.

        Version for piano: Enoch 1911, PPN 7264, 5 pages.

        Version for violin and piano: Enoch 1911, PPN
            7265.

        Selected performance

W366a   1904 (April); Paris; Salle Aeolian; Jeanne
         Leclerc, vocalist; Puyans, flute; Chami-
         nade, piano. See B284.

W367   Chanson Forestière. Text by L. Fortolis. Enoch,
        1904. PPN 5737. 5 pages. "Dans la harpe." Dedi-
        cated to Paul Wiallard.

        Selected performance

W367a   1907 (29 May); London; Aeolian Hall; Chami-
         nade, piano. See B290.

W368   Meneut. Text by Pierre Reyniel. Enoch, 1904. PPN
        5740. 4 pages. "Dans votre robe." Dedicated to
        Madame Ronchini.

W369   Départ. Text by Armand Silvestre. Enoch, 1904. PPN
        5914. 3 pages. "Sur la route." Dedicated to Ma-
        demoiselle Baume.

W370   N'Est-Ce Pas? Text by Armand Silvestre. Enoch,
        1904. PPN 5918. 5 pages. "N'est-ce pas." Dedi-
        cated to Marie Capoy.

W371   Son Nom. Text by Pierre Reyniel. Enoch, 1904. PPN
        5920. 5 pages. "Son nom rayonne de lumière." Ded-
        icated to Gaëtane Vicq.

W372   Dites-Lui. Text by Pierre Reyniel. Enoch, 1905. PPN
        5950. 4 pages. "Dites-lui que je l'attends." Ded-
        icated to Blanche de Preyval.

W373   Voix Du Large. Text by Charles de Bussy. Enoch,
        1905. PPN 5983. 8 pages. "Perdus sur l'océan
        amer." Dedicated to R. Chanoine-Davanches.

W374   Ses Yeux. Text by Pierre Reyniel. Enoch, 1905. PPN
        6026. 4 pages. "Elle a des yeux pâles." Dedicated
        to Madame Astruc-Doria.

W375   Avenir. Text by Charles de Bussy. Enoch, 1905. PPN
        6037. 5 pages. "Quand les printemps." Dedicated
        to Edmond Wangermez.

W376   Amour Invisible. Text by Charles de Bussy. Enoch,
        1905. PPN 6047. 5 pages. "Comme une torche." Ded-
        icated "à M. Lassalle de l'Opéra."

        Selected performances

        W376a   1907 (29 May); London; Aeolian Hall; Lydia
                 Obree, vocalist; Chaminade, piano. See
                 B291.

        W376b   1908 (24 October); New York; Carnegie Hall;
                 Ernest Groom, baritone; Chaminade, piano.

        W376c   1908 (12 December); Boston; Symphony Hall;
                 Ernest Groom, baritone; Chaminade, piano.

W377   La Lune Paresseuse. Text by Charles de Bussy.
        Enoch, 1905. PPN 6050. 5 pages. "Dans un rayon de
        crépuscule." Dedicated to Marie Lasne.

        Selected performance

        W377a   1907 (29 May); London; Aeolian Hall; Lydia
                 Obree, vocalist; Chaminade, piano. See
                 B291.

W378 La Reine De Mon Coeur. Text by Charles de Bussy. Enoch, 1905. PPN 6232. 7 pages. "La reine de mon coeur." Dedicated to Madame Revello.

    Selected performance

    W378a 1908 (24 October); New York; Carnegie Hall; Yvonne de St. André, mezzo soprano; Chaminade, piano.

W379 Un Souffle A Passé. Text by Pierre Reyniel. Enoch, 1906. PPN 6310. 4 pages. "Un souffle a passé." Dedicated to Arthur Michaud.

W380 Chanson De Neige. Text by L. Fortolis. Enoch, 1906. PPN 6485. 5 pages. "O neige, blanche neige." Dedicated to Irma Rastit.

W381 Chanson Naive. Text by Pierre Reyniel. Enoch, 1907. PPN 6514. 5 pages. "La petite chanson."

W382 Les Heureuses. Text by Charles Fuster. Enoch, 1909. PPN 6981. 5 pages. "Les fleurs ont des yeux de femmes." Copy of 1st edition at Stanford University is inscribed to Suzanne Astruc by the composer.

W383 Lettres D'Amour. Text by Emma di Rienzi. Enoch, 1910. PPN 7062. 4 pages. "Dormez tranquillement." Dedicated to Madame Th. Hervix-Kephalinidi.

W384 L'Ondine Du Léman. Text by L. Fortolis. Enoch, 1910. PPN 7065. 5 pages. "Au bord du Léman." Dedicated to Madame Paul Vitteau. This melody may have been originally intended for "Grisélidis," a short libretto by Silvestre that he had offered her, but which she turned over to Massenet. The latter produced a "Conte Lyrique" with that title, which premiered in November 1901.

W385 Voeu Suprême. Text by Pierre Reyniel. Enoch, 1910. PPN 7196. 4 pages. "Oh! dormir." Dedicated to Marie Monnier.

W386 Je Voudrais. Text by Pierre Reyniel. Enoch, 1912. PPN 7479. 5 pages. "Je voudrais être une fleur." Dedicated to Marie Capoy.

W387 Attente (Au Pays de Provence). Text by Philippe d'Ohsson. Enoch, 1914. PPN 7726. 5 pages. "Je ne sais à quoi je rêve." Dedicated to Gabrielle Fourquez-Ciampi.

W388 Chanson De Mer. Text by Philippe d'Ohsson. Enoch, 1914. PPN 7729. 8 pages. "Roule, tangue." Dedicated to Edmond Rambaud.

W389 Le Thrône Du Vieux Roi. Text by Louis Tiercelin. Enoch, 1914. PPN 7746. 7 pages. "Le vieux roi n'a

plus sa petite reine." Dedicated "à Mme. Ph. Paul
Vitteau, de l'Opéra-Comique."

Selected performance

W389a   1928 (5 February); Rouen; Mustel's; festival of Chaminade works organized by
Marie Capoy; Marie Capoy, vocalist; Thérèse Mauger, piano. See B429.

W390   Le Village. Text by L. Mercey. Enoch, 1915. PPN
7779. 5 pages. "Le village était joli."

W391   Sonne, Clairon (Marche Militaire). Text by L. Mercey. Enoch, 1915. PPN 7781. 5 pages. "Sonne clar-
ion!"

W392   L'Anneau Du Soldat. Text by M. Colombaz. Enoch,
1916. PPN 7809. 4 pages. "L'anneau que vous m'a-
vez donné." Dedicated "à mon amie Mme. Marie
Capoy."

PUBLISHED WORKS: COLLECTIONS

WC1   Pianoforte Album. Boston: White-Smith Music Publishing Company, 1898. 93 pages. Libellules, Op.
24; Serenade, Op. 29; Guitare, Op. 32; Valse-Caprice, Op. 33; Pas des Amphores, from Op. 37;
Scarf Dance, from Op. 37; Callirhoë, from Op. 37;
Pierrette, Op. 41; La Lisonjera, Op. 50; Scaramouche, Op. 56; Les Sylvains, Op. 60; Arabesque,
Op. 61.

WC2   Six Etudes Artistiques. Hamelle, 1912. 40 pages.
Etude-Printanière, [Op. 1]; Presto, [Op. 2]; -
Scherzo-Etude, [Op. 3]; Caprice-Etude, [Op. 4];
Chaconne, [Op. 8]; Etude Symphonique, [Op. 28].

WC3   Six Etudes de Concert: Deuxième Recueil. Enoch, [c.
1912]. 58 pages. Etude Symphonique, Op. 28; Etude
Mélodique, Op. 118; Etude Pathétique, Op. 124;
Etude Romantique, Op. 132; Etude Humoristique,
Op. 138; Etude Scolastique, Op. 139.

WC4   Petite Suite. Enoch, 1928. PPN 8665. 15 pages. No.
1: Air Italien [= Au Pays Bleu], Op. 170; No. 2:
Chanson Russe, Op. 98 No. 5; No. 3: Sérénade Espagnole, Op. 150.

WC5   Three Piano Works. New York: Da Capo, 1979. Reprint
of Enoch editions of 1895. Sonata in c minor, Op.
21; Etude Symphonique, Op. 28; Six Concert Etudes, Op. 35.

WC6   Album of Songs. Da Capo, 1984. Reprint of G. Schirmer edition of 1893. 95 pages. L'Absente; Amoroso; Amour D'Automne; L'Anneau D'Argent; Auprès De

Ma Vie; Chanson Slave; Colette; L'Eté; La Fiancée Du Soldat; Fleur Jetée; L`Idéal; Madrigal; Plaintes D'Amour; Rêve D`Un Soir; Les Rêves; Ritournelle; Rosemonde; Souhait; Sur la Plage; Tu Me Dirais.

UNPUBLISHED WORKS

WU1   Les Amazones, Symphonie Dramatique. Orchestral version of Op. 26; see W29.

WU2   Andante. Violin & piano. Has no title, only tempo indication. AUTOGRAPH: Family, dated September 1884. F major.

WU3   Andante Tranquillo. Violin & piano. Has no title, only tempo indication. AUTOGRAPH: Family.

WU4   Au Clair De La Lune (Incipit). Voice & piano. Incomplete, as piano staves are blank except at end. AUTOGRAPH; Family.

WU5   Ballade à La Terre. Voice & piano. Text by Henri Weinert. 5 pages. "Donc, ils ont peur." AUTOGRAPH: Family.

WU6   Callirhoë. Orchestral version of complete ballet, Op. 37; see W49.

WU7   La Capricieuse. Piano. 6 pages. Probably a very late work, c. 1935-44. AUTOGRAPH: Family.

WU8   La Chaise à Porteurs. Orchestral version of Op. 55 No. 2; see W74.

WU9   Comme Autrefois--Le Bon Vieux Temps. Piano. 4 pages. Probably a very late work, c. 1935-44. AUTOGRAPH: Family.

WU10   Concerto-Légende Pour Violon. Violin & piano. 25 pages. AUTOGRAPH: Family.

WU11   Les Deux Ménétriers. Orchestral version of song; see W277.

WU12   Deux Pièces, Op. 79. No. 1: Le Matin; No. 2: Le Soir. Orchestral version of two-piano pieces; see W106-07.

WU13   Egmont, Scène Dramatique, based on Goethe. Orchestra, chorus, & soloists. Mentioned in a family letter listing manuscript materials of orchestral pieces. Composed before April 1907; see B289.

WU14   L'Eté. Orchestral version of song; see W303.

WU15   Le Gladiateur. Piano. 4 pages. Possibly an early
        work. AUTOGRAPH: Family. In the hand of a copy-
        ist, or in a very student-like hand of the com-
        poser.

WU16   Hymne. Orchestra, chorus, & soloists. A newspaper
        article of the 1920s or 1930s mentions this piece
        being performed in Fribourg.

WU17   Idylle Arabe. Orchestral version of Op. 55 No. 3;
        see W75.

WU18   Légende Du Vieux Manoir. Piano. 4 pages. Probably a
        very late work, c. 1935-44. AUTOGRAPH: Family.

WU19   Marche Hongroise. Two pianos. Composed February
        1880 or earlier. AUTOGRAPH: Bibliothèque Nation-
        ale.

        Selected performance

        WU19a   1880 (8 February); Paris; Salle Erard; J.
                 Colombier and Chaminade, piano. See B13.

WU20   Meneut. Orchestral version of Op. 5; see W7. AUTO-
        GRAPH: Family.

WU21   Ne Nos Inducas In Tentationem. Voice & piano. Com-
        posed April 1878 or earlier.

        Premiere

        WU21a   1878 (25 April); Paris; home of Le Couppey;
                 Vergnet, male vocalist; Chaminade, piano.

WU22   O Salutaris. Voice (soprano or tenor), violin, &
        organ. 5 pages. Dedicated to Charlotte Ginistry.
        Possibly the piece performed at her first Com-
        munion, in Le Vésinet, in mid 1860s. AUTOGRAPH:
        Family.

WU23   Orientale. Orchestral version of Op. 22; see W24.

WU24   Sérénade. Orchestral version of Op. 29; see W33.

WU25   Sérénade D'Automne. Orchestral version of Op. 55
        No. 4; see W76.

WU26   La Sévillane. Orchestral version of the Overture
        (Op. 19), and the remainder of the 1-act opera,
        in piano-vocal score. See W18.

WU27   Souvenirs D'Enfance. Piano. 3 pages. Probably a
        very late work, c. 1935-44. AUTOGRAPH: Family.

WU28   Les Tambourinaires, Danse Provençale. Piano. AUTO-
        GRAPH: Family.

WU29   <u>Tarentelle</u>. Orchestral version of Op. 35 No. 6; <u>see</u>
         <u>W46</u>.

WU30   <u>Zingara</u>. Orchestral version of Op. 27 No. 2; <u>see</u>
         <u>W31</u>.

Discography

Key to Abbreviations: B = baritone; C = contralto; F = flutist; P = pianist; R = piano roll; S = soprano; T = tenor; V = vocalist; Vcl = cellist; Vn = violinist. Cross-references with a "B" pertain to the "Bibliography."

INDIVIDUAL WORKS

Air de Ballet, Op. 30

        Delta TQD 3037; see D219.

D1   Duo-Art 56649 (R). Clarence Adler (P).

        Gramophone 5552; see D231.

D2   Hamochord HB 2021. G. Meller (P).

        Summit LSU 3037; see D249.

Amour D'Automne

D3   Cantilena 6241. Jean Lassalle (V).

D4   Odeon 33908. Jean Lassalle (V).

L'Angelus

D5   Lumen 2-22-005. Balbon (V), Marc Hadour (P).

L'Anneau D'Argent

D6   Berliner 32273 (7"). [John Charles] Thomas (V).

D7   Club 99.76. Robert Couzinou (V).

D8   Club 99.2. Lucien Fugère (V).

D9   Columbia D13077 (France, 10"). Matrix L1020. Lucien Fugère (V), Elie Cohen (P).

D10   Edison 7400-R. Paul Dufault (V).

D11   EMI C053-12540. Michel Dens (B).

D12   G & T 3-32550 (7"). Henri Weber (V), with orchestra.

D13   G & T 3-32257 (7"). Henri Weber (V), with orchestra.

D14   Gramophone P442 (France, 1919, black label, 10").
       Suzanne Brohly (S). Reverse: <u>Stances</u> (Flégier).

D15   Gramophone 03156. Matrix 3510f. Clara Butt (V).

D16   Gramophone K6792 (France, 10"). Gordon (V).

D17   Gramophone 3865. G. Lonsdale (V).

D18   Gramophone DA973 (Great Britain, 10"). Matrix Bb
       11345I. John McCormack (T); in English. Reverse:
       <u>Bird-Songs at Eventide</u> (John Coates [T]).

D19   Gramophone IR303 (Ireland, 10"). John McCormack (T),
       Edwin Schneider (P).

D20   Gramophone 33681 (Paris, 1908, black label, 10").
       Matrix 5528b. Lucile Panis (S).

D21   Gramophone E195 (Great Britain, 10"). G. Thornton
       (V).

D22   HMV B-3699 (Great Britain, 10"); matrix 30-5246.
       Margarita Carlton (C).

D23   HMV 1303. John McCormack (T). Reverse: <u>Bird-Songs
       at Eventide</u> (John Coates, [T]).

D24   HMV 3103. Lucile Panis (C). Reverse: <u>Valse</u> (Frou
       Frou).

D25   Odéon 238247 (France, 10"). H. Chardy (V).

D26   Odéon 166666 (France, 10"). Ninon Vallin (S), Jean-
       Baptiste Fauredesch (P). Reverse: <u>Sais-Tu</u>? (Fon-
       tenailles).

D27   Olympic ORL 222. Clara Butt (C).

D28   Pacific 2255. Jean Lumière (V), Jacque-Simonot (P).

D29   Pathé STX 108. Mathé Altéry (V), orchestra conduc-
       ted by J. Metehen.

D30   Pathé PA 972. André Baugé (V).

D31   Pathé X93080. André Baugé (V).

D32   Pathé Saphir 3314. André Baugé (V).

D33   Pathé DTX/PLM 30159. Michel Dens (B).

D34   Pathé PD 131. Michel Dens (B), André Joseph (P).

D35   Pathé 33 DTX 30.I59. Michel Dens (B), orchestra
        conducted by Georges Tzipine.

D36   Pearl GEM 155/160. John McCormack (T).

D37   Plaisir Musical 30.159. "Chants d'Amour." Michel
        Dens (B), orchestra conducted by Georges Tzipine.
        Also works by Saint-Saëns, Martini, Denza, Gounod,
        Tosti, Chopin, Monti, Léoncavallo, Schubert,
        Liszt, Messager, and Godard.

D38   Polydor 522527 (France, 10"). Robert Couzinou (V).

D39   Rococo 5076. Pierre Bernac (B).

D40   Rococo 5347. Blanche Deschamps-Jehin (C).

D41   Rubini GV 901. John McCormack (T).

D42   Ultraphon AP 1569 (France, 10"). Pierre Bernac (B).

D43   Zonophone X-83048. Matrix 5041. Marie De L'Isle (V),
        with orchestra.

Arabesque, Op. 61

        EMI C069-16140; see D205.

Arlequine, Op. 53

   D44   Ace of Diamonds SDD 369. J. Partridge (P).

   D45   Argo ZRG 596. J. Partridge (P).

   D46   Pathé 52041B. Georges Truc (P).

Au Pays Bleu

   D47   G & T 2-32910 (London, 1903). Pol Plançon (B).

Aubade

        Gramophone B2499; see D209.

Automne, Op. 35 No. 2

   D48   Allegro 815. [Ronald] Smith (P).

   D49   Broadcast Twelve 5009-A. Maurice Cole (P).

   D50   Decca LK 4241. A. Semprini and Orchestra.

   D51   Duo-Art 58277 (R). Clarence Adler (P).

        Duo-Art 094 (R); see D226.

EMI C069 16140; see D205.

D52   Gramophone AM 3623 (10"). S. Crooke (P).

D53   Gramophone C1966 (Great Britain, 12"). De Groot's
       Orchestra.

D54   Gramophone C2064 (Great Britain, 12"). Matrix Cc
       20253. Mark Hambourg (P). Reverse: Chopin Prelude
       No. 17.

D55   Gramophone 5819. Matrix 8063. Mark Hambourg (P).

D56   Gramophone MBLP 6004. L. Johnson (P).

D57   Gramophone C057-25719. J. Meinders (P).

D58   Gramophone C3570. Matrix 2EA 11459-1. Melachrino
       Orchestra, conducted by George Melachrino. Re-
       verse: Melachrino First Rhapsody.

D59   Gramophone C2746. Reginald Reynolds (Weber Pianola
       Piano).

D60   HMV HQS 1287. John Ogdon (P).

D61   London 43004. Mantovani Orchestra.

D62   Meridien E77018 (c. 1979). Albert Ferber (P). "Meri-
       dien Anthology of Piano Favorites and Encore Pie-
       ces No. 1." Also works by Debussy, Fauré, Satie,
       Ibert, and Poulenc.

       Pianola 8756 (R); see D248.

D63   Pye NPLB 082. W. Atwell (P).

       Sterno 1463; see D213.

Autrefois, Op. 87 No. 4

   D64   Coronet SR4M 4693. G. Sherman (P).

   D65   Gramophone DB 21183 (Great Britain, 12"). Shura
          Cherkassky (P). Reverse: Liszt Consolation No. 3.

   D66   L'Oiseau-Lyre DSL 07 (c. 1975). Shura Cherkassky
          (P). "Cherkassky Kaleidoscope." Also works by
          Strauss, Saint-Saëns, Rameau, Schubert, Albéniz,
          Godowsky, Hofmann, Rubinstein, Tchaikovsky, Glaz-
          unov, and Mozskowski.

   D67   Orion ORS 7261. S. Kramer (P).

Berceuse

   D68   Decca D125D3. Joan Sutherland (S).

D69   Decca 3 390-106. Joan Sutherland (S); Richard Boynge
       (P). "Serenate musicali." Also works by Adam, Bel-
       lini, Campana, Cimara, Dalayrac, F. David, Del-
       ibes, Donizetti, Fauré, Godard, Gounod, Hahn,
       Lalo, Léoncavallo, Mascagni, Massenet, Meyerbeer,
       Ponchielli, Respighi, Rossini, Saint-Saëns, Tho-
       mas, and Verdi.

D70   London OSA 13132. Joan Sutherland (S).

Callirhoë, Air de Ballet, Op. 37

       Pianola 8683 (R); see D245.

Callirhoë Suite, Op. 37

D71   Parlophone E11062 (Great Britain, 12"). Victor Olof
       Salon Orchestra. Pas des Echarpes, Danse de Cal-
       lirhoë, Andante, and Valse.

Caprice Espagnole, Op. 67

D72   Duo-Art 61459 (R). Paquita Madriguera (P).

D73   Gemini Hall RAP 1010 (c. 1975). Michael May (P).
       "Woman's Work: Works by Famous Women Composers."
       Also works by F. Caccini, La Guerre, Anna Amalia
       (Princess of Prussia), Anna Amalia (Duchess of
       Saxe-Weimar), Paradis, Farrenc, Hensel, Malibran,
       Lang, C. Schumann, Viardot, Héritte-Viardot,
       Bronsart, Andrée, Poldowski, L. Boulanger, and
       Tailleferre.

Chanson Bretonne, Op. 76 No. 5

       EMI C069 16140; see D205.

Chanson Slave

D74   Discophilia DIS 752. Jeanne Gerville-Reache (C).

D75   Discophilia KIS KGG3. Jeanne Gerville-Reache (C).

       Gramophone RLS 724; see D210.

D76   Gramophone RLS 7105. Jeanne Gerville-Reache (C).

D77   Rococo R14. Jeanne Gerville-Reache (C).

D78   Victor 87035. Jeanne Gerville-Reache (C).

Concertino, Op. 107

D79   Avant 1015. Hobermann (F), Stannard (P).

D80   Award Artist AA 5766. William Kincaid (F), [Nicolai]
       Sokoloff (P).

D81   Claves Cla P704 (c. 1977). Peter-Lukas Graf (F),

Michio Kobayashi (P). "Joueurs de Flûte." Also works by Hüe, Enesco, Gaubert, Roussel, and Messiaen.

D82   Coronet S-1724. Pellerite (F), Indiana University Wind Ensemble.

D83   Gramophone C1302. Matrix CR 3137. John Amadio (F), with orchestra.

D84   HMV 9706 (US, 12"). John Amadio (F), with orchestra. Reverse: Hofmann Konzertstück-Finale, Op. 98.

D85   Musica Mundi VMS 1608. Karl-Bernhard Sebon (F), Berlin Radio Symphony Orchestra, cond. Uros Lajovic.

D86   RCA RL 25109 (c. 1977). James Galway (F), Royal Philharmonic Orchestra, cond. Charles Dutoit. "James Galway: French Flute Concertos." Also works by Ibert, Poulenc, and Fauré.

D87   VSM 2 C187-30.681/82. Karlheinz Zöller (F), Bruno Canino (P). "Musique de Salon." Also works by Borne and Fauré.

Concertstück, Op. 40

D88   Orion ORS 78296 (c. 1979). James Johnson (P), Royal Philharmonic Orchestra, cond. Paul Freeman. Also works by Dohnanyi.

D89   Turnabout TV 34754 (1980). Rosario Marciano (P), Orchestra of Radio Luxembourg, conducted by Louis de Froment. Also works by Tailleferre and Anna Amalia (Duchess of Saxe-Weimar).

Courante, Op. 95 No. 3

Gramophone 5553; see D232.

Danse Créole, Op. 94

Duo-Art 097 (R); see D227.

D90   Duo-Art 64228 (R). Carolyn Cone Baldwin (P).

Gramophone 5555; see D234.

Gramophone B2240; see D208.

Pianola 4748 (R); see D239.

D91   Sterno 1463. Alfred Newman (P).

D92   Victor 45050-B. Frank La Forge (P).

Ecrin

D93   Duo-Art 12906-S (R). Dallmeyer Russell (P), with the accompaniment of the high-voice version (in C).

Elévation, Op. 76 No. 2

D94   Duo-Art 58348 (R). Clarence Adler (P).

       Duo-Art 0297 (R); see D230.

L'Eté

D95   Belcantodisc BC 208. Emma Albani (S).

D96   Columbia A1527. Matrix 39284. Walter Laurence (V), with orchestra.

D97   Edison (Unissued), Master No. 3065-C (10"); recorded 27 May 1914. Clementine De Vere (S); sung in English.

D98   EMI-His Master's Voice RLS 7705 (c. 1982). [Emma Albani] (V). "A Record of Singers," Part I: The Castrato Voice; The Old School; English-Speaking Singers.

D99   G & T 33593 (Berlin, 1906). Blanche Marchesi (S).

       Gramophone RLS 724; see D210.

D100   Historic Record Society 1046-A. Emma Albani (S).

D101   Pathé 50332. Matrix 30491. Emma Albani (S).

D102   Rococo 5255. Emma Albani (S).

D103   Rococo R30. Blanche Marchesi (S).

D104   Victor 97-A. Matrix TTP 1490. Blanche Marchesi (S).

D105   Victor 70051. Lucy Isabella Marsh (S), with Victor Orchestra.

Etude Mélodique, Op. 118

D106   Rare Recorded Editions SRRE 140. K. Brady (P).

Etude Romantique, Op. 132.

       Duo-Art 091 (R); see D225.

Feuilles D'Automne, Op. 146

       Duo-Art 066 (R); see D224.

La Fileuse, Op. 35 No. 3

       EMI C069 16140; see D205.

Gavotte, Op. 9 No. 2

>Genesis GS 1024; see D207.

Cinquième Gavotte, Op. 162.

>Duo-Art 0203 (R); see D228.

Guitare, Op. 32

>Duo-Art 011 (R); see D220.

Impromptu, Op. 35 No. 5

>EMI C069 16140; see D205.

>Victor 70040; see D218.

Intermède, Op. 36 No. 1

>D107   FHM 8002. I. Beyer and H. Dagul (P.duet).

La Lisonjera, Op. 50

>D108   Brunswick 15001 (recorded 1926). Matrix 3721 2. Leopold Godowsky (P).

>D109   Columbia A2141. Matrix 46346. Prince's Orchestra.

>Columbia 1658D; see D203.

>D110   Duo-Art 57947 (R). Charles Gilbert Spross (P).

>Fono FSM 53036; see D206.

>Genesis GS 1024; see D207.

>Gramophone 5557; see D236.

>International Piano Archive 113; see D211.

>D111   Musical Heritage Society MHS 1139. Hans Kann (P). "Salon Music."

>Pianola 8702 (R); see D246.

>Turnabout TV 34754; see D215.

>D112   Victor 19564-A. Hans Barth (P).

>D113   Victor 20346-A. Hans Barth (P).

>Victor 20376; see D217.

>Victor 70040; see D218.

Madrigal

D114   Gramophone B744 (Great Britain, 10"); matrix 4 2768.
       Hubert Eisdell (T).

D115   Odeon 3528. Mlle. Simiane (S).

D116   Victor 953. Geraldine Farrar (S). Reverse: Tosti
       Serenata.

D117   Victor 64288. Rita Fornia (S); Rosario Bourdon (P).

Marche Américaine, Op. 131

Duo-Art 012 (R); see D221.

Le Matin, Op. 79 No. 1

Tiffany T2000; see D214.

Ultraphon AP 807; see D216.

Le Noël des Oiseaux

D118   Gramophone 232608 (France, green label, 10"). Marcel
       de Creus (T).

D119   Gramophone 232610 (France, green label, 10"). Marcel
       de Creus (T).

L'Ondine, Op. 101

Duo-Art 061 (R); see D223.

D120   Duo-Art 5514-4 (R). Rudolph Ganz (P).

Pas des Amphores, from Op. 37

D121   Duo-Art 59437 (R). Charles Gilbert Spross (P).

D122   HMV 45093. Victor Orchestra, cond. Charles Kellogg.
       Reverse: Kreisler Liebesfreund.

Pianola 8661 (R); see D243.

Pas Des Echarpes, from Op. 37

D123   Bluebird B-10993-B. Gray Gordon and his Tic-Tac Rhy-
       thm.

D124   Brunswick 50101A. Leopold Godowsky (P).

Columbia 1658D; see D203.

Columbia 9157; see D204.

D125   Connoisseur CSQ 2065. Virginia Eskin (P).

D126   Decca 18200B. Matrix DLA 2780A. Meredith Wilson and
        His Orchestra.

D127   Duo-Art 58256 (R). Charles Gilbert Spross (P).

        Fono FSM 53036; see D206.

D128   General 1205-B. Matrix 1687. Don Baker (P).

        Gramophone 5553; see D232.

        International Piano Archive 113; see D211.

D129   Majestic 149-A. Majestic Symphony Players/Orchestra.

        Parlophone E11062; see D71.

D130   Pathé 5382. Matrix 66900. Rudolph Ganz (P).

D131   Pathé 40175. The Great Lakes String Quartet.

        Pianola 8561 (R); see D241.

        Ultraphon AP 807; see D216.

D132   Victor 19564-B. Hans Barth (P).

D133   Victor 55030. Frank La Forge (P).

D134   Victor 35022-A. Arthur Pryor's Band.

D135   Victor 16690-B. Vienna Quartet.

        Victor 20346; see D217.

Pièce Dans Le Style Ancien, Op. 74

        EMI C069 16140; see D205.

Pierrette, Op. 41

        Columbia C9157; see D204.

        Delta TQD 3037; see D219.

D136   Duo-Art 69550 (R). Harold Bauer (P).

D137   Duo-Art 59947 (R). Coenraad V. Bos (P).

        Genesis GS 1024; see D207.

        Gramophone B2240; see D208.

        Gramophone 5556; see D235.

D138   Parlophone R818 (Great Britain, 10"). R. da Costa
        (P).

D139   Pathé 66424-RA. Lilian Bryant (P).

Pianola 8662 (R); see D244.

Summit LSU 3037; see D249.

Ritournelle

D140   Victor 17301-B. Alan Turner, vocalist; Victor Orchestra.

Romanza Appassionata, Op. 31 No. 2

Northeastern 222; see D212.

Ronde D'Amour

D141   Club 99.2. Lucien Fugère (B).

D142   Columbia D13044 (France, 10"). Lucien Fugère (B).
Reverse: Martini Plaisir D'Amour.

D143   Columbia DF 451 (Belgium, 10"). Edmond Rambaud (T),
orchestra cond. Elie Cohen.

D144   Gramophone 227. Suzanne Brohly (C). Reverse: "La
Lettre," from Offenbach's La Périchole.

D145   Gramophone GC 33788. Suzanne Brohly (C), with orchestra.

D146   Gramophone 33589 (black label, 10"). Marie De L'Isle
(V).

D147   Zonophone X83115. Matrix 9087. Marie De L'Isle (V);
with orchestra.

Scherzo, Op. 35 No. 1

EMI CO69 16140; see D205.

Sérénade, Op. 29

D148   Alco G15963. Maurice Cole (P).

Genesis GS 1024; see D207.

Pianola 8535 (R); see D240.

Sérénade Espagnole, Op. 150

D149   Angel SZ 37630. Itzhak Perlman (Vn), Samuel Sanders
(P).

D150   Camerata CMTX 1504. T. Nishizaki (Vn).

D151   CBS M37280. Yo-Yo Ma (Vcl), Patricia Zander (P).

D152   Columbia CQ 564 (Italy, 10"). A. Abussi (Vn).

D153   Columbia D13031 (Italy, 10"). R. Benedetti (Vn).

D154   Columbia 5029 (Great Britain, 10"). Y. Bratza (Vn).

D155   Columbia A3449. Matrix 79942. Eddy Brown (Vn); Josef
        Bonime (P).

D156   Columbia CQ 7021 (Italy, 10"). A. Poltronieri (Vn).

D157   Columbia 35819. Matrix CO-28666. Wladimir Selinsky
        and his String Ensemble.

D158   Decca F6179 (Great Britain, 10"). Alfredo Campoli
        (Vn). Reverse: Moszkowski-Sarasate Guitarre.

D159   DGG DG LPM 17166. T. Bisztricki (Vn), F. Shroder
        (P).

D160   DGG DG 133008. T. Bisztricki (Vn), F. Shroder (P).
        Also works by Tchaikovsky, Hubay, Kodaly, Zsolt,
        Dvorak, Rachmaninoff, Debussy, and Liszt.

D161   DGG DG 2538 016. Christian Ferras (Vn), G. Ambrosini
        (P). "Les bis de Christian Ferras." Also works by
        Dinicu, Dvorak, Kreisler, Massenet, Mendelssohn,
        Rimsky-Korsakov, Sarasate, Schubert, and Schumann.

D162   Edison 82172-L. Matrix 5061-B-23. Albert Spalding
        (Vn); André Benoist (P).

D163   Fidelio F001. J[oseph] Gingold (Vn).

D164   Gramophone DA 280 (Great Britain, 10"). Fritz
        Kreisler (Vn).

D165   Hamgaroton SLPX 12437. P. Csaba (Vn), Z. Kocsis (P).

D166   HMV 724. Fritz Kreisler (Vn), Carl Lamson (P). Re-
        verse: Granados Spanish Dance.

D167   HMV 729. Hugo Kreisler (Vcl). Reverse: [F.] Kreisler
        Viennese Folk-Song Fantasy.

D168   Kiwi LC 4. V. Aspey (Vn) and M. Till (P).

D169   London R10137. Matrix DR 13764-1A. Ossy Renardy
        (Vn), Ernest Lush (P).

D170   Melodiya D1185-6. G. Barinova (Vn).

D171   Nipponophon 15255. Kathleen Parlow (Vn).

        Northeastern 222; see D212.

D172   Parlophone 85881 (France, 10"). G. Will (Vn).

D173   Parlophone 80757 (France, 10"). G. Wullems (Vn).

D174   Pathé 020706B. Alexander Debruille (Vn).

D175   Pathé X98002. Manuel Quiroga (Vn).

D176   Perfect 11503-B. Alexander Debruille (Vn).

D177   Polydor 522840 (France, 10"). S. Filon (Vn).

D178   Polydor 67022 (Germany, 12"). Erica Morini (Vn) and
       Michael Raucheisen (P). Reverse: Lalo Symphonie
       Espagnole, fourth movement.

D179   Regal 9595-B. Rudolph Polk (Vn?).

D180   Schallplatte Grammophon 69824. Matrix 2261/2 bg.
       Erica Morini (Vn); Michael Raucheisen (P).

D181   USSR 25538. E. Grach (Vn).

D182   Victor 64503. Fritz Kreisler (Vn), Carl Lamson (P).

D183   Victor 66040. Fritz Kreisler (Vn); Hugo Kreisler
       (P).

D184   Westminster WM/WMS 1011. Erica Morini (Vn), L. Pom-
       mers (P).

Si J'Etais Jardinier

D185   Odéon 250383 (10"). Pierre Dupré (B). Reverse: P. Du
       Pont Les Sapins.

D186   Vega V30 S856. Aimé Doniat (V), orchestra cond. by
       Marcel Cariven.

D187   Vega V45 P1938. Aimé Doniat (V), orchestra cond. by
       Pierre Spiers.

D188   Victor 620. Geraldine Farrar (S). Reverse: Hahn Si
       Mes Vers Avaient Des Ailes.

D189   Victor 87322. Geraldine Farrar (S).

Sonata, Op. 21

D190   Educo 3146. Judith Alstadter (P). "Romantic Women
       Composers." Also works by Carreño and Backer-
       Grondahl.

       EMI C069 16140; see D205.

       Genesis GS 1024; see D207.

D191   Pelican LP 2017. Nancy Fierro (P).

Les Sylvains, Op. 60

D192   Duo-Art 63648 (R). Ernesto Berumen (P).

Duo-Art 046 (R); see D222.

Gramophone 5554; see D233.

D193   HMV 55031. Frank La Forge (P). Reverse: Chopin Berceuse.

Pianola 8711 (R); see D247.

Tarantelle, Op. 35 No. 6

EMI C069 16140; see D205.

Trahison

D194   Orion 82434. Christina Carroll (V). "The Art of
Christina Carroll, Volume II: Popular and Art
Songs." Also works by J. Kern, Fauré, Bizet,
Brahms, Lehar, and Romberg.

Trio, Op. 11

D195   Vox SVBX 5112 (c. 1979). Macalester Trio. "Chamber
Works by Women Composers." Also works by F. Hensel, Amy Beach, Clara Schumann, Carreño, Tailleferre, and Lili Boulanger.

Tu Me Dirais

D196   Club 99.82. Geraldine Farrar (S).

D197   Gramophone 33020. Geraldine Farrar (S).

D198   Odeon 33241. Marie De L'Isle (S).

Valse Arabesque, Op. 98 No. 4

Gramophone B2499; see D209.

Troisième Valse Brillante, Op. 80

Duo-Art 0207 (R); see D229.

Valse Caprice, Op. 33

Genesis GS 1024; see D207.

Pianola 8635 (R); see D242.

Valse Carnavalesque, Op. 73

D199   Duo-Art 6936-4 (R). Rudolph Ganz (P), doing an accompaniment roll of the first piano part.

Tiffany T2000; see D214.

Viens, Mon Bien-Aimé

D200   Odeon 36639. M. Udellé (V).

Voisinage

D201   Gramophone 233058 (France, green label, 10"). Matrix
       15935u. Cezac (S), with orchestra.

D202   Gramophone K447 (France, 10"). Cezac (S). Reverse:
       Alix Martell (C) singing Wachs Le Sentier Couvert.

ANTHOLOGIES

D203   Columbia 1658D. Matrix W147393. Columbia Symphony,
       conducted by Robert Hood Bowers. La Lisonjera, Op.
       50; Pas Des Echarpes, from Op. 37.

D204   Columbia C9157. Plaza Theatre Orchestra. Pas Des
       Echarpes, from Op. 37; Pierrette, Op. 41.

D205   EMI C069 16410 (c. 1980). Danielle Laval (P). "Pi-
       èces Pour Piano--Cécile Chaminade." Sonata, Op.
       21; Arabesque, Op. 61; Impromptu, Op. 35 No. 5;
       Automne, Op. 35 No. 2; Tarantelle, Op. 35 No. 6;
       Pièce Dans Le Style Ancien, Op. 74; Scherzo, Op.
       35 No. 1; Idylle, Op. 76 No. 3; Chanson Bretonne,
       Op. 76 No. 5; and Fileuse, Op. 35 No. 3.

D206   Fono FSM 53036. Rosario Marciano (P). La Lisonjera,
       Op. 50; Pas Des Echarpes, from Op. 37.

D207   Genesis GS 1024 (c. 1973). Doris Pines (P). "Jewels
       From La Belle Epoque." Sonata, Op. 21; Sérénade,
       Op. 29; La Lisonjera, Op. 50; Gavotte, Op. 9 No.
       2; Pierrette, Op. 41; Valse Caprice, Op. 33. Also
       works by Backer-Grondahl.

D208   Gramophone B2240 (Great Britain, 10"). Una Bourne
       (P). Danse Créole, Op. 94; Pierrette, Op. 41.

D209   Gramophone B2499 (Great Britain, 10"). Una Bourne
       (P). Aubade, Op. 140; Valse Arabesque, Op. 98 No.
       4.

D210   Gramophone RLS 724. Jeanne Gerville-Reache (C).
       Chanson Slave. E. Albani (V). L'Ete.

D211   International Piano Archive 113. Leopold Godowsky
       (P). La Lisonjera, Op. 50; Pas Des Echarpes, from
       Op. 37.

D212   Northeastern 222 (1985). Arnold Steinhardt (Vn),
       Virginia Eskin (P). Romanza Appassionata, Op. 31
       No. 2; Sérénade Espagnole, Op. 150. Also works by
       Tailleferre, Lili Boulanger, Marion Bauer, and Amy
       Beach.

D213   Sterno 1463. A. Newman (P). <u>Automne</u>, Op. 35 No. 2;
         <u>Danse Créole</u>, Op. 94.

D214   Tiffany T2000 (195-). Rudolph Ganz (P) and Parthenis
         Vogelback (P). "Two Piano Concert." <u>Le Matin</u>, Op.
         79 No. 1; <u>Valse Carnavalesque</u>, Op. 73. Also works
         by Franck, Poulenc, Saint-Saëns, R. Schumann, and
         A. Benjamin.

D215   Turnabout TV 34685 (1979). Rosario Marciano (P).
         "Piano Works by Women Composers." <u>Pas Des
         Echarpes</u>, from Op. 37; <u>La Lisonjera</u>, Op. 50. Also
         works by La Guerre, Paradis, Szymanowska, Cibbini-
         Kozeluch, F. Hensel, C. Schumann, I. von Bronsart,
         Backer-Grondahl, Carreño, Tailleferre, A. Beach,
         and Bacewicz.

D216   Ultraphon AP 807 (France, 10"). Paris Symphony. <u>Pas
         Des Echarpes</u>, from Op. 37; <u>Le Matin</u>, Op. 79 No. 1.

D217   Victor 20346 (10"). Hans Barth (P). <u>Pas Des
         Echarpes</u>, from Op. 37; <u>La Lisonjera</u>, Op. 50.

D218   Victor 70040. Frank La Forge (P). <u>Impromptu</u>, Op. 35
         No. 5; <u>La Lisonjera</u>, Op. 50.

CHAMINADE AS PERFORMER

D219   Delta TQD 3037. <u>Air De Ballet</u>, Op. 30; <u>Pierrette</u>,
         Op. 41. Probably the same release as D249.

D220   Duo-Art 011 (R) (London, 1913-14). <u>Guitare</u>, Op. 32.
         Issued in the US as No. 6480(0).

D221   Duo-Art 012 (R) (London, 1913-14). <u>Marche Améri-
         caine</u>, Op. 131.

D222   Duo-Art 046 (R) (London, 1913-14). <u>Les Sylvains</u>, Op.
         60.

D223   Duo-Art 061 (R) (London, 1913-14). <u>L'Ondine</u>, Op.
         101. Issued twice in the US as No. A-114, and No.
         D-797.

D224   Duo-Art 066 (R) (London, 1913-14). <u>Feuilles D'Au-
         tomne</u>, Op. 146.

D225   Duo-Art 091 (R) (London, 1913-14). <u>Etude Romantique</u>,
         Op. 132.

D226   Duo-Art 094 (R) (London, 1913-14). <u>Automne</u>, Op. 35
         No. 2.

D227   Duo-Art 097 (R) (London, 1913-14). <u>Danse Créole</u>, Op.
         94.

D228   Duo-Art 0203 (R) (London, 1913-14). Cinquième Gav-
        otte, Op. 162.

D229   Duo-Art 0207 (R) (London, 1913-14). Troisième Valse
        Brillante, Op. 80.

D230   Duo-Art 0297 (R) (London, 1913-14). Elévation, Op.
        76 No. 2. Issued three times in the US as No.
        74047, No. A-117, and No. D-805.

D231   Gramophone 5552 (London, 1901, 10"). Air De Ballet,
        Op. 30.

D232   Gramophone 5553 (London, 1901, 10"). Pas Des
        Echarpes, from Op. 37; Courante, Op. 95 No. 3.

D233   Gramophone 5554 (London, 1901, 10"). Les Sylvains,
        Op. 60.

D234   Gramophone 5555 (London, 1901, 10"). Danse Créole,
        Op. 94 No. 2.

D235   Gramophone 5556 (London, 1901, 10"). Pierrette, Op.
        41.

D236   Gramophone 5557 (London, 1901, 10"). La Lisonjera,
        Op. 50.

D237   Gramophone 5552-57 have been reissued on a cassette,
        Archive Documents ADC 11.

D238   Pianola [number unknown]. On a concert of 20 May
        1910, Chaminade is reported to have performed the
        two-piano version of Callirhoë, Op. 37, and of
        Valse Carnavalesque, Op. 73. The second piano part
        was played live, but the first piano part was a
        Pianola piano roll that she had recorded. See
        B402.

D239   Pianola 4748 (R) (before 1906). Danse Créole, Op.
        94.

D240   Pianola 8535 (R) (before 1906). Sérénade, Op. 29.

D241   Pianola 8561 (R) (before 1906). Pas Des Echarpes,
        from Op. 37.

D242   Pianola 8635 (R) (before 1906). Valse Caprice, Op.
        33.

D243   Pianola 8661 (R) (before 1906). Pas Des Amphores,
        from Op. 37.

D244   Pianola 8662 (R) (before 1906). Pierrette, Op. 41.

D245   Pianola 8683 (R) (before 1906). Callirhoë, Air de
        Ballet, Op. 37

D246   Pianola 8702 (R) (before 1906). <u>La Lisonjera</u>, Op. 50.

D247   Pianola 8711 (R) (before 1906). <u>Les Sylvains</u>, Op. 60.

D248   Pianola 8756 (R) (before 1906). <u>Automne</u>, Op. 35 No. 2.

D249   Summit LSU 3037. <u>Air De Ballet</u>, Op. 30; <u>Pierrette</u>, Op. 41. Probably the same release as D219.

Bibliography

Cross-references with a "D" pertain to the "Discography," and with a "W," "WC," or "WU" to "Works and Performances."

THROUGH 1889

B1   Assemblé Nationale, 1875.

        Review of Chaminade performing a Mozart Violin Sona-
        ta, with Marsick, at Le Vésinet: "If my admiration
        was great for the magnificent skill of the master,
        it was no less so for this child . . . so brilliant-
        ly and truly talented."

B2   "Concerts et Auditions Musicales." Revue et Gazette
        Musicale de Paris 44 (6 May 1877): 142.

        Notice of a chamber-music concert at the Salle Pley-
        el. Performing in a piano trio by Widor, Chaminade
        is judged "a young musician who acquitted herself of
        the task not only in her excellent musicianship but
        also in her obvious virtuosity."

B3   La France, [Early May] 1877.

        Review of the previous concert: "From the very start
        Mlle. Chaminade established her artistic reputation;
        the enthusiasm of the many spectators at the Salle
        Pleyel was as spirited as it was sincere."

B4   J. D. "Chronique Musicale." Espérance du Peuple (Nan-
        tes), c. 1877.

        Publication review of her Etude, Op. 1: "This deli-
        cate first fruit of a precocious talent, which is
        still maturing, is filled with pleasant modulations.
        They are fine embroidery on a melodic canvas, with a
        tender and sweet effect. . . . The entire piece
        offers satisfying work. . . . One will find it an
        étude that is both pleasing to the ear and perfect
        for the fingers." See W3.

B5   "Gazette de la Musique." <u>L'Evénement</u>, [27] April 1878.

       Review of Chaminade's first concert devoted to her
       own works, on 25 April: "The day before yesterday M.
       Le Couppey held a matinee devoted exclusively to the
       works of one of his pupils, Mlle. Cécile Chaminade.
       The program consisted of fifteen pieces, either
       songs or piano works, accompanied or performed by
       the author. I don't think I've ever experienced a
       more charming impression. . . . I prefer the piano
       pieces, which display a dense, taut workmanship, as
       well as an astonishing mastery of harmony. I espe-
       cially took note of a <u>Menuet</u> in the style of the
       18th century." <u>See</u> W3a, <u>W4a</u>, W6a, W7a, W8a.

B6   Guillemot, Jules. "Concerts: Salons de M. Lecouppey--
       Oeuvres Inédites de Mlle. Chaminade." <u>Le Constituti-</u>
       <u>onel</u>, [28] April 1878.

       Review of 25 April concert: "Let's note once again
       the presentation of new works of a very young lady,
       Mlle. Chaminade. It was at M. Lecouppey's that this
       gracious musician, with an extreme lightness of
       touch, performed some piano pieces of elegant and
       delicate design." <u>See</u> W3a, W4a, W6a, W7a, W8a.

B7   <u>La Revue Théatrale Illustrée</u>, [28] April 1878.

       Review of 25 April concert: "Mme. Fuchs and M. Ver-
       gnet . . . lent their assistance to Mlle. Chaminade,
       who herself performed with a remarkable <u>brio</u> a very
       original <u>Menuet</u>, and were warmly applauded in <u>Rose-</u>
       <u>monde</u>, <u>La Chanson du Fou</u>, <u>Papillons</u>, and <u>Te Souvi-</u>
       <u>ens-tu</u>, fresh inspirations revealing a talent that
       is serious and in full possession of itself." <u>See</u>
       W3a, W4a, W6a, W7a, W8a, W259a, W261a, W298a, W335a.

B8   Oswald, François. <u>Le Gaulois</u>, [30] April 1878.

       Review of 25 April concert: "A very young girl,
       Mlle. Cécile Chaminade, who composes with a great
       deal of skill and performs with remarkable virtuosi-
       ty, performed yesterday, at her professor's, M. Le-
       couppey, a series of new compositions that were very
       well liked. Of note were the encored <u>Chanson du Fou</u>
       . . . , <u>Papillons</u> . . . , an <u>Etude</u> in A-flat, a <u>Cap-</u>
       <u>rice-Etude</u>, and a <u>Menuet</u> performed by the author.
       This <u>Menuet</u>, in which we noticed a very successful
       fugue, is dedicated to M. Ambroise Thomas, who at-
       tended the recital and appeared very satisfied with
       it." <u>See</u> W3a, W4a, W6a, W7a, W8a, W259a, W335a.

B9   [D. C.] "Publications Musicales." <u>La Revue Théatrale</u>
       <u>Illustrée</u>, last half 1878.

       Publication review of 5 songs issued by Maho: "Like
       the previous productions of this brilliant virtuoso,
       they attest to a truly remarkable musical tempera-
       ment, which is served by an extremely high level of

inspiration and consummate skill. . . . <u>Ninette</u>,
<u>Sous Ta Fenêtre</u>, . . . <u>Papillons</u>, . . . <u>L'Heure du
Mystère</u>, . . . [and] <u>Te Souviens-Tu</u>? will be in the
repertoire of all the concerts and all the salons
this year." <u>See</u> W257-61.

B10   "Concerts Annoncés." <u>Le Ménestrel</u> 46 (1 February
        1880): 71.

        Announcement of a concert for 8 February, at the
        Salle Erard, featuring the works of Chaminade. <u>See</u>
        W9a, W11a, and W14a.

B11   "Concerts Annoncées." <u>Le Ménestrel</u> 46 (8 February
        1880): 79.

        Announcement of the concert taking place that day.
        <u>See</u> W9a, W11a, W14a.

B12   Ginisty, Paul. "Les Concerts: Salle Erard--Auditions
        des Oeuvres Musicales de Mlle. Cécile Chaminade."
        <u>Gil Blas</u>, [10] February 1880.

        Review of concert of 8 February: "Sunday there took
        place, at the Salle Erard, a very successful concert
        in which Mlle. Cécile Chaminade gathered the elite
        of the musical world for the presentation of her new
        works. . . . The most important piece on the reci-
        tal was a remarkable <u>Trio</u> in g minor . . . , which
        was spiritedly performed with incomparable virtuo-
        sity by Messieurs Marsick, Hekking, and the com-
        poser." <u>See</u> W9a, W11a, W14a.

B13   "Concerts." <u>L'Art Musical</u> 19 (12 February 1880): 51-
        52.

        Lengthy review of concert of 8 February: "She per-
        formed seven piano pieces of notable merit, whose
        quality is attributable to freshness of melodic
        ideas as well as conciseness and clarity of style. .
        . . Vocal music occupied a good portion of the reci-
        tal. . . . The concert ended with the <u>Marche Hon-
        groise</u> for two pianos, performed magnificently by
        Mlle. J. Colombier and the author, Mlle. Chaminade,
        who must be quite satisfied with the total result,
        for the audience appluaded as much for the musician
        as for the pianist, which is not saying a little.
        This young artist is embarking on a career through
        the grand door and we will often have the opportu-
        nity to speak of her talent." <u>See</u> W9a, W11a, W14a,
        WU19a.

B14   A. M. "Nouvelles Diverses: Concerts et Soirées." <u>Le
        Ménestrel</u> 46 (15 February 1880): 85-86.

        Extensive review of concert of 8 February: "Her <u>Trio</u>
        in g minor . . . is written with a hand already firm
        and assured and reveals a skill that is profound and
        serious. The ideas are felicitous but their develop-

ment is not always logical. . . . Also, perhaps
Mlle. Chaminade was not able to separate them sufficiently from her virtuosic skill, notably in the
Scherzo, which almost seems more like a fantasy for
piano than a piece of chamber music. But whatever
the case, this trio is a substantial composition,
with real value. . . . The vocal mélodies . . . are
no less remarkable than the instrumental pieces. . .
. Overall, let us note once again that Mlle. Chaminade enjoyed a great and deserved success." See W9a,
W11a, W14a, W261b, W262a.

B15   "Concerts et Auditions Musicales." Revue et Gazette
       Musicale de Paris 47 (22 February 1880): 62.

       Brief review of concert of 8 February: "Mlle. Cécile
       Chaminade and her compositions enjoyed a great suc-
       cess at the matinee. . . . One heard a Trio in g
       minor, a Pièce Romantique, a Barcarolle, a Menuet,
       and several songs. There is talent and youth in all
       of them; but Mlle. Chaminade will have to curb a
       certain exuberance of form, and sacrifice less to
       virtuosity, especially in the ensemble music." See
       W9a, W11a, W14a, W261b, W262a.

B16   "Concerts et Auditions Musicales." Revue et Gazette
       Musicale de Paris 47 (4 April 1880): 110.

       Review of concert of 27 March, at the Société Na-
       tionale de Musique, which included the Trio and sev-
       eral songs and piano pieces, as well as works by
       other composers. "The Trio . . . , despite inexperi-
       ence and awkward harmonies, is of genuine interest;
       the personality of the young artist is already ap-
       parent in it. . . ." See W9b, W10a, W14b.

B17   E. G. "Concerts et Soirées." Le Ménestrel 46 (4 April
       1880): 143.

       Review of concert of 27 March. The Trio is judged
       interesting, very well constructed, and well-per-
       formed. See W9b, W10a, W14b.

B18   Le Petit Journal, 5 April 1881.

       Brief review of concert of 4 April, at the Salle
       Erard, of the Société Nationale de Musique: "The
       Suite d'Orchestre of Mlle. Cécile Chaminade, who has
       a bright future ahead of her, generated great ap-
       plause. Her work, well orchestrated and finely chi-
       seled, contains very fresh melodies and a broad and
       powerful chorale. . . . Our congratulations." See
       W7b, W19-22a.

B19   A. M. "Nouvelles Diverses: Concerts et Soirées." Le
       Ménestrel 47 (10 April 1881): 150.

       Review of concert of 4 April: "Very successful was
       the last number of the program, the Suite d'Orches-

tre in four parts by Mlle. Chaminade. Eliciting
great applause were the last two: a very nice Scherzo, and a solemn Chorale that has the cymbals striking a blow on every note of the main theme, of which
we do not approve." See W7b, W19-22a.

B20   Ruelle, Jules. "Concerts." L'Art Musical 20 (14 April
1881): 114.

In this largely unfavorable review of the entire
program of 4 April, Chaminade's Suite d'Orchestre is
given very brief mention and deemed as unworthy as
most of the other works performed. See W7b, W19-22a.

B21   A. M. "Nouvelles Diverses: Concerts Et Soirées." Le
Ménestrel 47 (17 April 1881): 159.

Review of two recent concerts in which Chaminade
participated as pianist. The Trio is judged "remarkable" and the Menuet singled out for its "excellent
qualities." See W7b, W14c.

B22   Gil Blas, 3 June 1881.

Publication review of the Trio, Op. 11, which talks
more about Chaminade's gifts in general than this
work in particular. "A remarkable pianist and a composer whose talent is already recognized, Mlle. Chaminade has a bright future assured if her future
compositions are of the level of this trio, which I
heard performed this winter, with the greatest pleasure, by its author and Messieurs Marsick and Delsart." See W14.

B23   "Nouvelles et Correspondances, France." L`Art Musical
21 (19 January 1882): 23.

Announcement of a series of four chamber music concerts (18 January, 1 and 13 February, and 1 March),
at the Salle Pleyel, in which Chaminade will participate.

B24   "Matinée Le Couppey." L'Art Musical 21 (26 January
1882): 29.

Review of concert of 22 January, devoted largely to
the works of Chaminade. They include Berceuse ("an
old acquaintance"), Libellules ("a charming short
piece"), Gavotte, and Caprice Etude, all of which
the composer performed. In addition, two other pianists performed her Scherzo, "which wins the honor of
being encored." See W6b, W8b, W12a, W26a.

B25   Voltaire, 23 February 1882.

Announcement of private performance of opera, La
Sévillane, at Chaminade family's home (69, rue de
Rome), on that day. See W18a.

B26   L'Ordre, 24 February 1882.

Notice of performance of 23 February: "A brilliant
gathering occurred yesterday at the home of M. Chaminade. . . . The attraction of the evening was the
performing of an opéra-comique of Mlle. Cécile Chaminade. . . . [Its] success assumed the proportions
of a musical event, and it is, we are assured, prom-
ised to the Opéra-Comique." See W18a.

B27   [Maz, Albert]. "Revue Musicale: Audition de la Sévillane." Feuilleton de l'Ordre, 25 February 1882.

Detailed, article-length review of performance of 23
February: "[We are] persuaded that the great success, so deserved, that marked its first performance
will encourage M. Carvalho to mount this work, wor-
thy in every way of his attention. . . . Her music
is original without being tormented, and her truly
inspired ideas are framed in a skillful way without
being affected, clear without being banal. Mlle.
Chaminade . . . is . . . a musical temperament of
the first order. . . . We have singled out the entire first part of the Overture as being extremely
distinguished. . . . La Ronde des Alguazils is, in
our opinion, one of the best pieces in the score: a
chorus that is highly original and admirably con-
structed. . . . In short, a very interesting soirée,
illuminating a composer of real merit. . . . Remember this name--it is destined to make rapid progress
in an artistic career." See W18a.

B28   Le Petit Journal, 25 February 1882.

Brief review of performance of 23 February: "La Se-
villana [sic], a 1-act opéra comique, . . . has a
wealth of inspiration that is truly remarkable." See
W18a.

B29   Ordonneau, Maurice. "P. S." Le Gaulois, [25] February
1882.

Brief review of performance of 23 February: "Unfortunately I don't have the room to discuss the private, intimate performance of a charming opéra comique, La Sévillane. . . . This work, very well
written, . . . is highly deserving of a staged pro-
duction." See W18a.

B30   De Jennius. La Liberté, 26 February 1882.

Brief notice of performance of 23 February: "Great
success for the artists and the authors. Someday we
will have the opportunity to applaud this charming
work when it is staged." See W18a.

B31   Kerst, Léon. <u>Voltaire</u>, 26 February 1882.

>   Substantial review of performance of 23 February:
>   "After having written a number of chamber pieces in
>   which the construction and the ideas are in perfect
>   equilibrium, she is now seeking to tackle the thea-
>   ter and invited the critics to hear her first
>   essay." One discerns a feeling for the theater that
>   will no doubt mature with experience. If the review-
>   er were director of the Opéra-Comique he would not
>   hesitate to mount the work. <u>See</u> W18a.

B32   <u>La Marseillaise</u>, [26] February 1882.

>   After praising the talents of the librettist, this
>   account of the performance of 23 February discusses
>   the composer: "Mlle. Chaminade, known as a distin-
>   guished virtuoso and a composer of pleasant roman-
>   ces, has proven that she could do more. Her score
>   reveals numerous qualities: lofty melody, finely
>   crafted orchestration, and, throughout, very distin-
>   guished music." <u>See</u> W18a.

B33   <u>Le Mot D'Ordre</u>, [26] February 1882.

>   Review of performance of 23 February, echoing the
>   assessments in other reviews: "Her music is of very
>   high quality, including melody, freshness of ideas,
>   and orchestration that is fine and ingenious. Many
>   pieces were encored. . . . We predict a brilliant
>   musical future for Mlle. Chaminade." <u>See</u> W18a.

B34   <u>Le Réveil</u>, [26] February 1882.

>   Review of performance of 23 February: "The music,
>   full of originality and charm, of freshness and fee-
>   ling applied to an interesting libretto, earned the
>   approval of everyone in the audience. Most of the
>   pieces were encored." <u>See</u> W18a.

B35   <u>Gil Blas</u>, 28 February 1882.

>   Review of performance of 23 February: "Once again, a
>   public performance by a female author. This time,
>   it's a young lady, whose name . . . has already
>   begun to see the light of day in the musical world.
>   . . . An opéra comique entitled <u>La Sévillane</u> . . .
>   was a complete success, performed before an elite
>   and knowledgeable audience. . . . The music of Mlle.
>   Chaminade is imprinted with a style that needs only
>   experience to become totally personal. Many pieces
>   were encored, among others a charming chorus of Al-
>   guazils. . . . " <u>See</u> W18a.

B36   <u>Le Bulletin Musical</u> 2 (1 March 1882).

>   Précis of the performance of 23 February: "A premi-
>   ere in a salon on Thursday, at M. Chaminade; the
>   principal pieces of a 1-act opéra comique, <u>La Sévil-</u>

lane, were sung. . . . A complete success. Many
pieces encored. When is the premiere at rue Favart?"
See W18a.

B37   La Vérité, 1 March 1882.

Warm review of performance of 23 February: "La Sévillane was received very well. The music of Mlle.
Chaminade is distinguished by an abundance of melody
and a power of conception that is surprising in a
young lady. . . . We sincerely hope to hear La Sévillane later on one of our grand stages." See W18a.

B38   Terzetto. La Renaissance Musicale 2 ([1] March 1882).

Providing a list of each piece and its interpretor,
this review of La Sévillane concludes: "The music of
Mlle. Chaminade has elegance, grace, and a striking
delicacy of feeling. Several pieces were encored,
including a delightful chorus of alguazils that was
not part of the original program." See W18a.

B39   D'Auriac, E.-Mathieu. "Paris et Départements." Le Ménestrel 48 (5 March 1882): 109.

Notice of the performance of 23 February; it con-
sists entirely of the review that appeared in Le
Monde Artiste. Especially praised are the overture,
the serenade, and the chorus of alguazils. See W18a.

B40   M. CH. "Paris et Départements." Le Ménestrel 48 (12
March 1882): 117.

Brief review of Chaminade participating in a chamber
recital. Her Trio No. 1 is included, and the Presto
movement is singled out for praise. See W14d.

B41   Le Figaro, [15] March 1882.

Announcement of forthcoming concert, on 19 March, at
Cirque d'Eté, that includes the first Suite d'Orchestre. See W19-22b.

B42   "Nouvelles Diverses: Concerts Annoncés." Le Ménestrel
48 (19 March 1882): 127.

Announcement of performance that day of the Suite
d'Orchestre. See W19-22b.

B43   Le Petit Journal, 21 March 1882.

Very brief review of concert of 19 March: "The Suite
d'Orchestre . . . was very warmly received. The Intermezzo was roundly applauded, and the public demanded an encore of the Scherzo, whose skillful
grace won total approval." See W19-22b.

B44   Darcours, Charles. "Notes de Musique." Le Figaro, 22
March 1882.

Review of concert of 19 March. Chaminade is a "pianist whose style and brilliant execution have already placed [her] among the best. . . ." Regarding composition, "Mlle. Chaminade comes from a school in which melodic invention is not considered the mark of the inept. It has grace and infuses the phrases with a contour that is in no way banal." See W19-22b.

B45   La Marseillaise, 22 March 1882.

Brief review of concert of 19 March, which deems the Suite "a great success," and discerns the same qualities that are present in La Sévillane. "The Scherzo, particularly successful, earned the honor, well deserved, of an encore." See W19-22b.

B46   Le Mot D'Ordre, 22 March 1882.

Brief review of the concert of 19 March. The Suite was a great success, "and reinforces the qualities that characterize [the music] of Mlle. Chaminade: fresh ideas, and refined and ingenious orchestration." See W19-22b.

B47   Le Bulletin Musical 2 ([22] March 1882).

Mixed review of the Suite d'Orchestre. Finding the first movement the weakest, the reviewer praises the second (Intermezzo) as the best, mostly on the basis of its fine orchestration. "The public seemed to prefer the Scherzo. Let's say that the public was right; but I maintain my preference for the Intermezzo. The Choral . . . , which was previously performed at the Société Nationale, is a very noble creation, and one is astonished that such a piece could germinate in the brain of such a gracious and delicate young lady as Mlle. Chaminade." See W19-22b.

B48   "Concerts." L'Art Musical 21 (23 March 1882): 91.

Review of concert of 19 March, in which the Suite is accorded a very brief assessment: "Mlle. Chaminade garnered great applause with a very original Suite d'Orchestre." See W19-22b.

B49   Maz, Albert. L'Ordre, 24 March 1882.

Lengthy review of the Suite. Within a concert of orchestral works by young composers, the principal attraction was Chaminade's Suite d'Orchestre. "A new triumph" for her, whose orchestral style combines "solid musical instruction" with "an astonishing delicacy of touch that is totally individual." After an assessment of each movement, the reviewer labels the work a great success and looks forward to a re-acquaintance, in the near future, on the opera stage. See W19-22b.

B50   "Nouveaux Concerts." Le Monde Artiste 22 (25 March 1882).

Brief assessment of concert of 19 March: "We derived great pleasure from the Suite d'Orchestre." See W19-22b.

B51   Jouve, L. Le Bulletin, 26 March 1882.

Review of concert of 19 March. Chaminade is accorded brief mention; her "charming" Scherzo received a very warm reception. See W19-22b.

B52   La Renaissance Musicale 2 (26 March 1882).

Review of concert of 19 March: "The Suite d'Orchestre . . . contains some excellent sections. If the Marche and the Intermezzo are a little confused, on reflection the Scherzo is of a singular clarity. . . . The final Choral contains, notably, a passage written for the trombones and recalled by the cellos, which is handled very well." See W19-22b.

B53   La France, 12 April 1882.

Brief review of 19 March concert, in which the Suite D'Orchestre is judged "very interesting." It was recently published by Léon Grus. See W19-22b.

B54   L'Opinion, 18 April 1882.

Review of concert of 15 April, in which Chaminade was a participant. "This young lady composes charming things at an age when one can barely comprehend the masters. She is also a force on the piano." Te Souviens Tu is included on the program. See W261c.

B55   Le Peuple Français, [18] April 1882.

Brief notice of the concert of 15 April, in which Chaminade is singled out for special mention.

B56   Le Mot D'Ordre, 22 April 1882.

Brief review of concert of 15 April: "We particularly applauded Mlle. Cécile Chaminade, who is not content to be a composer of great talent--witness La Sévillane--but is also a virtuoso of the first rank."

B57   D'Auriac, E.-Mathieu. Le Monde Artiste 2 (25 April 1882).

In this concert of 22 April involving several performers, Chaminade is reviewed in one line: "Mlle.

Chaminade was warmly applauded, first as pianist and then as composer."

B58   Le Mot D'Ordre, 7 May 1882.

Review of concert of 6 May: "We should mention every piece, but we must especially take note of the success occasioned by a Menuet of Mlle. Cécile Chaminade. Very original, very fresh, and very distinguished, this Menuet, whose orchestration is very polished and deliberate, was encored by a public of connaisseurs." See W7c.

B59   Le Petit Journal, 7 May 1882.

Very brief review of 6 May concert, when orchestral version of Menuet performed. Deemed "brilliant," the piece is encored. See W7c.

B60   "Nouvelles et Correspondances," L'Art Musical 21 (11 May 1882): 150.

The reviewer is very complimentary, praising both the delicacy and the orchestration of the Menuet. "Mlle. Chaminade, despite her sex and her age, has assumed her place today among the most respected modern composers." See W7c.

B61   Dolmetsch, Victor. "Nouvelles Diverses: Concerts et Soirées." Le Ménestrel 48 (14 May 1882): 191.

Explaining the selection procedures of the Société Nationale and then proceeding to an evaluation of the concert of 6 May, this review gives brief mention of each work on the program. The Menuet is considered a "pleasant" work. See W7c.

B62   La Marseillaise, 18 December 1882.

Review of concert of 17 December, which includes the Suite D'Orchestre, Op. 20. The Scherzo receives special praise. See B19-22c.

B63   Le Progrès Artistique 5 (22 December 1882).

Favorable review of concert of 17 December: "The Suite d'Orchestre that we heard discloses an original temperament and a deep knowledge of the orchestral art. . . . Her new work only increases the hopes we had already envisioned for her future and her talent. At this moment, this young composer holds a place of honor in our new school." See B19-22c.

B64   D'Auriac, E.-Mathieu. Le Monde Artiste 22 (23 December 1882).

Review of concert of 17 December: "M. Pasdeloup presented, for the first time, with great success, a

Suite d'Orchestre of Mlle. Cécile Chaminade. Seduced
by the originality that characterizes a part of the
work, and struck by the breadth of the Choral that
occurs last, the public did not skimp in its applause. How many in the audience were far from reali-
zing that this symphony [sic], which reveals an un-
common talent in orchestration, was written by a
young lady! Such a debut holds great promise for the
future." See B19-22c.

B65   Dubreuilh, Gaston. "Concerts et Soirées." Le Ménestrel
       49 (24 December 1882): 30.

       Review of concert of 17 December: "The Suite d'Or-
       chestre . . . testifies to an imagination that is
       original and a technique that is very skillful. The
       Marche and the Choral are very well orchestrated;
       the Intermezzo is especially notable for the extreme
       elegance of its melodic contours; and the Scherzo,
       trim and rhythmic, seduces one as much by the cle-
       verness of its motifs as it does by the disposition
       and variety of its timbres." See B19-22c.

B66   "Concerts du Dimanche." L'Art Musical 22 (18 January
       1883): 21.

       Announcement of forthcoming orchestral concert (20
       January), which will include two excerpts from La
       Sévillane: Chorus of the Alguazils and the Ronde des
       Mariés, the latter for the first time. See W18.

B67   "Concerts Populaires." L'Art Musical 22 (29 March
       1883): 101.

       Announcement of concert of 31 March, featuring the
       Overture to La Sévillane. See W18.

B68   Crespel, M. Clairon, [26] February 1884.

       Lengthy review of concert of 25 February. "Yester-
       day, at the Salle Erard, Mlle. Chaminade had invited
       the press to hear her opéra comique, La Sévillane. .
       . . The music of Mlle. Chaminade is admirably well
       constructed, written by someone who knows her trade.
       The Romance of Don Louis is the most melodic piece
       of the score; it will be one of the highlights if
       the work appears on the stage some day. I am less
       enamored of the Duo between Rita and Don Louis,
       which seemed a bit common. The Trio contains a char-
       ming opening phrase. . . . A nice Trio, very pleas-
       ant to hear, closes the score." The reviewer hopes
       that the opera will be staged. See W18b.

B69   "Les Théâtres--A La Salle Erard--" Le Matin, 27 Febru-
       ary 1884.

       Review of program of 25 February. ". . . Her music
       has genuine worth. It is pleasant and well written;
       it lacks neither feeling nor spirit. One paid par-

ticular attention to a romance--the <u>Romance de Don Luis</u>, which would shine in the theater; perhaps it will be on every piano before long. Other passages seemed to be lacking a bit in originality. . . . [The evening] was a great success . . . . We wish all good things to Mlle. Chaminade." <u>See</u> W18b.

B70   Abraham, Emile. <u>Le Petit Journal</u>, 28 February 1884.

Brief review of "brilliant concert" of 25 February. "The very gracious pianist-composer presented a recital of several of her works, including excerpts from an opéra comique, <u>La Sévillane</u>, with the assistance of distinguished artists. Especially notable were a romance for soprano, a serenade for tenor, and a trio whose texture reveals skill in the service of exquisite inspiration." <u>See</u> W18b.

B71   <u>Le Réveil</u>, 28 February 1884.

Flattering review of concert of 25 February. Included are a <u>Trio</u> [No. 1], an <u>Intermezzo</u>, a <u>Menuet</u> (encored), a <u>Barcarolle</u>, <u>Libellules</u>, and excerpts from <u>La Sévillane</u>, considered "animated, playful, and full of melodies elegantly scored. We are surprised that none of our operatic directors has produced it yet." <u>See</u> W7d, W9c, W14e, W18b, W20e, W26b.

B72   <u>Le Gaulois</u>, 28 February 1884.

Favorable review of concert of 25 February, which concludes, "Mlle. Chaminade marches, among contemporary female composers, in the footsteps of Mme. de Grandval and Mlle. Holmès."

B73   D'Auriac, E.-Mathieu. <u>Le Monde Artiste</u> 24 ([29] February 1884).

Review of concert of 25 February. Responding favorably to the all-Chaminade program, the writer observes: "This recital was a clear success, every piece was enthusiastically received, and we are persuaded that a score as charming as that of <u>La Sévillane</u> would be very welcome in the theater." <u>See</u> W18b.

B74   "Audition des Oeuvres de Mlle. Cécile Chaminade." <u>Le Bulletin Musical</u> 4 ([1] March 1884).

In this complimentary review of the concert of 25 February, the writer makes clear his preference for the <u>Trio</u>: "Never has the young composer risen so high under the combined influence of inspiration and skill. Without excessive developments or pretentious affectations, this <u>Trio</u> constitutes nothing less than a truly beautiful work, classical in form and romantic in its abundance of ideas." <u>See</u> W14e.

B75   A. L. D. Le Progrès Artistique 6 (7 March 1884).

       Substantial review of the concert of 25 February.
       The Trio in g minor is praised for its Andante and
       Scherzo. It shows "remarkable clarity in its presen-
       tation of ideas and its developments. However, . . .
       the piano part has a tendency to eclipse its part-
       ners," which is attributed to the composer being a
       pianist. Regarding the excerpts from La Sévillane,
       "it is very embarrassing to discuss a theatrical
       work for which one has only heard excerpts at the
       piano. . . . I'll content myself with pointing out
       the Romance de Don Louis . . . , the Air de Rita,
       and the Duo that follows. The overall plan I was
       able to discern leads me to believe that these vari-
       ous excerpts would be put in relief with the orches-
       tra, given the author's skill in orchestration." See
       W14e, W18b.

B76   Moszkowski, Moritz. "Ein Brief [von] Paris." Deutsches
       Montags-Blatt (Berlin), 17 March 1884.

       The writer, later to be Chaminade's brother-in-law,
       begins by claiming that women participate more ac-
       tively in concert life in Paris than elsewhere. Cha-
       minade is then singled out for attention, with a
       review of her concert of 25 February. "In these sev-
       eral works, not only did [she] show herself a sov-
       ereign master of the technical side of her art, but
       rather a composer with a strongly marked, attractive
       individuality. This showed mainly in the Scherzo of
       her Piano Trio, in especially piquant harmonies in a
       Trio from her opera La Sévillane, and furthermore in
       a few solo piano pieces." See W14e, W18b.

B77   "Nouvelles Diverses: Concerts Annoncés." Le Ménestrel
       51 (22 February 1885): 93.

       Announcement of upcoming concert featuring Sérénade
       and Zingara. See B31a.

B78   Le Gaulois, 23 February 1885.

       Brief review of Sérénade and Zingara: "These two
       pieces, well written and pleasantly scored, are or-
       chestral transcriptions of two genial piano works by
       the young artist. This part of the program was very
       successful." See B31a.

B79   Morsac, G. "Nouvelles Diverses: Concerts et Soirées."
       Le Ménestrel 51 (1 March 1885): 103.

       Review of Sérénade and Zingara: "Written very ele-
       gantly, with a fluid orchestration, they were well
       received." See B31a.

B80   "Nouvelles Diverses: Concerts et Soirées." Le Ménes-
       trel 51 (29 March 1885): 135.

Brief mention of Mendels and Lefort having recently devoted a chamber music concert to the work(s) of Chaminade; no specific titles are provided.

B81   "Concerts." L'Art Musical 24 (31 March 1885): 44.

A listing of the program of Benjamin Godard, at the Cirque d'Hiver, on 29 March, which included Chaminade's Suite d'Orchestre. See W19-22d.

B82   G. M. "Nouvelles Diverses: Concerts et Soirées." Le Ménestrel 51 (5 April 1885): 143-44.

In a review of Godard's concert of 29 March, Chaminade's Suite is termed "simple and in good taste." See B19-22d.

B83   Album du Gaulois, 15 December 1885, 8-9.

Short biographical account: "Still very young, Mlle. Cécile Chaminade has focused attention on herself by the diversity of her compositions. . . . Her published works number 31." This is followed by a description of her output.

B84   "Nouvelles Diverses: Paris et Départements." Le Ménestrel 52 (3 January 1886): 39.

Brief notice of a performance of the Trio, at the Société de Musique Française. See W14f.

B85   "Concert Chaminade." Le Figaro, 5 February 1886.

Detailed review of concert of 4 February, at Salle Erard, devoted exclusively to her works. The concert included her second Trio, the Andante of which "recalls a little the famous romance of Mignon, 'Connais-tu le pays'." Several songs were performed as well. In addition, "M. Marsick performed a Romanza on his magnificent instrument, a Bohémienne, and a Scherzo, accompanied by the composer." Chaminade is praised for both her compositional and performing skills. "Overall, lovely soirée; a lovely concert consisting of eight miniature masterpieces." See W36-37a, W40a.

B86   Berliner Tageblatt, 16 February 1886.

Review of concert of 4 February: "In all her works a feeling for the German masters is evident, resulting in clear, transparent expression. . . . Furthermore, the Intermezzo and Pas des Cymbales, orchestral pieces transcribed for two pianos, were very interesting; we are to hear them here next winter. Fräulein Chaminade intends to perform a few of her compositions in Berlin next spring." See W20f, W48a.

B87   "Nouvelles Diverses: Concerts et Soirées." Le Ménestrel 52 (11 April 1886): 152.

Brief notice of a Marsick recital, in which special
mention is made of Chaminade's Scherzo.

B88   "Nouvelles Diverses: Paris et Départements." Le Ménestrel 52 (9 May 1886): 186.

During the 1884-85 season of Les Concerts Modernes,
under Benjamin Godard, Chaminade works were performed 3 times (maximum number for any composer is
10).

B89   Nivelle, Jean de. "Un Maître du Piano." Le Soleil, 11
August 1886.

In a lengthy article on Le Couppey upon his retire-
ment, Chaminade is mentioned briefly: "Regarding one
of his pupils . . ., hasn't she already achieved
renown for her very original compositions, many of
them charming?"

B90   "Nouvelles Diverses: Paris et Départements." Le Ménestrel 52 (24 October 1886): 380.

Announcement of program for the 23rd anniversary of
the Concerts Populaires (Pasdeloup), on 31 October,
which will include the Tarentelle. See W46a.

B91   [Leduc, Alphonse]. "Nouvelles Diverses: France." L'Art
Musical 25 (31 October 1886): 159.

Another announcement of the Tarentelle concert. See
W46a.

B92   Dolmetsch, Victor. "Nouvelles Diverses: Paris et Départements." Le Ménestrel 52 (7 November 1886): 395.

Review of the Tarentelle: "The texture of this piece
would perhaps be better suited to the virtuosity of
a soloist than to the layers of an orchestra, but
this does not indicate any less of a fresh inspiration or genuine skilll on the part of the composer."
See W46a.

B93   [Héler, A.]. "Revue des Concerts: Concerts Populaires." L'Art Musical 25 (15 November 1886): 163-64.

Another review of the Tarentelle: Comparing the
piece to a very successful work by Tchaikovsky heard
on the program, the reviewer considers the Tarentelle to be out of its element. "This piece . . . is
merely an unfortunate orchestral transcription of a
virtuosic fantasia." See W46a.

B94   "Nouvelles Diverses: Paris et Départements." Le Ménestrel 53 (12 December 1886): 15.

Announcement of a forthcoming program involving many
performers, in which Chaminade is to present several

piano works: Automne, Scherzo, Fileuse, Marine, Guitare, and Air de Ballet. See W34a, W38a, W41a, W42a,
W43a, W56a.

B95   "Nouvelles Diverses: Concerts et Soirées." Le Ménes-
       trel 53 (30 January 1887): 72.

       Two of Chaminade's mélodies included on a recital of
       Mme. Laborde's vocal students, in which the composer
       participates.

B96   J. "Nouvelles Diverses: Concerts et Soirées." Le Mén-
       estrel 53 (13 February 1887): 87.

       The Trio No. 2 presented at a concert of the Société
       Nationale de Musique: "[The piece], without display-
       ing much relief, is written in an assured and ele-
       gant manner." See W40.

B97   Boutarel, Amédée. "Nouvelles Diverses: Concerts et
       Soirées." Le Ménestrel 53 (1 May 1887): 176.

       On her recital at the Salle Pleyel, the pianist Mme.
       Roger-Miclos performed one or more Chaminade solo
       pieces on a program devoted to modern works.

B98   A. R. "Nouvelles Diverses: Paris et Départements." Le
       Ménestrel 53 (25 December 1887): 415.

       The pianist Louis Livon gave a fine rendition of
       Chaminade's Toccata on the eighth program of the
       Association Artistique in Marseille. See W57a.

B99   Cisvenn, Karl. "Revue Musicale." Gazette du Midi (Mar-
       seille), [15] March 1888.

       Chaminade, who has come to Marseille to direct the
       rehearsals for her ballet Callirhoë, performs seve-
       ral pieces at a séance on 11 March at the Livons,
       all very well received. Among them are Marine, Menu-
       et, Intermezzo, Pas des Cymbales, Zingara, and Au-
       tomne. Assessing her talent, the reviewer declares
       that "Mlle. Chaminade strikes me as a musical Geor-
       ges Sand. This is a woman who thinks and writes like
       a man. . . ." See W7e, W20g, W31b, W42b, W47b, W48b,
       W56b.

B100   Silvio. "Chronique Musicale: Une Matinée Musicale In-
       time Chez Mme. Livon--Mme. Chaminade." Le Petit Pro-
       vençal (Marseille), [15] March 1888.

       Another account of the Livon musicale, also serving
       to introduce Chaminade the composer and pianist to
       Marseille in advance of the imminent Callirhoë pre-
       miere. Very impressed with her talents, the reviewer
       deems her a composer "of the first rank, highly in-
       dividual," and then details the fine points of her
       style. See W7e, W20g, W31b, W42b, W47b, W48b, W56b.

B101   La Vedette (Marseille), [15] March 1888.

Brief account of musicale at the Livons' on 11
March. In addition to the piano pieces, Chaminade
took part in several of her songs, including Magdeleine, Ritournelle, Madrigal, and Chanson Slave.
See W262c, W263b, W265b, W266b.

B102   L. M. "Causerie Musicale: 23eme Concert de l'Association Artistique." Journal de Marseille, 16 March
1888, 2-3.

Review of the 23rd program of the Association Artistique, which performed the Overture to La Sévillane
and Zingara. Of the former, the reviewer singles out
"its Spanish character that excludes, however, the
banalities common to the genre," but goes on to cri-
ticize the abrupt ending, which is all too common a
trait in young composers. Zingara is "delicious in
every way." The remainder of the rather lengthy article is devoted to the Livon musicale, in which
Chaminade's compositions earn high praise. See W18d,
W31c.

B103   Silvio. "Chronique Musicale: Salle Vallette--23e Concert Classique." Le Petit Provençal (Marseille),
[16] March 1888.

Musically detailed review of the same program described above. "The Overture, with a very spirited
opening, is done well in a style befitting the pro-
logue of an opéra-comique. Local color is brought
out very nicely--that is, sufficiently picturesque
without exaggerated rhythms and crude sounds. I have
only one complaint to make . . . that of ending too
abruptly . . . which has been inaugurated by the new
school in composition. I confess I have not accus-
tomed myself to it yet." In the very favorable assessment of Zingara, the reviewer points out the
recapitulation, where the brasses have a novel effect: "I repeat, it is unexpected and exquisitely
placed." See W18d, W31c.

B104   Prégentil, R. "La Soirée à Marseille: Grand-Théâtre,
Callirhoë." Le Soleil du Midi (Marseille), 17 March
1888.

Review of premiere of Callirhoe, on previous evening. Expressing pride at having such an important
musical event take place in his city, the reviewer
judges the ballet "a great success" and generally
praises the talents of the composer. "I will add
immediately that upon leaving the theater, one was
almost murmuring the word 'masterpiece,' and we are
still under the charm of this bright, brilliant
music, whose powerful orchestration seems to flow
from the pen of an experienced master." See W49a.

B105   Silvio. "Chronique Musicale: Mlle. Chaminade--Callir-
        hoë." Le Petit Provençal, [17] March 1888.

        In a lengthy article written after the premiere of
        Callirhoë, the reviewer discusses the city's gradu-
        ally changed perception of Chaminade since her ar-
        rival a few weeks earlier--from one known only for
        music for dilettantes to an acknowledged grand mas-
        ter. The reviewer is extremely impressed by her tal-
        ents. Although he must defer a full assessment of
        the ballet, he sums up its achievement thus: "What
        charming and agreeable things in the score of Cal-
        lirhoë--Delibes or Widor would have gladly signed
        his name to it, and a colorist like Massenet would
        not fail to render homage!" See W49a.

B106   Delonchamps, G. "Spectacles." Gazette du Midi, 18
        March 1888, 3.

        In this substantial account of Callirhoë considera-
        ble space is devoted to the story and to the dance
        itself. The assessment of the music is mostly posi-
        tive, although the reviewer believes that the music
        does not adequately depict the archaic Greek time in
        which the work is set. See W49a.

B107   Frisch, Henry. "Callirhoë: I--Une Répétition Génér-
        ale." Journal de Marseille, 18 March 1888, 3.

        The first part of a trio of articles, appearing to-
        gether, on Callirhoë (see also B108-09). An eye-
        witness narrative, in the present tense, of the
        dress rehearsal. The style is literary and is in-
        tended to heighten the reader's expectation for the
        work itself and for the following two articles. In
        its subjectivity and obvious appeal to the emotions
        it seems unusual for a newspaper. See W49a.

B108   De Bohern, Noël. "Callirhoë: II--Mlle. Chaminade et Le
        Ballet de Callirhoë." Journal de Marseille, 18 March
        1888, 3.

        This second part, more traditional, recounts briefly
        the backround of the Rougier-Chaminade collaboration
        on Callirhoë. It then provides a personal and pro-
        fessional history of the composer. "One day we will
        surely see one of her works performed on the grand
        stage of the Opéra."

B109   Manuel. "Callirhoë: III--La Représentation." Journal
        de Marseille, 18 March 1888, 3.

        The concluding part contains an assessment of the
        work, although the writer asserts that the actual
        review will appear in the "Causerie Musicale" col-
        umns. The article opens with a refutation of the
        widely-held belief that women are incapable of com-
        posing. The proof is Callirhoë, a work that displays
        "a powerful conception, knowledge of harmony, skill

in orchestration, [and] . . . melody that is always distinguished and limpid; this is the work of a master." At the end of the performance "Mlle. Chaminade was literally covered with flowers, palms, and wreaths." See W49a.

B110   "Nouvelles Diverses: Concerts et Soirées." Le Ménestrel 54 (18 March 1888): 96.

One or more Chaminade piano pieces were included on the program of Cécile Monvel.

B111   Pepito. "Grand-Théâtre: La Première de 'Callirhoë'." L'Etincelle (Marseille), [18] March 1888.

A preliminary evaluation of Callirhoë, which deems it a great success ("without precedent"). A large segment of the article details the verses underlying a part of the ballet. See W49a.

B112   Philip. "Mlle. Chaminade," Le Petit Marseillais, 18 March 1888, 2.

Lengthy, informative interview with the composer in Marseille, which begins with the tantalizing lines, "Do you know Mlle. Chaminade? do you know who she is?" We learn, for instance, of the genesis of the Rougier-Chaminade collaboration and of her plans in the immediate future.

B113   Pradelle, Jules. "Chronique Musicale: Grand-Théâtre." Le Sémaphore de Marseille, [18] March 1888.

Favorable review of Callirhoë, and of a concert of the Cercle Artistique. Chaminade's music for the ballet is lauded for its grace, charm, and feeling. It evinces great harmonic skill, and does not offend with an excess of orchestral color. "The success of the work is without precedent in Marseille." See W49a.

B114   Ball, A. "Théâtres et Concerts," Le Soleil du Midi (Marseille), 19 March 1888, 4.

Brief notice of other Chaminade works performed in a concert subsequent to the Callirhoë premiere: the Scherzo and Choral from the Suite d'Orchestre. "The Scherzo was pleasing by virtue of its playfulness; the Choral, however, has a vocal breadth of considerable worth." See W21e, W22e.

B115   "Courrier des Théâtres: Grand Théâtre." Le Mondain, [20] March 1888.

Mixed review of Callirhoë: "In truth, this score . . . contains delicious motifs, such as that of the 'Pastorale' for oboe, and the 'Valse Finale.'. . . The 'Pas des Echarpes' and the 'Danse Orientale,' whose rhythm is . . . insufficiently accentuated,

produced an equally favorable impression on the public. Alongside these musical perfections are motifs
lacking originality, which could very easily be sup-
pressed without detracting from the success of the
work, whose orchestration is perfect and whose harmony is sophisticated and well fashioned." See W49a.

B116   "Causerie Musicale: Callirhoë." Journal de Marseille,
        22 March 1888.

        In this lengthy review various strengths and weak-
        nesses are discussed. The "delightful Scherzetto"
        and the Scène Pastorale are considered "the two
        pearls of the score." The writer would like to see
        more heightened musical description, as this is a
        staged work with particular local color; performed
        in the concert hall, as a suite, there is no problem
        in this regard. Overall, the work is dubbed "origi-
        nal" and "charming." See W49a.

B117   Cisvenn, Karl. "Revue Musicale--CLXIV--Callirhoë."
        Gazette du Midi, [23] March 1888.

        An excellent, thought-provoking assessment of Cal-
        lirhoë in relation to the French musical scene. This
        is one of the few articles on Chaminade that men-
        tions Wagner. Very impressed with the work, the wri-
        ter states that the composer "belongs to that modern
        school that strives to satisfy the spirit in par-
        ticular; but with her, the ear is always charmed as
        well." Her vigorous conception of a piece is a trait
        not always found in the stronger sex. After briefly
        assessing the individual movements, the reviewer
        notes the great variety in "this remarkable score."
        He then convincingly refutes the potential criticism
        that the music does not adequately depict the an-
        cient Greek setting of the story: "This criticism .
        . . is as well-founded as if one were to blame Fey-
        deau for not having written Salambô in the Carthagi-
        nian dialect." See W49a.

B118   Comettant, Oscar. "Revue Musicale." Le Siècle (Paris),
        [25] March 1888.

        Reporting the brilliant success of Callirhoë in Mar-
        seille, the writer expresses the hope that the bal-
        let will be presented soon at the Eden-Théâtre in
        Paris. See W49a.

B119   "Nouvelles Diverses: Concerts et Soirées." Le Ménes-
        trel 54 (25 March 1888): 104.

        On 6 March, one or more Chaminade works were per-
        formed at the annual concert of the pianist Gabri-
        elle Turpin.

B120   Rostand, Alexis. "Nouvelles Diverses: Paris et Dépar-
        tements." Le Ménestrel 54 (25 March 1888): 103.

Of moderate length, this assessment provides a bal-
anced and perceptive view of Callirhoë. It praises
several general stylistic traits, including its
grace, its harmony, and its orchestral color, although the last is deemed a bit too gentle for this
type of work. "The most well-received movements of
this symphonic score are the Pas des Amphores and
the Pas des Echarpes, almost of a Classical turn."
The audience also warmly applauded "an adorable
fairy-like Scherzo, in duple meter, which accompa-
nies the pursuit of the Amours . . . , a lovely Pastorale, and the Valse Finale." See W49a.

B121   Pradelle, Jules. "Callirhoë." Il Trovatore [Milan],
        [25] March 1888.

        This review is taken from the Pradelle article cited
        above; see B113. See W49a.

B122   S. Lucien B. "Grand-Théâtre." L'Etincelle (Marseille),
        [26] March 1888.

        This review concentrates on the ballet itself and on
        the dancers. Only in the last paragraph is notice
        taken of the composer, "the idol of the Marseille
        artistic world for the past two weeks."See W49a.

B123   Silvio. "Chronique Musicale--Sur Le Sens du Terme
        'Symphonique' Appliqué au Ballet Callirhoe de Mlle.
        Chaminade." Le Petit Provençal, [28] March 1888.

        Long, interesting article written after the seventh
        performance of Callirhoë. Chaminade gave the sub-
        title "symphonique" to the work. The author explains
        the connotations of this term, especially in rela-
        tion to the symphonic poem, and concludes that Cal-
        lirhoë fits the description. Rather than merely pro-
        viding rhythmic backdrop for the dances, the music
        attempts to depict the poetic intentions of the lib-
        retto and to evoke orchestrally a sense of the an-
        tique. Furthermore, the score contains recurring
        motifs, which help to underscore the relationship of
        the two main characters as well as provide unity.
        Overall the harmonic and melodic structures are
        praised. In a subsequent article (see B124), the
        author will tackle the issue of music's ability to
        evoke local color. See W49.

B124   Silvio. "Chronique Musicale: Un Mot Sur La Couleur
        Locale et La Convention du Coloris Antique Dans La
        Musique Moderne." Le Petit Provençal, [30] March
        1888.

        Adopting the definition of local color from Les Il-
        lusions Musicales by Johannes Weber, the author pro-
        ceeds to discuss Callirhoë. The difficulty is how to
        depict ancient times when one cannot utilize an an-
        cient musical style. Chaminade succeeds admirably in
        overcoming this inherent difficulty through subtle

musical means, especially through line, color, and sonority. The result still evokes the Greek era, and does it beautifully, but not through the usual means of inserting popular tunes of the given culture into one's general compositional style. See W49.

B125　Lassalvy, P. "Deuxième Correspondance--Grand Théâtre," Le Progrès Artistique 11 (c. early April 1888).

This review comes after the tenth performance of Callirhoë in Marseille. "The music of Mlle. Chaminade is in the modern style; it is skillful, polished, and difficult, but it does not lack harmony. It is especially the freshness of inspiration that we have admired in this young talent. We are persuaded that an arrangement of the principal sections of this work into a suite will be very successful at the Colonne or Lamoureux concerts." See W49.

B126　"Grand-Théâtre de Marseille." La Nation (Bordeaux), 7 April 1888.

Report on Callirhoë in Marseille, which focuses on the novelty of artistic decentralization that this event represents. See W49a.

B127　"Nouvelles Diverses: France." L'Art Musical 27 (15 April 1888): 55.

Notice of the Callirhoë premiere. "The new work has been a great success, and the entire local press sings Dithyrambic praises to her honor, of which the majority, we understand, are absolutely deserved." See W49a.

B128　J. H. "Le Concert 'C. Chaminade' au 'Cercle Catholique'." L'Escart (Anvers), [19] April 1888.

Substantial review of 18 April Anvers concert, with the premieres of Les Amazones and Concertstück, and other works: excerpts from La Sévillane, and the mélodies Madrigal and Chanson Slave. Chaminade is not totally unknown in Anvers, as some of her songs were performed at a Société de Musique concert. "Mme. Cécile Chaminade is a musician of style, possessing skill and distinction. That is to claim a lot, and these qualities might appear astonishing in a woman, but they are definitely a part of Mlle. Chaminade, and to a great degree." With regard to Les Amazones, the flight of Himris and Gandhar is compared to the ride to the abyss in The Damnation of Faust, and to the ride of the Valkyries. "In this time of musical troubles and complications, in which every new arrival strains himself to imitate Wagner, Mlle. Chaminade's music provides a character that is fundamentally French, faithful to its nature. . . This 'flight' is indeed a French 'ride'." The Duo is praised for its turbulent and dramatic setting. In general, her music has sentiment without being cloy-

ing; "it is less effeminate than Massenet's, for
example." The Concertstück "contains nice ideas,
elegantly and naturally developed. We heard a remarkable series of scales, linked successively with
truly original harmonies ['tonalités'], blending
with the solo instruments and complementing them."
Chaminade sets a good example to the young of the
stronger sex. See W18e, W29a, W58a, W262d, W266c.

B129   V. M. "Katholieke-Kring: Concert Chaminade." Het Handelsblad (Antwerp), [20] April 1888.

Review of concert of 18 April, which says nothing
about the Concertstück. The concert was a real musical event and very well-attended despite the bad
weather. Overall Chaminade's music has spirit, feeling, and color; her orchestral style is vigorous.
Les Amazones is a work that displays her talents.
Again, the flight of Himris and Gandhar is compared
to Wagner's ride of the Valkyries. Praise is also
reserved for the Trio and chorus from La Sévillane.
See W18e, W29a.

B130   "Théâtres et Concerts." La Patriote (Anvers), [20]
April 1888.

Account of 18 April concert: "This younng and brilliant pianist, . . . almost unknown in Anvers, has,
in one evening, captured a niche in the artistic
world for her remarkable talent. Every piece on the
program was appluded with enthusiasm, and the young
artist received an ovation from all the musicians."
See W58a.

B131   L. M. Journal de Marseille, 20 April 1888.

Rather than a review, this article is a continuation
of the ongoing discussion in Marseille newspapers on
the question of musical representation of local
color, as in Callirhoë. The writer mentions his colleagues at the Gazette du Midi and Le Petit Provençal, singling out Silvio. See B105-06, B117, and
especially B123-24.

B132   "Anvers." Le Guide Musical 34 No. 17 (26 April 1888):
133.

Drawn in large part from newspaper reviews (see B128
and B130), this substantial account is often detailed, and very complimentary. Sections of Les Amazones compare favorably with Wagner and Berlioz but
always retain a French sensibility. "The Concertstück for piano and orchestra, performed by the author, who displays a remarkable pianistic talent in
the service of composition, contains attractive
ideas, developed elegantly and naturally." See W58a.

B133   "Nouvelles Diverses: Concerts et Soirées." Le Ménestrel 54 (29 April 1888): 144.

Brief notice of a recital by Louise Steiger, pianist, on 18 April at the Salle Pleyel, which included one or more pieces by Chaminade.

B134   Berliner Courier, c. late April 1888.

Report on Chaminade's recent successes: "A ballet from her pen, entitled Callirhoë, was a success at the Marseille Opera, and was unanimously well received by critics and the public. Just as lustrous was the reception of her work, Les Amazones, a Cantata [sic] for chorus, soloists, and orchestra, which premiered at the Cercle Catholique. On this occasion Fräulein Chaminade also appeared as pianist and distinguished herself as such mainly through her rendition of her Concertstück with orchestra." See W18e, W29a, W58a.

B135   Le Figaro, 20 June 1888.

After conveying Chaminade's success with Callirhoë in Marseille, this brief article continues: "Today we are reproducing, on page 8, an excerpt from this important work, a Danse Pastorale . . . , an interesting sample of the distinguished talent of Mlle. Cécile Chaminade." See W54.

B136   "Autographe de Mlle. Cécile Chaminade." L`Art Musical 27 ([July] 1888): 226.

Chaminade sent the journal an excerpt from Les Amazones. The accompanying letter, dated "Le Vésinet, 16 June," was published as well: "It gives me great pleasure to send you a few lines of the autograph for you to reproduce in L'Art Musical. The excerpt that I'm sending is drawn from my dramatic symphony, Les Amazones, for orchestra, soloists, and chorus." See W29.

B137   "Audition d'Oeuvres de Mlle. C. Chaminade." Courrier de Lyon, [last half 1888].

Review of a program devoted to Chaminade's works, at the hall of the music publisher E. Clot. The composer was one of the performers. "Of the two movements drawn from the first Trio, we especially liked the second, with its playful and spirited grace." Of the four songs performed, La Fiancée du Soldat "is a sort of legend with the allure of a popular chant"; Chanson Slave "is very curious in its dark accents in the low register"; but Madrigal "and especially Ritournelle are ravishing inspirations, full of freshness and feminine charm, and it is certain that they will be heard often in all the salons." Eight piano pieces completed the program; the reviewer preferred Sérénade, Air de Ballet, and Pas des Echarpes. Overall, the recital was deemed a great success. See W14g, W33b, W34c, W52a, W56c, W57b, W262e, W265c, W266d, W267a.

B138   "Concerts et Soirées." Le Ménestrel 55 (20 January 1889): 23.

Announcement of Lamoureux concert that afternoon, at Cirque d'Eté, which includes "Concertstück, for piano and orchestra (first hearing), performed by the composer (Mlle. C. Chaminade)." See W58b.

B139   [Darcours, Charles?]. "Les Concerts du Dimanche." Le Figaro, 21 January 1889.

Review of 20 January concert. Chaminade is mostly an unknown commodity to the Parisian public; except for her successful ballet Callirhoë, performed in Marseille, her works have hardly been performed, except at the clannish Société Nationale de Musique. "Mlle. Chaminade deserves better than that . . . . Still very young, she already possesses considerable credentials, and has familiarized herself with all genres. . . . The Concertstück that she performed yesterday is a work that is interesting, serious, and brief, with a well-conceived structure, orchestrated without excess but not without vigor, containing certain passages that are especially well written. I will single out a passage that returns twice, in which the piano, above a pattern in the orchestra, executes a rapid ascending scale that it repeats like an ostinato, and whose effect is both highly ingenious and felicitous. As virtuoso and as composer, Mlle. Chaminade enjoyed a great success." See W58b.

B140   Claris. "Concerts Lamoureux." Le Progrès Artistique, [c. 25 January 1889].

Review of composer performing Concertstück. While praising the form and the overall level of creativity, the reviewer asserts that "the orchestration seemed a bit dense; sometimes it covers the piano. If relieved a bit of its tiring sonorities, the piece will quickly take its place in the category of brilliant concert pieces to recommend to virtuosos who do not wish to totally sacrifice the music to digital gymnastics. Mlle. Chaminade interpreted her composition with consummate virtuosity and was recalled with warmth." See W58b.

B141   Petit-Jean. Le Soleil, [25] January 1889.

Brief notice of Concertstück at Lamoureux Concerts, stating that the work and the concert were a great success. See W58b.

B142   Boutarel, Amédée. "Concerts et Soirées--Concerts Lamoureux." Le Ménestrel 55 (27 January 1889): 31.

Mixed review of <u>Concertstück</u>: "The <u>Concertstück</u> of Mlle. C. Chaminade, performed with real virtuosity by the composer, seemed to us to have an extreme propensity for violent sonorities, and as a result, not exempt from errors in taste. One can be energetic without putting the brass and percussion in the forefront, and it is not necessary in every case to have the piano's chords that are always a bit weak proceed without transition to highly eccentric sonorities in the orchestra. For the rest, there are some ideas in the <u>Concertstück</u> of Mlle. Chaminade, and the public displayed great warmth toward the composer and the performer." <u>See</u> W58b.

B143   "Les Grands Concerts." <u>La Semaine Artistique et Musicale</u>, [c. 27 January 1889].

Flattering review of the <u>Concertstück</u>, "a work of value, perhaps a bit short, but well developed. Written in one movement, in quadruple meter, with, of course, ritards and accelerandos, it unfolds with an ease indicating on the part of the author a clarity of thought and a sureness of hand seldom encountered. The general feeling of the work is one of grace and charming delicacy; the phrases are of a poetic cast and an exquisite delicacy. There is a little of the color of Weber and Delibes, but without the least imitation. And it is orchestrated in an incomparable manner. Mlle. Chaminade, in this regard, evidently has nothing else to learn. She is absolute master of this very important aspect of her art; Massenet would not have done better." <u>See</u> W58b.

B144   De Jennius, from <u>La Liberté</u>, as quoted in "Nouvelles Diverses: Concerts et Soirées." <u>Le Ménestrel</u> 55 (17 February 1889): 56.

One or more Chaminade works were included on a program devoted exclusively to the works of female composers, rendered by the pianist Mme. Roger-Miclos. Among the other composers are Augusta Holmès, [Pauline] Viardot, and Grandval.

B145   Darcours, Charles. "Notes de Musique." <u>Le Figaro</u>, 20 February 1899, p. 6 cols. 1-2.

Review of the recital devoted to works by women composers (<u>see</u> B144). Chaminade did not perform.

B146   "Quatorzième Concert Populaire." <u>Angers Revue</u>, [late February 1889].

This is a review of the <u>Concertstück</u>, presumably in Angers (<u>see</u> B147-48). The reviewer generally praises the work, singling out specific passages, such as the "brilliant" opening. We are in the presence "of a work that is strong and virile, too virile perhaps, and that is the reproach I would be tempted to address to it. For me, I almost regretted not having

found further those qualities of grace and gentle-
ness that reside in the nature of woman, the secrets
of which she possesses to such a degree." See W58c.

B147   "Chronique Musicale: 18ème Concert Populaire." Le Patriote de L'Ouest (Angers), [late February 1889].

Review of Louise Steiger's performance of Concertstück. Noting that the composer recently performed
this piece at the Lamoureux concerts, the reviewer
praises the work for its virility, its energy, and
its orchestration. "Don't expect a concerto for
piano and orchestra. Not at all. This is a symphonic
piece, in one movement, with piano obbligato. Perhaps there are a few abuses of the brass. Perhaps,
quite simply, we don't get enough strings. Variety
of rhythm, no banal passages, here and there new
effects--these are sufficient to assure Mlle. Chaminade a secure place among the composers of our
time." See W58d.

B148   "Concertstück." Anjou Artiste (Angers), [late February
1889].

The most interesting part of this article is its
quotation from the Parisian newspaper, Le Monde Artiste, when it reviewed the composer's recent performance of Concertstück: "The new work . . . is
written with a rare assurance; without being absolutely original, it's never ordinary; the orchestration is varied, but a bit heavy-handed. Despite this
fault, which experience will correct, the work . . .
is extremely interesting. It has varied rhythm and
is never sentimental. If its sonorities were occasionally less brutal it would recall L'España of
Emmanuel Chabrier." See W58b, W58c.

B149   "Nouvelles Diverses: Concerts et Soirées--Concerts
Divers et Matinées." Le Ménestrel 55 (10 March 188-
9): 79.

Steiger's performance of Concertstück in Paris: "Interesting work, but with a form a bit tormented,
[it] was performed very well. . . ." See W58d.

B150   "Nouvelles Diverses: Concerts et Soirées." Le Ménestrel 55 (24 March 1889): 96.

On 4 April, at the Salle Erard, excerpts from La
Sévillane will be included on the annual concert of
an amateur choral society, the Société de Sainbris.
See W18f.

B151   "Nouvelles Diverses: Concerts et Soirées." Le Ménestrel 55 (31 March 1889): 104.

Chaminade will participate in a chamber concert, on
2 April, organized by the violinist Marcel Herwegh.
See W40b.

B152   "Concerts Herwegh." Le Monde Musical 1 ([5] April
        1889).

        Brief report on the chamber concert given 2 April,
        in which Chaminade's Trio [No. 2] is performed. Both
        the piece and its rendition are praised. See W40b.

B153   "Nouvelles Diverses: Concerts et Soirées." Le Ménes-
        trel 55 (7 April 1889): 112.

        Very brief notice of the chamber concert. See W40b.

B154   "Nouvelles Diverses: Concerts et Soirées." Le Ménes-
        trel 55 (21 April 1889): 127.

        Review of the Société de Sainbris choral concert. "A
        lovely chorus from La Sévillane . . . concluded this
        soirée." See W18f.

B155   Massiac, Théodore. "Cécile Chaminade." La Semaine Ar-
        tistique et Musicale, [October 1889].

        Extensive, valuable article, including biography,
        evaluation of her style and popularity, and enumera-
        tion of notable performances. Harking back to her
        private performance of La Sévillane several years
        ago (see W18a), the writer notes how many young lad-
        ies are engaged in music and how many are provided
        poor training and guidance. But Chaminade is obvi-
        ously one who has succeeded. She can be compared
        with two other female composers, Grandval and Hol-
        mès, among whom "she is certainly the most femin-
        ine." The one quality that sums up her music, and
        her playing, is "charm," although in the large works
        there is also vigor and strength. In concluding, the
        writer hopes "that she remain faithful to the French
        style, to that style of reason, of clarity, of in-
        spiration, of grace, of elegance, of grandeur--of
        wisdom and of order; to that style to which we owe
        so many masterpieces."

B156   "Courrier des Théâtres." Le Figaro, 12 December 1889,
        p. 3 col. 3.

        Announcement of forthcoming Lamoureux concert, on
        Sunday the 15th, which includes two Chaminade works:
        Scherzettino and Pas des Cymbales, both from Callir-
        hoë. See W48c, W82a.

B157   "Revue des Grands Concerts." Le Ménestrel 55 (15 De-
        cember 1889): 397.

        Announcement of Lamoureux concert that afternoon.
        See W48c, W82a.

B158   "Théâtres et Concerts." Le Petit Marseillais, [19]
        December 1889.

Report of 15 December Lamoureux concert, including Pas des Cymbales and Scherzettino. The writer mentions the warm reception of the pieces, and asserts that this should serve as an impetus to the new direction of the Grand-Théâtre, where Callirhoë was first performed, to remount the work. See W48c, W82a.

B159   Le Petit Provençal, [20] December 1889.

Report on Lamoureux concert, which expresses the wish that Callirhoë be produced again in Marseille. See W48c, W82a.

B160   Boutarel, Amédée. "Revue des Grands Concerts." Le Ménestrel 55 (22 December 1889): 406.

Mixed review of the Lamoureux concert: "The Scherzettino . . . is a charming piece, with orchestration that is equally ingenious and restrained. On the other hand, the Pas des Cymbales seems to contain many noisy effects and phrases whose melody is vulgar." See W48c, W82a.

1890 TO SEPTEMBER 1908

B161   L. M. "Nouvelles Diverses: France." L'Art Musical 29 (31 January 1890): 15.

One or more unspecified works of Chaminade on a program, organized by Rondeau, in which the composer participated.

B162   Gautier-Garguille. "Propos de Coulisses." Gil Blas, 31 January 1890, p. 3 col. 1.

Brief review of Chaminade concert, on 30 January at the Salle Erard, devoted to her works. The Concertstück is singled out as being very successful. Other works on the program were Marine, Pierrette, and Fileuse, "given a marvelous interpretation by Mlle. Chaminade." See W43b, W56d, W58e, W59a.

B163   "Nouvelles Diverses: Paris et Départements." Le Ménestrel 56 (2 February 1890): 40.

Announcement of a recital of a vocalist, Caroline Chaucherau, to take place on 4 February, in which Chaminade will participate.

B164   L. M. "Nouvelles Diverses: France." L'Art Musical 29 (15 February 1890): 23.

Brief announcement of forthcoming concert of the students of Fabre, which will include some compositions by Chaminade.

B165   J. T. "Nouvelles Diverses: Paris et Départements." Le
        Ménestrel 56 (23 March 1890): 95.

        Review of violinist Herwegh's concert on 14 March,
        in which Chaminade participated and one of her
        works, Bohémienne, was performed. "As always, Mlle.
        Chaminade showed herself to be a most distinguished
        composer and performer." See W37b.

B166   "Nouvelles Diverses: Paris et Départements." Le Ménes-
        trel 56 (27 April 1890): 136.

        Notice of Louise Steiger's piano recital, in which
        Chaminade participated. "Great success for all."

B167   "Nouvelles Diverses: Concerts et Soirées." Le Ménes-
        trel 56 (18 May 1890): 160.

        Bohémienne was performed on a program of the Société
        des Concerts du Conservatoire, on 5 May. See W37c.

B168   Reuss, Eduard. "Klavierstücke von Cécile Chaminade."
        [source unknown], [1890].

        Lengthy essay, including stylistic analysis of her
        works. The author reveals his predilection for salon
        works, and he views Chaminade as a master of this
        type of piece. He discerns "an incomparable grace
        and charm" in many of her pieces, and attributes her
        harmonic and structural skills to her teacher, Sav-
        ard. Automne is reminiscent of the style of Chabri-
        er. In addition, her compositions do not betray "fe-
        male traits," which affect the treatment of form and
        melody in most female composers. The writer points
        to Pas des Echarpes as a sterling piece. The article
        concludes with the author's earnest hope that Chami-
        nade will remain true to the smaller forms. See W42,
        W52.

B169   Gautier-Garguille. "Propos de Coulisses." Gil Blas, 24
        November 1890, p. 3 col. 2.

        Report on Callirhoë Suite, at Concerts Colonne: "It
        was quite successful. It is music that is delicate
        and fine, without a trace of sentimentality. Its
        ideas show a feminine side, in delicious contrast
        with the writing, which shows a sureness of hand
        totally masculine. In its entirety the work has a
        poetic, ravishing quality, and it has definitely en-
        tered the repertory of the Concerts du Châtelet."
        See W50a.

B170   "Chronique Musicale." Le Monde Musical 2 ([1] December
        1890).

        Review of Colonne Concert: "First hearing . . . of
        Callirhoë, orchestral suite of Mlle. C. Chaminade,
        who is, of all composers of the weaker sex, the one
        whose type pleases us the most. A great distinction,

a very skilled hand, a wealth of fresh ideas. Sometimes some hints of Léo Delibes, and this is no reproach. . . . . The Pas des Echarpes is for us the
best number. . . ." See B50a.

B171   "Chronique Musicale: Concerts Colonne." Le Progrès
Artistique, [1] December 1890.

The Callirhoë Suite is mentioned briefly and favorably. The reviewer concludes, "Mlle. Chaminade places herself, more and more, among the favorite composers of the public." See B50a.

B172   Darcours, Charles. "Notes de Musique." Le Figaro, 3
December 1890, p. 6 cols. 2-3.

Review of Callirhoë Suite: "The excerpts from Callirhoë . . . form a very interesting orchestral
suite. . . . It's the third [movement] . . . that we
prefer, in acccordance with the public, who demanded
another hearing. These four pieces, substantial in
their conciseness, are orchestrated `for the
effect,' but with curious ingenuity and perfect success." See B50a.

B173   Gazetta Musicale di Milano, [early December] 1890.

Announcement that Ricordi has acquired some Chaminade pieces and will publish them by the end of the
year (see W68-71). Also a report that the Callirhoë
Suite has just been performed at the Colonne Concerts in Paris. See B50a.

B174   M. "'Callirhoë' à Monte-Carlo." [Le Soleil du Midi]
(Marseilles), [1891].

Review of Callirhoë Suite performed at the Concerts
Classiques in Monte Carlo. "The newspapers of the
region mention the great success." Quotations from
Le Figaro and Le Gaulois, both Parisian newspapers,
also comment on the work's warm reception in its
first performance in Monte Carlo. See W50.

B175   Loret, Victor. "Critique Musicale: Musique Méconnue."
L'Echo de Lyon, 13 January 1891.

Writer looks forward to the re-mounting of the ballet Callirhoë in Lyon. See W49b.

B176   Ménard, L. Le Journal de Marseille, [February] 1891.

Callirhoë is expected to return to Marseille soon.
Meanwhile, the article takes note of the recent suc-
cess of the Suite, at the Colonne Concerts. See
W50a.

B177   "Callirhoë." Le Courrier de Lyon, 12 February 1891, 2-
3.

Announcement of the concert that evening, including a detailed synopsis of the story. See W49b.

B178   "Nouvelles Diverses: Paris et Départements." Le Ménestrel 57 (22 February 1891): 64.

Report of the Lyon performance of Callirhoë: "The work was mounted with care, and the orchestra, under the skilled hand of its director, Luigini, worked wonders." See W49b.

B179   "Nouvelles Diverses." L'Art Musical 30 (31 March 18-91): 47.

Brief mention of Le Noël des Marins being performed by the Société Chorale d'Amateurs, at the Salle Erard. See W66a.

B180   "Nouvelles Diverses: Concerts et Soirées." Le Ménestrel 57 (10 May 1891): 152.

At a soirée, several works by several composers were performed. Chaminade was represented by a few pieces, including Pas des Echarpes, Madrigal, and La Livry. See W52b, W69a, W266e.

B181   "Nouvelles Diverses: France." L'Art Musical 31 (15 January 1892): 14.

Announcement of Chaminade being awarded "Officier de l'Instruction Publique," on 1 January.

B182   "Nouvelles Diverses: Paris et Départements." Le Ménestrel 58 (17 January 1892): 24.

A performing series, entitled "Une heure de musique nouvelle," began 16 January and will run every Saturday afternoon, up to 2 April, with plans to include some works by Chaminade.

B183   Ménard, L. "Causerie Musicale." Journal de Marseille, 26 February 1892, 2.

Interesting review of a performance of the Concertstück, in Marseille, played by Louis Livon: "In form, the work of Mlle. Chaminade would imply a title of Fantasy for Piano and Orchestra. It would come close to the Rhapsodies so much in vogue today if it were based on nationalistic motifs. Whatever its title, it offers us an original composition, rich in color and of sustained interest. An expansive theme, like a leitmotif, permeates the score. . ." See W58f.

B184   "Nouvelles Diverses: France." L'Art Musical 31 (29 February 1892): 31.

Notice of the recent Concertstück performance in Marseille. See W58f.

B185   "Nouvelles Diverses: Paris et Départements." Le Ménes-
         trel 58 (29 May 1892): 176.

         Brief mention of Louise Steiger's second concert at
         the Salle Pleyel, in which Chaminade lent her per-
         forming assistance.

B186   "Mdlle. Chaminade." Globe (London), 24 June 1892.

         Review of first England concert, on 23 June: "Mdlle.
         Chaminade's skill as a pianist was evidenced in her
         performances of seven piquant and graceful piano-
         forte works, and also in her share of works for two
         pianists. Of these, the first--an Andante et Scher-
         zetto and a Pas des Cymbales--were the most success-
         ful. These are bright, original, and cleverly writ-
         ten. . . . Of the eighteen original compositions .
         . . none was weak or commonplace." See W82b, W48d.

B187   "Mdlle. Chaminade's Recital." Daily Chronicle (Lon-
         don), 24 June 1892.

         "Both as composer and executant her success was be-
         yond question."

B188   "Mdlle. Chaminade's Recital." Pall Mall Gazette (Lon-
         don), 24 June 1892.

         "It was a happy idea of the distinguished French
         composer . . . to give a concert in London entirely
         devoted to her own compositions. The programme was
         well calculated to show her talent to its utmost
         advantage. Her second trio . . . contains many ideas
         treated with fancy and skill. It is rare, indeed, to
         find this difficult form of composition so success-
         fully dealt with by a female composer." See W40c.

B189   "Mdlle. Chaminade's Concert." Standard (London), 24
         June 1892.

         "The name of Chaminade has appeared with increasing
         frequency of late in concert programmes, but proba-
         bly the majority of London amateurs were not aware
         that the tasteful songs, and light, though artistic,
         pianoforte pieces with which it has been associated
         were from the pen of a young French lady."

B190   [Bennett, Joseph.] Daily Telegraph (London), 25 June
         1892.

         "The entertainment proved a complete success."

B191   "An Interesting Concert." St Jame's Gazette (London),
         25 June 1892.

         "By several brilliant pieces for the pianoforte and
         by a few tender and expressive songs Mdlle. Chami-
         nade was already known in England. But none of her

orchestral works have been played in this country.
. . In some twenty works of varying degrees of interest Mdlle. Chaminade always maintains herself at
a high artistic level, to reach at times poetic
heights such as few composers are able to attain."

B192   "Mdlle. Cécile Chaminade." Daily News (London), 25
        June 1892.

        "Mdlle Chaminade . . . is best known here by her
        very charming songs. [She] showed herself at her
        best in those graceful little drawing-room pieces
        which have helped to gain her celebrity here, such
        as Pierrette, Pas des Echarpes, and other delicately
        written trifles . . . , and in her songs, seven of
        which were sung by Mr. and Mrs. Oudin." See W52c,
        W59b.

B193   "Mdlle. Chaminade's Concert." The Times (London), 25
        June 1892, p. 19 col. 3.

        A mixed review: "On the whole, the composer's pro-
        ductions stood the severe test better than might
        have been expected, for though few of them reach a
        very high level of art, yet their flow of melody is
        so fresh and spontaneous, and they are so cleverly
        devised, as well as so varied in character, that no
        sense of monotony is produced." The Concertstück, in
        a two-piano version, is judged "of no great origina-
        lity. . . . A Second Trio . . . shows considerable
        knowledge of form, and is most effectively written
        for the instruments; the themes are very original,
        but a want of interest in their development makes it
        impossible to bestow unqualified praise upon it."
        See W40c, W58g.

B194   The Observer (London), 26 June 1892, p. 7 col. 3.

        "Mdlle. Chaminade . . . exhibited great ability in
        the performance of pianoforte works, all composed by
        herself, and all, without exception, interesting."

B195   "Music and Musicians," Sunday Times (London), 26 June
        1892, p. 6 cols. 4-5.

        "The piano trio in A . . . proved to be an eminently
        graceful and interesting work, the andante being a
        particularly charming movement. . . . In the Fileuse
        she displayed a sympathetic touch, and in the Air de
        Ballet a delightful crispness of execution, the re-
        finement of her method being always conspicuous."
        See W43c.

B196   Morning Post (London), 27 June 1892.

        "Mdlle. Chaminade's concert included . . . a piano-
        forte trio from her pen. In this work the gifted
        young French lady gave evidence of distinct talent
        and not a little originality of thought. There is in

all her compositions a certain refined charm and
delicacy of expression." See W40c.

B197   "Music: The Week." The Athenaeum (London) No. 3375 (2
July 1892): 41.

"The most important of the instrumental items was a
pianoforte trio in A minor. . . . This is a work of
great merit, not only in the symmetry and consistency of its construction, but in the remarkably fresh
and spirited treatment of the subject matter. . . .
She is certainly the most gifted female composer who
has recently appeared." See W40c.

B198   "Mdlle. Chaminade." Queen (London), 2 July 1892.

"Some of her pianoforte pieces, such as her Sérénade, her Automne, and her La Fileuse, . . . most
daintily played by the composer, have gained almost
universal popularity, and some of the songs from her
pen . . . are almost equally well-known." See W33c,
W42c, W43c.

B199   Pictorial World (London), 2 July 1892.

"Quite an event . . . was Mdlle. Chaminade's concert
at St. James's Hall on Thursday."

B200   "Nouvelles Diverses: Etranger--Nouvelles de Londres,
29 Juin." Le Ménestrel 58 (3 July 1892): 213-14.

In this report from London, dated 29 June, the correspondent calls the recital "one of the most pleasant concerts of the season. . . . The public gave a
particularly warm reception to the Trio in a, Op.
34." See W40c.

B201   "Nouvelles Diverses: Paris et Départements." Le Ménestrel 58 (10 July 1892): 223-24.

On 3 July, a program performed by amateurs was presented at Versailles. Chaminade and other notable
musicians were in attendance, and two of her Choeurs
were performed.

B202   Guiraud, Omer. "Courrier Artistique." L'Express du
Midi (Toulouse), Thursday 17 November [1892].

Review of Callirhoë at Toulouse: "Her score contains
no less than twenty numbers, all written with her
customary mastery. . . . In a word, the score of
Callirhoë is distinguished by the grace and the quality of its melodic ideas, by its very elegant harmonies, and by its colorful orchestration. . . . The
public experienced a double pleasure: pleasure for
the ears and pleasure for the eyes." See W49c.

B203   "Nouvelles Diverses: Paris et Départements." Le Ménestrel 59 (1 January 1893): 6.

Report of a private musicale involving diverse performers, including Chaminade, who accompanied a few
of her songs.

B204   Barbadette, H. "Revue des Grands Concerts: Concerts et
Musique de Chambre." Le Ménestrel 59 (26 February
1893): 69.

Review of the first soirée of the White chamber-
music ensemble. Chaminade's Trio No. 2, in which the
composer performed, is deemed "a remarkable work."
See W40d.

B205   "Nouvelles Diverses: Paris et Départements." Le Ménestrel 59 (12 March 1893): 80.

Report on the required repertory for monthly performance examinations of the students of Mme. Dignat,
in Auteuil. Chaminade's name appears in the list of
modern composers.

B206   "Nouvelles Diverses: Paris et Départements." Le Ménestrel 59 (12 March 1893): 88.

Brief mention of Chaminade presenting some of her
"appealing compositions" at a soirée the week before
at Mme. Moreau-Sainti.

B207   "Nouvelles Diverses: Concerts Annoncées." Le Ménestrel
59 (9 April 1893): 120.

Announcement of Chaminade assisting at the forthcoming recital (11 April) of Marguerite Weyler.

B208   "Nouvelles Diverses: Paris et Départements." Le Ménestrel 59 (23 April 1893): 135.

One or more works of Chaminade appeared on a recent
program, part of a series organized by Mme. Clamage-
ran.

B209   "Mdlle. Chaminade's Concert." The Times (London), 3
June 1893, p. 7 col. 6.

Substantial but mostly negative review of her concert of 1 June: "The extraordinary popularity of
this young composer was illustrated in the very
large audience gathered . . . to hear a programme
consisting entirely of her works. Clever as these
are, they can hardly be held to stand successfully
the severe ordeal of being heard in a great quan-
tity. Mannerisms which are not perceived when two
songs or pianoforte pieces are heard in the course
of an ordinary concert become evident to the least
cultivated ears at the end of such an entertainment
as this. The audience, it is only fair to say, received every part of the programme with favour, and
two of the songs sung by Mr. Oudin--L'Amour Captif

and <u>Amoroso</u>--had to be repeated. These, as well as
<u>Viens, Mon Bien-Aimé</u>, charmingly sung by Mrs. Oudin,
were the most successful vocal numbers. . . ." <u>See</u>
W283a, W290b, W292b.

B210   "Concerts and Recitals." <u>The Athenaeum</u> (London) No.
3424 (10 June 1893): 742.

"The programme consisted entirely of her songs,
vocal duets, and <u>salon</u> pianoforte pieces, in which a
certain measure of sameness was noticeable, though
for the most part they were piquant and melodious,
and, in Mlle. Chaminade's native tongue, <u>spirituel</u>,
a term for which we have no exact equivalent."

B211   <u>Lille Artiste, Organe Artistique de la Région du Nord</u>
2 No. 147 (19 November 1893), cover.

Chaminade's picture appears on the cover of this
publication, which means, according to the magazine,
that she was performing in Lille around this time.

B212   Brun, Louis. "Deuxième Concert Populaire." (Lille),
[late November 1893].

Favorable review of Chaminade's program in Lille,
which included the <u>Callirhoë Suite</u>, at least three
piano works (<u>Arabesque</u>, <u>Elévation</u>, and <u>Air de Bal-
let</u>), and the <u>Concertstück</u>. "As composer and pianist, she positively thrilled her audience. Her orchestral suite is charming. . . . But a piece that
we think first rate is the <u>Concertstück</u>. . . . It is
music of the grand scale in which neither grace nor
fantasy is excluded. . . ." <u>See</u> W34d, W50d, W58,
W84b, W99a.

B213   "Nouvelles Diverses: Etranger." <u>Le Ménestrel</u> 60 (7
January 1894): 4.

Brief report of Chaminade's participation in a program in Tournai, which included songs, piano pieces,
and choruses.

B214   "Chronique Locale: Concert d'Abonnement." <u>Journal de
Genève</u>, 18 February 1894, 3.

Announcement of forthcoming subscription concert, in
Geneva, featuring Chaminade and a program devoted
mostly to her works, of mixed genres. It will include several piano pieces (e.g. <u>Deux Pièces dans le
Style Ancien</u>, <u>Elévation</u>, and <u>Les Sylvains</u>), songs
(e.g. <u>Les Deux Ménétriers</u>), the <u>Callirhoë Suite</u>, and
the <u>Concertstück</u>, for which she will conduct the
orchestra and Willy Rehberg will be soloist. <u>See</u>
W50c, W58h, W83a, W99b, W277a.

B215   Le Genevois, 20 February 1894.

Lengthy, flattering article, which includes a general discussion of Chaminade as well as an assessment
of the recent concert. As background, the legendary
statement of Ambroise Thomas is presented, as well
as a comparison of Chaminade with Georges Sand and
Chopin. The reviewer goes into great detail in his
evaluation of Les Deux Ménétriers. Callirhoë Suite
merits high praise as well. Concertstück "is very
interesting and we can appreciate the success that
it enjoyed at the Lamoureux Concerts . . . and at
the Association Artistique in Angers. . . . [It] was
directed with assurance by Mlle. Chaminade, a conductor with a beat that was clean, precise, and yet
supple, for whom a glance or a scant movement would
suffice to signal the cutoff to the various instruments. It was a charming sight, totally free from
the absurdities that the anti-feminists were pleased
to predict." See W50c, W58h, W277a.

B216   "Chronique Locale: Concerts." Journal de Genève, 22
February 1894, 3.

Announcement of another Chaminade program in Geneva,
this time to take place at the Conservatoire. Songs,
piano solos, and choruses for female voices will
constitute the program. Furthermore, on the 24th,
Chaminade will appear on a benefit concert for the
orchestra members and conduct Callirhoë Suite. See
W50.

B217   "Chronique Locale: Concerts." Journal de Genève, 24
February 1894, 3.

A second announcement of the benefit concert to take
place that evening.

B218   A. H. "Nos Correspondances: Etranger." L'Art Musical
33 (1 March 1894): 69.

Brief mention of Chaminade conducting and performing
several of her compositions in three musical events
in Geneva.

B219   Berknay, P. "Concert de Mlle. Chaminade." L'Echo [de
Lyon], 4 March 1894.

Review of concert on the series of the Société de
Musique de Chambre, in which Chaminade's works make
up the majority of the program, including the Trio
[No. 2?] and a few songs. "It is with eagerness that
the elite of Lyon's dilletantes went to make the
acquaintance of Mlle. Chaminade the pianist."

B220   "Concert de Mlle. Chaminade." Public (Lyon), 4 March
1894.

Assessment is very flattering, discussing Chaminade and her music in very general terms, without mention of specific pieces or compositional devices.

B221   "Echos des Spectacles: Concert Chaminade." L'Express de Lyon, 4 March 1894.

"The public gave a very warm reception to this artist, both composer and performer." This is the first time that Chaminade has appeared in person in Lyon.

B222   E. D. "Nouvelles Diverses: Etranger." Le Ménestrel 60 (4 March 1894): 70.

Brief report of Chaminade's activities in Geneva, "what one could call the 'Chaminade Festival,' at the Grand-Théâtre, for the public gave a warm reception to Mlle. Chaminade as pianist, composer, and orchestra conductor."

B223   "Concert de la Société Philharmonique." Eclaireur de L'Est (Reims), [17] March 1894.

Chaminade performs some of her own works on the third and last program of the season of the Société Philharmonique of Reims, for its honorary members. The reviewer has only one negative comment to make about the Concertstück: the title should be the French Morceau de Concert. She performed it very well, "this composition whose inspiration is always abundant and felicitous." Noël des Marins is praised for its delicacy. Tu Me Dirais is one of the songs presented. See W58i, W66b, W282b.

B224   Courrier de la Champagne (Reims), 17 March 1894.

Review of the Reims concert, in which the second half was devoted to Chaminade performing her works: "The Concertstück obtained the kind of great success that it receives everywhere it is performed. What originality in the timbral disposition, what profound knowledge of orchestration, what flights of fancy in the realm of the ideal!" Also favorable is the assessment of the two choral works, Noël des Marins and Noce Hongroise. See W58i, W65a, W66b.

B225   "Théâtres et Concerts: Société Philharmonique." Indépendante de Reims, 17 March 1894.

Another positive evaluation of the Reims concert: "The Concertstück is very interesting, and the orchestral accompaniment is colored in the spirit of the piece, without unexpected effects, without recognizable influences ['réminiscences']. It is, in a word, from the hand of a master, and all assembled were charmed by it." The two choral works received a similarly positive review. See W58i.

B226   "Bruits Qui Courent." <u>L'Art Musical</u> 33 (22 March
        1894): 96.

        Notice of a concert, on 21 March, devoted to Chami-
        nade works, in which the qualities of "originality
        and charm" were in evidence. In another notice, a
        work of Chaminade was presented the same day at a
        soirée organized by Louis Diémer.

B227   "Bruits Qui Courent." <u>L'Art Musical</u> 33 (12 April
        1894): 120.

        Report on a concert of Chaminade works, including <u>La
        Valse Carnavalesque</u>, <u>Barcarolle</u>, <u>Pardon Breton</u>, and
        <u>L'Anneau d'Argent</u>, the last labeled "truly exqui-
        site." Chaminade's recent tours are then listed,
        encompassing Belgium, Lyon, Geneva, and Reims. <u>See</u>
        W63a, W64b, W95a, W284b.

B228   "Nouvelles Diverses: Paris et Départements." <u>Le Ménes-
        trel</u> 60 (13 May 1894): 151.

        Notice of a recital presented by A. Dien, on which
        several works of Chaminade appeared.

B229   Petilleau, George. "Lettre d'Angleterre." <u>L'Art Musi-
        cal</u> 33 (31 May 1894): 172.

        In his letter dated 28 May, the writer describes the
        first program under the auspices of the Wolf Union
        Musical, which is attempting to promote French
        music. One or more pieces of Chaminade, as well as
        several by Widor, made up the program.

B230   "Mdlle. Chaminade's Concert." <u>The Times</u> (London), 5
        June 1894, p. 13 col. 4.

        Substantial, mixed review: "The programme of Mlle.
        Chaminade's third annual concert once more proved
        her to be a talented musician with considerable re-
        finement of style and a charming gift of melody. If
        her works seldom attain a very high artistic level,
        they never sink below a certain standard of excel-
        lence, and are at least graceful and often captiva-
        ting. In spite of the inevitable monotony of a con-
        cert made up of one author's works, a very large
        audience showed an appreciation which at times a-
        mounted to enthusiasm." Several songs were featured
        (e.g. <u>Madrigal</u>, <u>L'Anneau d'Argent</u>, and <u>Auprès de Ma
        Vie</u>), vocal duets (<u>Barcarolle</u> and <u>Duo d'Etoiles</u>),
        and solo piano works (<u>Pièce dans le Style Ancien</u> and
        <u>Valse Caprice</u>). <u>See</u> W39b, W85a, W94a, W96a, W266f,
        W268a, W284c.

B231   "Free Trade Hall: Mdlle. Chaminade's Concert." <u>The
        Manchester Courier</u>, [June 1894].

        The year of this review, and the next, is uncertain.
        "Mdlle. Chaminade possesses gifts that are closely

allied with genius . . . [they] are all associated
with daintiness, freshness, tunefulness, and vivaci-
ty. Melody is the foundation of all her work, . . .
allied with a sentimentality that befits and interprets lighter feelings and tenderer moods. That is
to say, all her work is eminently French in its
grace, in its piquancy, in its display of good
taste. . . ."

B232   "Free-Trade Hall: Miss Chaminade's Concert." (Manchester), [June 1894].

This review, which mentions at least twenty works,
of mixed genre, offers the following: "As a song
writer Miss Chaminade is an able and accomplished
representative of the modern French school . . . In
her pianoforte pieces [she] also created a very fav-
ourable impression; they are all endowed with grace
and fancy. As characteristic examples of her poeti-
cally fanciful style we may refer to the Serenade
and Pierrette." See W33d, W59c.

B233   "Bruits Qui Courent." L'Art Musical 33 (28 June 1894):
207.

Brief notice of the recital of students of Mlle.
Taconet, on 3 June, which included one or more works
of Chaminade.

B234   "Bericht aus Genf." Musikalisches Wochenblatt 25 (5
July 1894): 343.

Belated review, very favorable, of Chaminade's appearance in Geneva in February (see B215 above):
"This highminded composer was recognized not only as
interpretor of many of her piquant piano pieces, but
also as conductor. The most brilliant success of the
evening, however, was reserved for Herr Professor
Willy Rehberg, who performed Fräulein Chaminade's
Concertstück, under the direction of the composer,
with total mastery. The latter also appeared in a
soirée, as well as in a benefit concert for the orchestra members, and in both earned deserved
applause." See W58h.

B235   Solenière, Eugène de. La Femme Compositeur. La Critique, 1895, 16-18.

In this brief biographical account, the author pre-
dicts an even brighter future for Chaminade.

B236   Lorgnette, Jacques. "Festival Chaminade." Journal du
Havre, [1895].

Review of a concert dedicated to the works of Chaminade, in Le Havre, in the hall of the Lyre Havraise.
Several piano works, which she performed, were presented; the Concertstück was performed by Mlle. Ber-
the Duranton. See W58.

B237   U. C. D. B. [= Une Chaise des Baignoires]. "Concerts
        Classiques." Le Mondain, (Marseilles) [1895].

        This review is tongue-in-cheek, approaching the sar-
        castic. "What a hall! What bravos!"--and so begins
        the account of a concert in which Chaminade conduc-
        ted the orchestra in a performance of the Callirhoë
        Suite. "But the high point of the concert was, you
        won't doubt it, Mlle. Cécile Chaminade, who directed
        the orchestra, its vanities, and its works, with a
        notable brio and an exquisite rose dress. Her bouncy
        and decisive entrance had already made the majority
        of the audience well disposed toward her. In the
        course of the Suite taken from Callirhoë . . . the
        enthusiasm mounted and it could not help but erupt
        at the last notes of Pas des Cymbales, so strangely
        rhythmic. It did erupt. In vain would a rogue in-
        sinuate that Mlle. Chaminade holds the baton like a
        fishing rod. This young moron is wasting his time,
        and our musicians, delighted at being guided by this
        light hand, make valiant efforts. . . . I demand a
        rescue medal for them." The program also included
        orchestral versions of Sérénade D'Automne and Chaise
        à Porteurs, in which "our excellent musicians chami-
        naded [`chaminadèrent'] no less cheerfully. . . .
        One of our major music dealers was conspicuously
        beaming. No matter--we will long remember Mlle. Cé-
        cile Chaminade, for she is mostly good, that one."
        See W50d, W74b, W76b.

B238   "Courrier des Théâtres et Concerts," (Toulon), [1895].

        Favorable review of first performance of Callirhoë
        in Toulon: "The success of Callirhoë was complete
        last evening. . . The beautiful combinations with
        which Chaminade painted her skillful score were ar-
        ticulated beautifully by the musicians of the or-
        chestra." Singled out for praise were the prelude,
        the march, and the pastoral scene. See W49d.

B239   "Nouvelles Diverses: Paris et Départements." Le Ménes-
        trel 61 (7 April 1895): 112.

        Brief announcement of an upcoming concert, on 16
        April, at the Salle Pleyel, in which Chaminade will
        assist in the performance of ensemble music.

B240   A. P. "Revue des Grands Concerts." Le Ménestrel 61 (28
        April 1895): 133.

        Brief notice of one or more Chaminade pieces having
        been performed in a recent recital given by the pia-
        nist Clotilde Kleeberg.

B241   "Nouvelles Diverses: Paris et Départements." Le Ménes-
        trel 61 (5 May 1895): 144.

Report of a recital presented by the students of
Mme. and Mlle. Véros de la Bastière, at the end of
which several emiment figures, including Chaminade,
performed.

B242   H. B. "Nouvelles Diverses: Paris et Départements." Le
Ménestrel 61 (19 May 1895): 160.

Notice of a series of four chamber concerts given by
a violinist, Jeanne Meyer. One (or both) of Chaminade's trios were presented within the series.

B243   "Nouvelles Diverses: Paris et Départements--Concerts
et Soirées." Le Ménestrel 61 (2 June 1895): 176.

Chaminade's song Si J'Etais Jardinier was performed
at a recent benefit concert, organized by H. Logé.
See W296.

B244   "Mdlle. Chaminade's Concert." The Times (London), 8
June 1895, 7.

Mixed review of Chaminade's London concert: "The
annual concerts given by this popular composer are
to be regarded as a parallel to those small picture
exhibitions by means of which some painters dispose
of their year's productions. This year's songs, to
judge from the specimens brought out yesterday afternoon in St. James's Hall, are a good deal above
the average level of Mlle. Chaminade's work; in one
Sur la Plage, a deeper note of emotion is struck,
and Le Noël des Oiseaux, though very conventional,
is certainly attractive." Other works included on
the program are Nocturne Pyrénéen, Viatique, and
Partout. See W88a, W286a, W297a, W313a, W316a.

B245   "Chronique Musicale: Le Concert Chaminade." (Lausanne), [1896].

Review of the first of two Chaminade concerts in
Lausanne. Among the many works on the program are Le
Soir and Le Matin. The reviewer finds the Trio [No.
2] the best work. "The compositions of Mlle. Chaminade are characterized by a modernism that many lis-
teners will have found a bit excessive here and
there. Of course, ideas that are melodic and poetic
abound, but it seems that the composer keeps herself
in check against her own training and that the
criticism she fears most is that of sentimentality.
She avoids it with extreme care. . . . For it is
truly grace and originality that are the dominant
characteristics of her charming works." See W40e,
W106a, W107a.

B246   "Spectacles et Concerts: Concerts Chaminade." (Lausanne), [1896].

Review of Chaminade's two concerts of her works,
which were very successful: "Mme. Chaminade has

carved out a small domain for herself in the vast kingdom of the art, where caprice, fantasy, elegant banter, and a very modern outlook reclothed in classical garb have assured her great success. Her style is temperate and clear, a far cry from the musical unintelligibility that certain innovators of the young French school give us as the finest of the fine, the ultimate expression of art."

B247[1]   "Cécile Chaminade." Le Miroir des Modes, [1896]: 440-42.

Lengthy biographical account, with many photos of her home at Le Vésinet, including interior shots of her working area. It tells of her recent tours, including trips to Rumania, Serbia, and Greece; in Athens she did a benefit for the music conservatory. Chaminade prefers the poetry of Armand Silvestre, finding his verses the texts par excellence to set to music.

B248   "Nouvelles Diverses: Paris et Départements." Le Ménestrel 62 (26 January 1896): 32.

Review of the concert of Laure Taconet, vocalist, which included one or more mélodies of Chaminade.

B249   "Nouvelles Diverses: Paris et Départements." Le Ménestrel 62 (23 February 1896): 63.

Brief announcement of a forthcoming concert, on 25 February, of Stéphane Elmas, pianist, which will present one or more works of Chaminade.

B250   Martin, J. Nos Auteurs et Compositeurs Dramatiques. Flammarion, 1897.

Biographical dictionary of contemporary (or mostly contemporary) French figures, in which Chaminade's entry occupies two pages. On the first is a photo, with a brief account of her training and her important pieces. It states that she is completing a "drame lyrique" in collaboration with Armand Silvestre. The second page lists all her works for piano solo, to date.

B251   "Mdlle. Chaminade's Concert." The Times (London), 12 June 1897, p. 8 col. 6.

Substantial review of her concert of 10 June, at St. James's Hall, which begins: "The annual concert given by this popular composer has a mercantile rather than an artistic character, since the occasion exactly resembles those exhibitions of feminine ap-

---

[1]After the book manuscript was completed, new information revealed that the date of this entry should be at least late 1899, as her first East European tour was in that year.

parel which the purveyors of such things are wont to
hold on their return from Paris. The new fashions in
songs are remarkably like the productions of the
last few years, and the young lady who selects any
one of them for performance need not fear that she
will shock her friends by anything at all unusual."
Among the songs are Veux-Tu, Sans Amour, Tu Me Dirais, Madrigal (dubbed "hackneyed"), and Chanson
Slave. Among the new piano works was Autrefois, "the
best written . . ., in imitation of the style of the
last century harpsichord writers." See W120a, W262g,
W266g, W282c, W318a, W324a.

B252   "Musikalisches aus Leipzig." [Swiss source?], 31 July
        [1897].

        A review of the Concertstück, performed by Willy
        Rehberg. The piece is characterized as "a Breughel
        vision of hell with Wagnerian sonorities," which "is
        concealed behind the inconspicuous title of Concert-
        stück for piano and orchestra. It should not be con-
        sidered possible for Fräulein Chaminade to construct
        this Wagnerian work and also perform it. Professor
        Willy Rehberg, of Geneva, rendered the piano part of
        this interesting work, to tumultuous applause from
        the audience. Rehberg's other pieces, Liszt's Ave
        Maria and Schawenka's Staccato-Etüde, appeared very
        tame compared to the devilish piano writing of Fräu-
        lein Chaminade." See W58.

B253   "Nouvelles Diverses: Etranger." Le Ménestrel 63 (5
        December 1897): 390.

        Announcement that the Society of Musical Art, in New
        York, is launching a series of concerts that feature
        French works. "The second is to be composed of the
        Portrait de Manon, by Massenet, . . . and of Callir-
        hoë, the ballet by Mlle. Cécile Chaminade." However,
        a check of New York newspapers of this period, espe-
        cially The New York Times, reveals no performance of
        Callirhoë. See W49.

B254   Ae. Sd. "Komponistin Cécile Chaminade." Neues Frauen-
        blatt No. 12 (1898): 233.

        Review of a recital by Chaminade devoted to her
        works, in Berlin. The reviewer notes the long pro-
        gram (27 numbers) and observes that her style has
        much in common with Moritz Moszkowski. He raises the
        issue of why there are so few good women composers,
        and concludes that Chaminade is a member of this
        small group. Among the pieces performed are the Trio
        [No. 2], which is praised, as well as several solo
        piano works (e.g. Toccata, Arabesque), two-piano
        works (e.g. Pas des Cymbales), and songs (e.g. Via-
        tique). See W40f, W48e, W57c, W84c, W313b.

B255   Quidam. "Chronique Locale: Petits Portraits--Mlle.
        Cécile Chaminade." L'Union Républicain du Havre,
        [1898].

        Favorable review of Chaminade's recital, devoted to
        her own works, including the Concertstück, Romances
        sans Paroles, and Pièces Humoristiques. "Originality
        in composition, charm in performance--such are the
        two masterful qualities of Mlle. Chaminade. Her mus-
        ical writing, always correct, is both attractive and
        full of surprises. It is not trite, and, on the
        other hand, not excessive. At the piano, the young
        artist possesses power and digital agility, as well
        as feelings that communicate." Furthermore, she is
        held in high esteem by the British court, where she
        has been a frequent guest. See W58, W98-103c, W117-
        22a.

B256   Hughes, Rupert. "Women Composers." Century Magazine 55
        (March 1898): 768-79.

        Within a discussion of why there have been few women
        composers, and a survey of contemporary practition-
        ers, Chaminade emerges as the focus of the article.
        Her life and a stylistic critique of some works oc-
        cupy approximately half of the essay. "The most pro-
        minent woman composer, and on many accounts deser-
        vedly so, is Mlle. Cécile Chaminade. Many musical
        people who were familiar with the compositions of
        `C. Chaminade' have been surprised to learn that
        music of such ability belongs to a woman."

B257   "Nouvelles Diverses: Etranger." Le Ménestrel 64 (10
        April 1898): 110.

        Notice of a recital under the auspices of the Royal
        Conservatory in Parma, in which several French works
        occupy a major portion of the program. Chaminade's
        Madrigal is included, along with pieces by Saint-
        Saëns, Massenet, Bizet, and Berlioz. See W266.

B258   "Nouvelles Diverses: Paris et Départements." Le Ménes-
        trel 64 (17 April 1898): 119.

        Brief account of a program of religious music at
        Mme. Vincent-Carol, which included one or more vocal
        works of Chaminade.

B259   "Nouvelles Diverses: Paris et Départements." Le Ménes-
        trel 64 (29 May 1898): 175.

        Notice of a recital of Berthe Duranton, at the Salle
        Erard, in which Chaminade participated.

B260   "Nouvelles Diverses: Etranger." Le Ménestrel 64 (5
        June 1898): 182.

        Chaminade's name is mentioned as one of the pianists

who gave a recital at the Salle Bechstein, in Berlin, during the past concert season; see B254.

B261   Hiaulmé, Léon. "Mlle. Cécile Chaminade." La Sarthe (Le Mans), 3 July 1898.

The impetus for the article is the great success of Chaminade's recent recital in Le Mans. The discussion turns to her life and her fame. In listing her notable compositions, the author mentions only her orchestral pieces. Regarding her renown, "Strange thing--it is abroad that the name of Mlle. Chaminade has become very popular. In England, her works are on every piano. . . . In Germany, Switzerland, and Belgium the passion is the same, and the `Chaminade Festivals' always attract a big crowd. Finally, in America, the renown of the artist has gotten to the point where there are already four clubs that bear her name, and, very recently, she was offered a fortune to cross the Atlantic."

B262   "Le Concert Chaminade." Le Mondain (Roanne), [1899].

Review of a benefit concert in Roanne in which Chaminade participated, with the proceeds aiding the local Alliance Française.

B263   "Concert Populaire." Mémorial des Vosges (Epinal), [1899].

Review of a program of Chaminade performing her own works, including the Trio [No. 2] and the songs La Fiancée du Soldat, Viens Mon Bien-Aimé, Madrigal, and Villanelle. "We had the very rare pleasure in Epinal of hearing . . . a composer interpret her own works. . . . Mlle. Chaminade, whose reputation as pianist is universally established, provided us one of those artistic joys that one usually finds only in Paris." See W40g, W266h, W267b, W290c, W306a.

B264   "Woman's Work in Music." The Etude 17 (February 1899); 36.

A feature appearing regularly in The Etude, "Woman's Work in Music" focuses on the activities of women's clubs in America. As Chaminade clubs are emerging all over the country around this time, this column furnishes useful background information as to their nature, scope, and organization.

B265   Boutarel, Amédée. "Nouvelles Diverses: Paris et Départements." Le Ménestrel 65 (5 March 1899): 80.

Notice of one or more Chaminade compositions included on a recital of Mme. Tassu-Spencer, at the Salle Pleyel, who performed on the new chromatic harp that does not have pedals.

B266   Journal de St.-Quentin, [29] May 1899.

Favorable review of a concert that included Chaminade performing several of her compositions. Included are Capriccio for Violin and Piano, Viatique, A
Travers Bois, Ritournelle, and Trahison. See W17a,
W86a, W265d, W308a, W313c.

B267 "Mdlle. Chaminade's Concert." The Times (London), 12
June 1899, p. 4 col. 5.

Mostly negative review of Chaminade's recital on 9
June, at St. James's Hall: "Each year the forms in
which the songs are cast seem fewer and more conventional, and the same tendency may be noticed in the
direction of self-repetition which so regrettably
marks the work of some popular painters." Among the
songs were Nuit d'Eté, Immortalité, Reste!, and Au
Pays Bleu. See W326a, W332a, W336a, W338a.

B268 Perry, Edward Baxter. "Sophie Menter and Cécile Chaminade." The Etude 17 (November 1899): 348-49.

Lengthy article devoted to two women who are termed,
respectively, the greatest living woman pianist and
the greatest living woman composer. The second half
of the essay concentrates on Chaminade, whom the
American author heard in recital in Berlin. On the
program were 35 pieces, consisting of a Trio [No.
2], 8 works for "four hands," 15 songs, and the remainder for solo piano. "Considered from the standpoint of modern virtuosity, Chaminade can not [sic]
be considered in the strict sense a great pianist. .
. . [Her] abilities as a composer far exceed her
powers as a performer. . . . [It] is in her songs
that Chaminade reaches her highest level. These are
all melodious and, in the best sense of the term,
effective; but should never be sung except in
French." A portion of the article goes on to point
out the unjustly severe criticism that was meted out
by the Berlin critics, which rests on three main
points: "first, the genuine German conviction that a
woman can do nothing ably . . . ; second, the race
prejudice against everything French in general, and
French music and musicians in particular; and third,
a little irritation that the performer had the ef-
frontery to remain single until well on toward middle life, and to possess little, if any, physical
beauty." See W40h.

B269 "Nouvelles Diverses: Etranger." Le Ménestrel 66 (14
January 1900): 14.

Brief notice of three recent concerts performed at
the Odeon in Athens, in which one or more works of
Chaminade was presented.

B270 Middleton, Ethelyn Friend. "The Idol of the Girls: A
Personal Glimpse of Mademoiselle Chaminade." The
Ladies Home Journal 17 (February 1900): 7.

Lengthy article, based on an interview with the composer that discusses her background, working habits,
personality, and recent professional activities.
"Mlle. Chaminade every year makes extended concert
tours in Austria, Germany and England, and perhaps
every year gives fewer concerts in France." She is
reported "latterly [to have] been deeply engaged on
an opera."

B271   H-r. "Concert Chaminade-Lallemand." [German-language
        source], 19 March 1900.

        Review of a Chaminade concert: "Even though Fräulein
        Chaminade is not in the first rank of contemporary
        keyboard interpretors, we do not, nevertheless, hes-
        itate to claim, we have much more than a virtuoso
        before us; we have a complete artist with an in-
        spired conception of piano literature. The impres-
        sion that the renowned artist conveyed here will not
        have been fleeting."

B272   Radiguer, Henri. "Cécile Chaminade." Le Petit Poucet,
        Journal des Concerts Militaires et Civils 6 No. 5
        (1900).

        A flattering biography, and one of the few to men-
        tion her various publishers. Now she is completing
        the Six Poèmes Evangéliques, and is also in the
        midst of a "drame lyrique," on a text of A. Silves-
        tre. Her larger works are emphasized, rather than
        songs and piano works. See W141-46.

B273   "Mlle. Chaminade on Piano Playing." The Musical Stan-
        dard (Great Britain) 13, No. 331, Illustrated Series
        (5 May 1900): 276.

        An article devoted exclusively to the composer's
        advice regarding specific practicing and performing
        techniques. These comments first appeared in Girl's
        Realm.

B274   Courrier du Havre, [1901].

        Review of a concert, in Le Havre that included two
        choral works of Chaminade: Sous L'Aile Blanche des
        Voiles and Pardon Breton. Regarding the latter,
        "This . . . piece, sung in a wonderful manner, was
        very much noticed by the audience because of its
        characteristic color, its pervasive charm, and its
        extreme sentimentality. It is, besides, one of the
        best works of C. Chaminade, which he [sic] composed
        on the delicate poem of . . . Armand Silvestre." See
        W63c, W64c.

B275   Thomas, Fannie Edgar. "Chaminade: A Picture of the
        Eminent French Composer." Boston Evening Transcript,
        11 December 1901, 16.

A moderately lengthy article. It discusses little of importance, instead dwelling on Chaminade's physical appearance and her residence in Le Vésinet.

B276   Ebel, Otto. Women Composers: A Biographical Handbook of Women's Work in Music. Brooklyn: F. Chandler, 1902, 34-36.

A fairly standard account for a biographical dictionary, with a substantial, although in no way complete, works list. "Refinement and elegance of detail, as well as piquant melody and originality in rhythm, are the leading characteristics of all the compositions by this lady. . . . [At] the present time there are very few male composers France can boast of whose works compare with those of Chaminade's, and not one whose compositions are so widely known and played as hers, and find such a ready sale."

B277   Shippen, Kathleen M. "Mademoiselle Chaminade." The Philharmonic (Chicago) 2 No. 1 (February 1902): 1-5.

A fanciful, rather extensive narrative centered around her extremely successful trip to Constantinople, in which she received a prestigious award from the Sultan (the Chefekat).

B278   "Conseils Pour L'Exécution de Nos Morceaux." Musica 1 (October 1902): 16.

This page contains a paragraph of instructions for performing the song Ecrin, which is published in the musical supplement of the same issue of Musica. See W359.

B279   D'Oussouville, G. "Petits Portraits: Madame Chaminade." [Marseille source], [1903].

Report of a performance of Callirhoë in Marseille, at the Salle Beauveau. Some biography of Chaminade is provided, as well as statistics on major performances of the ballet: in Marseilles, 17 times in 1888 after the premiere that year, and repeated numerous times; in Lyon, 20 times; in Bordeaux and Toulon, 15 times each. See W49.

B280   "Nouvelles Diverses: Etranger." Le Ménestrel 69 (4 January 1903): 6.

A French singer, Mme. Alexander-Marnis, is on a tour of several cities of the United States, and one or more songs by Chaminade is part of the repertoire.

B281   Challice, Rachel. "Madame C. Carbonel Chaminade." Madame (England) (24 January 1903): 175.

Very informative article on Chaminade's life and career, which is based mostly on a recent interview at Le Vésinet. For example, we learn the approximate date of her marriage (mid 1901), as well as of her foreign tours and her most recent compositional projects.

B282   Elson, Arthur. <u>Woman's Work in Music</u>. Boston: L. C. Page & Co., 1904. Reprint: Longwood Press, 1976, 174-77.

A standard biographical account precedes an assessment of her works. "Her career has been one of constant progress and constant triumph. . . . She has been especially in demand for the performance of her own concerto. . . . Her works have become widely known, and her name is now a familiar one, not only in France, but in England, Continental Europe, and America. . . . It is undoubtedly her songs that have made her fame so wide-spread."

B283   D'Ohsson, Philippe. "Les Femmes du XXe Siècle: Madame Cécile Chaminade." <u>L'Echo Musical</u> 2 (1904).

A short biography, which includes some interesting information, including the number of Chaminade clubs in America and a list of her famous songs in France.

B284   "Le Mois Musical: Récitals Chaminade." <u>Musica</u> 3 (May 1904): 320.

Brief review of two recitals featuring works of Chaminade. The first included the <u>Trio No. 2</u>, a few works rendered by the composer and the pianist Gabrielle Turpin, and an unpublished song, <u>Portrait</u>. On the second, the <u>Concertino</u> was performed with piano. <u>See</u> W40i, W154a, W366a.

B285   Le Petit Miousicographe. "Cécile Chaminade Enfant." <u>Miousic (Journal des Petits Musiciens)</u> (1 November 1904): 3-4.

In this magazine intended for children, an article on Chaminade's childhood spins fanciful yarns on a wispy framework. In addition to a few photographs, there are a couple of cartoons fabricated for the story.

B286   Maurel, André. "Le Mois Musical: Le Résultat de Notre Concours." <u>Musica</u> 4 (April 1905): 63.

A piece by Chaminade had been one of a group of six anonymously-presented pieces by diverse composers in the contest. The others are Gaston Serpette, Saint-Saëns, Massenet, Rudolphe Berger, and Debussy.

B287   Chaminade, Cécile (as told to William Armstrong). "How to Sing and Play My Compositions." <u>The Ladies Home Journal</u> 22 (November 1905): 19.

In this lengthy article the composer concentrates on technical and interpretive tips for singers to enable them to master her songs. She provides a graded list of songs, and then a combined graded list of songs and piano pieces.

B288   Bulletin of New Music for the Pianola, Pianola Piano, Aeriola, Orchestrelle, and Aeolian Grand. New York: Aeolian Co., March 1906.

Lists the ten most popular works by Chaminade on piano roll, according to sales figures: La Lisonjera, Callirhoë, Pierrette, Pas Des Echarpes, Pas Des Amphores, Automne, Les Sylvains, Sérénade, Valse Caprice, and Danse Créole. For each, Aeolian numbers are provided for the pianola roll, the metrostyle and autograph metrostyle roll, and for the Aeolian grand roll. See W33, W39, W42, W51, W52, W53, W59, W68, W83, W129. See also the "Discography" chapter.

B289   Mitchell, Percy. "The Composer of The Little Silver Ring." New Idea Woman's Magazine (New York) (May 1907): 26-30.

An excellent, in-depth picture of Chaminade the artist and composer. Among the myriad topics discussed are the Chaminade clubs, her fondness for the lyrics of Armand Silvestre, her incomplete opera, her childhood, her work habits, and her music.

B290   "Concerts." The Times (London), 31 May 1907, p. 10 col. 3.

"Among the many piano solos and songs given at Mme. Chaminade's concert . . . were a fair number which bore the label 'new.' This was not, however, the characteristic for which they were most remarkable; rather one was struck by the fact that the Valse Romantique, the Chanson Forestière, and others bearing the inscription, gave pleasant expression to the same kind of musical ideas as have brought to Mme. Chaminade's earlier compositions their wide popularity." See W162a, W367a.

B291   M. B. "'Flying Dutchman' at Covent Garden; Chaminade Introduces New Songs and Piano Pieces in London." Musical America (22 June 1907): 17.

"Cecile Chaminade . . . played several new piano pieces from her pen at her second matinee in Aeolian Hall. These were an Etude Mélodique, Conte Bleu No. 2, and a Caprice Humoristique, all of which bear unmistakable Chaminade hall-marks." The new songs were Amour Invisible, Voix Du Large, La Lune Paresseuse, and Plaintes D'Amour. See W160a, W165a, W281b, W376a, W377a.

B292   Bullett, Emma. "A Talk with Cecile Chaminade." The
        Brooklyn Daily Eagle, 14 July 1907, "News Special"
        Section, p. 4 cols. 1-2.

        A one-column account, based on an interview in
        Paris. The composer provides some valuable insights
        on her married life. She would like very much to
        visit America but does not wish to leave her mother,
        who is 82 years old.

B293   "Concerts." The Times (London), 22 October 1907, p. 6
        col. 3.

        Review of London program of 21 October, entirely of
        her own composition. "The advantage of an arangement
        of this sort is that every one knows what to expect
        and, what is even better, no one is disappointed. .
        . . For one reason why Mme. Chaminade does not dis-
        appoint her audience is that she understands her own
        limitations, and only writes what she knows she is
        capable of writing well. . . . Mr. Frederic Griffith
        played the Concertino for flute with delicacy." See
        W154b.

B294   Chapotot, Dr. E. "Notice Sur Mme. Cécile Chaminade."
        La Chanson (Lyon) 7 No. 3 (March 1908): 45-53.

        This article, of substantial length and detail, be-
        comes the basis for numerous subsequent accounts of
        Chaminade. A short introduction informs us that the
        article was first a lecture, delivered on the eve of
        her recital, in Lyon, at L'Hôtel de la Chanson, on
        20 February. The body discusses her life, her works,
        and her compositional habits. There follows a detai-
        led discussion of L'Anneau d'Argent, which is nota-
        ted later in the issue. See W284.

B295   "Chaminade to Tour America." Musical America 7 No. 23
        (18 April 1908): 2.

        Announcement of Chaminade's tour the following sea-
        son. "No European celebrity has been more sought
        after by American impresarii than Chaminade." The
        notice mentions that a violinist and baritone will
        accompany her; Chaminade ended up coming with two
        singers, and no violinist.

B296   "The Remarkable Career of Mme. Cecile Chaminade." Mus-
        ical America 7 No. 25 (2 May 1908): 3.

        A biographical account, with photographs, in antici-
        pation of her American tour next season.

B297   "Many Pianists Are to Come Next Year." Musical America
        8 No. 2 (23 May 1908): 1.

        Chaminade is given a few lines within this general
        article: "The announcement that Cécile Chaminade,
        the French pianist and composer, will make her first

visit to this country in the Fall has created wide-
spread interest. It already seems inevitable that
the limited number of appearances for which she has
been engaged will have to be extended to meet the
demands to hear her."

B298   "An Interview with Cecile Chaminade." The Musical Age
        62 No. 13 (25 July 1908): 293.

        Substantial excerpts from an interview, conducted by
        Charles Henry Meltzer, published in the New York
        American. Among the many statements by the composer,
        of particular interest are the following: "No, I did
        not enter the Conservatoire. My father and mother
        were rather afraid of the associations I might find
        there." She mentions later that "it is strange that
        so few women should have become famous as composers.
        The art of music seems peculiarly calculated to at-
        tract them. . . I am afraid women recoil from the
        hard work of mastering the technical difficulties of
        music."

        UNITED STATES TOUR: OCTOBER TO DECEMBER 1908

B299   Chaminade, Cécile (as told to William Armstrong). "How
        to Play My Compositions." The Ladies Home Journal 25
        (October 1908): 23.

        Abridged version, with new photo, of B287. Probably
        published again because of Chaminade's imminent
        visit to the United States.

B300   "Mme. Cécile Chaminade." The Musician 13 No. 10 (Oc-
        tober 1908): 446.

        This biography of Chaminade is in preparation for
        her American tour. It includes significant quotation
        from the composer, much of it taken from an earlier
        interview in the New York American; see B298.

B301   Eichelberger, S. Eccleston. "New Opera House the Cen-
        ter of Philadelphia's Musical Interest." Musical
        America 8 No. 22 (10 October 1908): 23.

        Chaminade's forthcoming appearance is listed under
        events in Philadelphia during the 1908-09 season.
        Helen Pulaski-Innes is the local manager.

B302   Mephisto. "Mephisto's Musings." Musical America 8 No.
        23 (17 October 1908): 5.

        Beginning "Do you believe in ghosts? I mean musical
        ghosts?", the column relates the story of Chaminade
        feeling the soul of Beethoven upon a visit to his
        house in Bonn. See p. 19 in the "Biography" chapter.

B303   "French Woman Composer Arrives." New York Herald, Sun-
        day 18 October 1908, p. 14 cols. 1-2.

        Announcement, with photo, of Chaminade's arrival in
        New York for the start of her concert tour.

B304   [Lynch, Miss.] "Mme. Chaminade in New York." The Sun
        (New York), Sunday 18 October 1908, sec. 1, p. 4
        cols. 1-2.

        A lengthy, very informative interview with Chami-
        nade, which becomes the basis of publicity articles
        in other American cities. Not only does she offer
        her impressions of New York but she also discusses
        her marriage, her favorites among her own composi-
        tions, her likes and dislikes among contemporary
        French composers, and her general plans for this
        tour.

B305   "Musical Notes and Comment." New York Daily Tribune,
        Sunday 18 October 1908, sec. 5 p. 5.

        Two pertinent items appear in this column. The first
        is an announcement of a vocal recital that after-
        noon, in which her Barcarolle will be performed. The
        other is a listing of the program she will present
        at her Carnegie Hall recital next Saturday, 24 Oc-
        tober. See W85c.

B306   "The Coming of Mme. Chaminade." The Boston Evening
        Transcript, 19 October 1908, 7.

        Announcement of Chaminade's arrival, with extensive
        quotation from the interview in The Sun; see B304.

B307   Greeley-Smith, Nixola. "World's Greatest Woman Com-
        poser, Who Cannot Speak English, Gives an Interview
        in Music." The Evening World (New York), 20 October
        1908, 3.

        The composer punctuates her interview with incipits
        of four of her pieces, which are notated in her own
        hand in the article. She claims that she has wanted
        to visit New York for the past fifteen years.

B308   "Madame Chaminade to Give Recital." Philadelphia
        Times, 23 October 1908.

        Announcement of Chaminade's two appearances in Phil-
        adelphia, followed by biographical background. It is
        erroneously stated that "although never married she
        is called Madame Chaminade because she is, she says,
        'wedded to her music.' This was the answer it is
        said she gave to Godard, who proposed to her three
        times."

B309   "Chaminade Busy Seeing New York." Musical America 8
        No. 24 (24 October 1908): 1 and 8.

Substantial article, mostly absorbed with her impressions of New York and her opinions on contemporary music.

B310   "Another Visiting Composer." Musical America 8 No. 24 (24 October 1908): 12.

Editorial using Chaminade's visit as a springboard to demonstrate how European composers have a much better attitude toward America than in the past.

B311   Aldrich, Richard. "Mlle. Chaminade's Concert." The New York Times, Sunday 25 October 1908, p. 13 col. 4. Reprinted in collection of Aldrich's reviews, Concert Life in New York, 1902-23, ed. Harold Johnson. Freeport, N.Y.: Books for Libraries Press, 1971, pp. 227-28.

This substantial review is mostly critical of Chaminade as both composer and pianist. "[She] enjoys a kind of artificial vogue in this country and no doubt in others, as one of the few women composers who have attained distinction and as perhaps the foremost now living of that small band. She has become a sort of tutelary saint of women's clubs, where her music is industriously studied, discussed, played and sung. . . . What she does . . . is small in compass, unpretentious in idea, aiming chiefly at attractive melody and rhythmic grace and claiming immediate acceptance by those whose knowledge and taste in music are not erudite. In a word, Mlle. Chaminade's music is salon music; but it is salon music with a distinction. . . . Her music is unpretentious, though it is sometimes developed to a length that the substance of its ideas does not warrant. . . . But it is one thing to write agreeable salon music and another to attempt to fill out an entire afternoon with it. . . . She plays as a composer; and the piano playing of a composer has a name of its own. . . . It is not difficult to believe that [her] music would not have sounded so dull in the hands of other pianists."

B312   De Koven, Reginald. "Chaminade's Debut an Artistic Event." The World (New York), Sunday 25 October 1908, 8.

More positive assessment of Chaminade's American debut. The author laments the fact that none of her large-scale, orchestral pieces were programmed, particularly since an entire program of one style becomes excessive ("Sweet, killing sweet," in a quotation from Elizabeth Barrett Browning). "She is a real artist in interpretation, especially in her accompaniments. Her playing is marked by grace and delicacy . . . and a fluent technique, but is nevertheless a trifle monotone from a certain lack of force and variety." A few of the numbers are praised, including <u>Pastorale</u>, <u>Thème Varié</u>, and <u>Valse Romantique</u>. <u>See</u> W124a, W161a, W162b.

B313   Krehbiel, Henry E. "Mme. Chaminade's Concert." <u>New York Daily Tribune</u>, Sunday 25 October 1908, 7.

Negative, often biting assessment of the concert of 24 October: "It was an amiable ebullition of dilettantism, viewed from either side of the footlights, very sincere in a small kind of artistic sincerity, very gentle and very, very saccharine. . . . There is in [her music] no variety of manner or mood, and as for the sentiment . . . or the spiritual content . . . one ought not to try to find hints of such things in the titles of her pieces--for they have nothing to do with the case. . . . Those who saw her yesterday saw her under pretty circumstances, and were charmed as much by her modest and graceful appearance and deportment as they were by her equally modest and graceful playing, which never extended beyond the modest and graceful frame around her music."

B314   "Mme. Chaminade's Concert: An Afternoon of Graceful Salon Music at Carnegie Hall." <u>The Sun</u> (New York), Sunday 25 October 1908, 9.

Another unfavorable, although much shorter, review: "The concert yesterday disclosed no element of depth of inspiration, but had features certain to interest those who look upon music as an after dinner recreation of the salon. Perhaps the piano compositions would have made a firmer impression if they had been well played. . . . "

B315   "Great Welcome to Mme. Chaminade." <u>New York Herald</u>, Sunday 25 October 1908, p. 11 cols. 6-7.

More an account than a review, this article takes no critical stand but rather describes the expectations and enthusiastic reactions of the audience in attendance.

B316   "Mme. Chaminade's Concert." <u>The Evening Post</u> (New York), 26 October 1908, 7.

Overall, a negative assessment of the Carnegie Hall concert. The reviewer does, however, single out a few works for praise--<u>Consolation</u>, <u>Pastorale</u> (reminiscent of Mendelssohn), and <u>L'Ondine</u> ("with ornaments à la Liszt"). "Mme. Chaminade's music is salon music. It has a certain feminine daintiness and grace, but it is amazingly superficial and wanting in variety. . . . But on the whole this concert confirmed the conviction held by many that while women may some day vote, they will never learn to compose anything worth while. All of them seem superficial when they write music. . . . Mme. Chaminade is even

more superficial in her playing than in her compositions." See W121b, W148a, W161a.

B317   "Cécile Chaminade's Debut." Musical Courier (28 Oc-
        tober 1908): 35.

        This review takes note of Chaminade's great popular-
        ity and of the tremendous financial success of the
        Carnegie Hall concert. Her melodic gifts are under-
        scored, and her pianistic skills, although not
        great, are adequate to the technically undemanding
        works.

B318   Humiston, William Henry. "Chaminade." Independent 65
        (29 October 1908): 976-78.

        Prompted by Chaminade's visit, this article is taken
        largely from the 18 October interview appearing in
        The Sun (see B304). The writer concludes with the
        wish that some of Chaminade's orchestral works could
        have been heard as well.

B319   "Chaminade Opens Her American Tour." Musical America 8
        No. 25 (31 October 1908): 1 and 8.

        Very lengthy account of her recital of 24 October:
        "Inasmuch as she does not pose as a concert pianist,
        it would be manifestly unjust to review her playing
        in the light of that of a virtuoso. It was as Chami-
        nade the composer that she appeared, and it was to
        hear her compositions with the 'personal touch' that
        people came." The subtleties and charm of her pieces
        would be more effective in a smaller setting. Also
        observed is a lack of variety. "Notably effective
        were Consolation, and the Pastorale, the first of
        the Contes Bleus, and the Valse Romantique." Earlier
        she had asserted that she might write a piece to
        commemorate her American trip. See W121b, W161a,
        W162b, W169.

B320   "Chaminade and the Low-Brow." Musical America 8 No. 25
        (31 October 1908): 11.

        Chaminade is the subject of an anecdote. Someone
        asks, "By the way, what is a Chaminade?," and dis-
        covers to his consternation that it is a female com-
        poser.

B321   "Mme. Chaminade, Greatest Woman Composer, Who is Now
        Visiting America, Tells of Her Dreams." The Washing-
        ton Post, 1 November 1908, "Magazine" section, p. 4.

        Very informative interview with Chaminade, dateline
        "New York, October 30." Perhaps most interesting are
        the composer's views on opera, both old and new, and
        on the creative abilities and opportunities of
        women.

B322   "Chaminade Club Prospectus" and "Philadelphia Orches-
       tra Program." Philadelphia Inquirer, 1 November
       1908, 8.

       The first notice announces the three concerts spon-
       sored by the Chaminade Club of Philadelphia, of
       which the composer's forthcoming public concert is
       one. The second item presents the program for the
       fourth pair of concerts of the Philadelphia Orches-
       tra, which includes four works of Chaminade.

B323   "Brilliant Composer Excited Over Her American Debut."
       Louisville Herald, 1 November 1908, sec. 5 p. 7.

       In anticipation of Chaminade's Louisville recital of
       9 November, this article features excerpts from New
       York interviews, in which she expressed her excite-
       ment at being in America and also her desire for the
       past fifteen years to make the long journey.

B324   "Chaminade Meets Her Brooklyn Namesakes." Musical Cou-
       rier 57 No. 19 (4 November 1908): 34.

       Prominent members of the Chaminade Club of Brooklyn
       are introduced to the composer in the Green Room of
       the Brooklyn Academy of Music after her concert
       there.

B325   "Chaminade is a Wonderful Woman." Louisville Post, 6
       November 1908.

       In anticipation of her Louisville appearance, this
       article provides standard biographical information.
       "Mme. C. Chaminade is ranked as the foremost woman
       composer, while her position as a piano virtuoso is
       among the recognized leaders."

B326   "Chaminade's Autograph." Philadelphia Times, [6] Nov-
       ember 1908.

       Article describing Chaminade's fondness for the pia-
       nola player-piano. The 36 rolls she has made for
       this mechanism all bear her autograph.

B327   "Mme. Chaminade Likes America." Philadelphia Press, 6
       November 1908, 8.

       An interview with the composer upon her arrival in
       Philadelphia, before her concert appearance that
       afternoon and the next evening with the Philadelphia
       Orchestra.

B328   "Mme. Chaminade on Visit." Ledger (Philadelphia), 6
       November 1908, 3.

       Brief article that provides some biographical back-
       ground. It also mentions that Chaminade will return
       to Philadelphia in a month, to give a recital under

the auspices of the local Chaminade Club (9 December).

B329   "Mme. Cecile de [sic] Chaminade." The Evening Bulletin (Philadelphia), 6 November 1908, 4.

Just a photograph, with a caption that details her concert appearances that afternoon and the next evening.

B330   "Applauding Music Lovers Hear Mme. Chaminade." Philadelphia North American, 7 November 1908.

Review of her program the evening before. Concertstück evinces "vigor and artistic quality . . . , although the passages for piano seemed ornamental rather than essential. The distinguished woman composer lacks both the physical power and the technique necessary to produce large musical effects in a huge auditorium like that of the Academy." The lighter pieces are "grace without greatness, true sentiment without lofty inspiration." See W58k.

B331   "Chaminade to Play in New York Again." Musical America 8 No. 26 (7 November 1908): 16.

Announcement that two later concerts have been arranged: her farewell performance, on 15 December in Carnegie Hall; and her only appearance in Boston, on 12 December.

B332   "Mme. Cecile Chaminade Appears with the Philadelphia Orchestra." The Evening Bulletin (Philadelphia), 7 November 1908, 5.

Mildly favorable review of Chaminade and her compositions: "The Concertstück is a somewhat ambitious composition in three movements, with a rather elaborate orchestration of some unusual effects. In this her lack of power was evident, and the impression she created was agreeable but mild, though she won the customary liberal applause. Upon her second appearance she gave a group of three short compositions for piano alone--Automne, Courante, and Quatrième Valse--playing them in an easy, unobtrusive manner, with admirable execution and sympathetic touch, winning the sincere admiration of the audience." The reviewer looks forward to more of her solo works, when she returns in a month. See W42d, W58k, W126a, W132a.

B333   "Philadelphia Orchestra." Philadelphia Inquirer, 7 November 1908, 13.

Mostly negative assessment. The reviewer feels that the selection of works did not do the composer justice. Furthermore, "the Concertstück, Op. 40, which although nominally in three movements, is played without any break, is a vague, formless, incoherent,

vacillating piece of work, without any thematic
backbone or logical harmonic development." And as a
pianist, "her technical equipment is of the slender-
est description." See W58k.

B334   "Philadelphia Orchestra." Ledger (Philadelphia), 7
        November 1908, 8.

        More positive review of the concert of 6 November.
        "Madame Chaminade . . . had chosen for performance
        in the Concertstück a composition which does not
        suffer by comparison with the musical handiwork of
        man. The three movements are telescoped, with no
        interval between, and her fleet-fingered, facile
        performance brought out with entire clarity of ut-
        terance the rippling continuity of the movement. . .
        . She plays, as she composes, like a woman sentient
        to every influence of nature." The Courante is
        "based on a sound and scholarly understanding of
        Bach," and the Quatrième Valse is termed "a deli-
        cious morceau." See W58k, W126a, W132a.

B335   "Chaminade Recital Monday." Louisville Evening Post, 7
        November 1908, 2.

        In advance of her upcoming recital on 9 November,
        this notice furnishes the program as well a few bits
        of biographical information.

B336   "Chaminade Coming." Minneapolis Journal, Sunday 8 No-
        vember 1908, "Dramatic & Social" section, p. 3.

        Short article announcing Chaminade's forthcoming
        recital in Minneapolis, on 17 November, and giving
        some biographical background.

B337   "Chaminade Tells How to Play Her Songs." Louisville
        Courier-Journal, 8 November 1908, sec. 2 p. 3.

        In anticipation of Chaminade's Louisville recital
        the next evening, this article presents excerpts
        from earlier magazine articles on the same subject
        (see especially B287).

B338   "French Composer Rouses Great Interest." The Chicago
        Sunday Tribune, 8 November 1908, "Drama" section, p.
        1 col. 1.

        A report on Chaminade's great success on the East
        Coast, followed by some biographical background
        taken from published sources.

B339   "In Musical Circles." Louisville Herald, 8 November
        1908, sec. 2 p. 9.

        This article consists chiefly of excerpts from Cha-
        minade's earlier article on how to sing her songs
        (see B287).

B340   Hogan, Agnes Gordon. "Woman's View of French Music."
        Philadelphia Record, 8 November 1908, 5.

        Article largely absorbed with an interview. Chami-
        nade speaks at length on French music and offers her
        impressions of the United States.

B341   "Mme. Chaminade at Macauley's Tonight." The Louisville
        Herald, 9 November 1908, 7.

        Notice of Chaminade's recital that evening.

B342   "Chaminade's Recital." Louisville Evening Post, 10
        November 1908, 3.

        Mostly favorable review of the Louisville recital:
        "[Her] appearance . . . was the occasion for one of
        the most enthusiastic welcomes that has ever been
        accorded a composer and pianist here. . . . As a
        composer Madame Chaminade's talents cover a wide
        scope, though it is in the more dreamy melodies that
        she is at her best. As a writer of songs, Madame
        Chaminade also shows her genius. . . . As a perfor-
        mer, [she] may not rank with Paderewski and other
        great pianists, but her technique is wonderful, and
        in all her numbers she showed the great artist."

B343   K. W. D. "Music and the Drama." Louisville Courier-
        Journal, 10 November 1908, 4.

        Very positive assessment of the Louisville recital:
        "Madame Chaminade is winning her way anew through
        the hearts of her admirers by her beautiful and poe-
        tic interpretation of her own works. The programme
        last night embraced 23 numbers, varying surprisingly
        when one considers that they all emanated from one
        mind." She is also praised for her graceful melodies
        and "a certain characteristic suavity." Her song
        writing "is specially felicitous."

B344   "Songbird Interprets for Mme. Chaminade." Cincinnati
        Post, 11 November 1908, 3.

        Brief announcement of Chaminade's upcoming recital,
        on 12 November at the Grand Opera House, when one
        can hear "the only world-famous woman interpret her
        own compositions," with the assistance of Yvonne de
        St. André, soprano.

B345   "American Artists to Assist Chaminade." The Musical
        Leader and Concert Goer 14 (12 November 1908): 11.

        Notice of Chaminade's final concert on her American
        tour, on 15 December, at Carnegie Hall.

B346   Gilman, Lawrence. "The World of Music: Chaminade and
        Others." Harper's Weekly 52 (14 November 1908): 28.

In this overview of the current concert season, the author weaves his assessment of Chaminade's talents, judged far short of stellar, into a discussion of women as composers. Chaminade is one of the most popular, but she lacks true artistic genius. "So to Mme. Chaminade, maker of adored and ingenious music, let us offer gladly the salutation that is due the skillful and self-respecting craftsman, the music-maker of true and honorable talent."

B347   "Cecile Chaminade to Feature Week." Milwaukee Sentinel, 15 November 1908, part 3 p. 5.

Article announcing Chaminade's recital the next evening. It includes the standard biographical outline.

B348   "Chaminade is Not 'Puma of Pianoforte'." Indianapolis Star, 15 November 1908, p. 17 col. 5.

Announcement of her forthcoming concert in Indianapolis, on 3 December. Most of the notice is devoted to a substantial quotation from The Ledger regarding her Philadelphia appearance.

B349   "Chaminade Recital Tuesday Evening." The Minneapolis Journal, Sunday 15 November 1908, "Dramatic & Social" section, p. 13.

Announcement of her recital at Minneapolis Auditorium, 17 November, which details the program—identical to that given in New York—and furnishes some background. The anonymous writer displays healthy skepticism when he describes the information to come as "facts and alleged naive and illuminating remarks."

B350   Hughes, Rupert. "Mme. Chaminade and John Philip Sousa Talk About Music; The Distinguished French Composer and the American March King Reveal the Sources of Their Inspiration." The New York Herald, Sunday 15 November 1908, "Magazine" section, part II, pp. 9-10.

The famous music critic, at times affecting a mocking tone, and his two guests meet at the Waldorf-Astoria for a discussion that forms the basis of this extensive article. "The public has need and room for both the song of the cannon and the song of the distaff, and it has done well to select these two persons as the wearers of the two crowns. Mr. Sousa writes like a manly man and Mme. Chaminade like a womanly woman." Sousa begins by asking Chaminade whether she prefers to be a woman or a composer; she would rather be a composer. She discusses French composers, the circumstances surrounding the composition of L'Anneau D'Argent, and women having a career in music. Of American composers she is acquainted with the works of MacDowell and impressed with the music of Mrs. H. H. A. Beach, whose pieces

she heard in London. Sousa invites Chaminade to conduct his band right away. She is both tempted and
taken aback, and soon takes rather abrupt leave of
the group. See W284.

B351   "Mme. Chaminade to Charm Song Lovers Tuesday." The
        Minneapolis Sunday Tribune, 15 November 1908, p. 24
        col. 5.

        The flavor of this article, announcing her forth-
        coming recital on the 17th, is much more romanti-
        cized than that in its local cousin (see B349).

B352   "Chaminade Wins Favor." Milwaukee Sentinel, 17 Novem-
        ber 1908, 7.

        In this mostly positive assessment of her concert of
        16 November, Chaminade is praised as a "great pian-
        ist," but the program lacks variety. "It seems . . .
        that an ability such as displayed by Mme. Chaminade
        might be brought to better climax in the handling of
        the work of several masters." She was shown in best
        light in the Valse Romantique and the Troisième
        Valse. The songs "do not offer a vast tonal range"
        to the singer. "Ernest Groom and Yvonne de St. André
        are tested only from a Chaminade viewpoint. Each
        succeeds." See W108a, W162c.

B353   Maclean, Stuart. "Music: Chaminade Recital." The Min-
        neapolis Journal, 18 November 1908, 14.

        A witty, sometimes harsh review of her recital of 17
        November. "Minneapolis and his wife" filled the
        hall, although "perhaps it would be neater to say
        Minneapolis and her husband, because the husbands
        were in the minority." He describes almost mockingly
        her motions and appearance upon approaching the
        piano and then performing. Furthermore, "Mme. Chami-
        nade is no great pianist." Her piano compositions
        are treated as mere parlor works. Her songs, such as
        L'Anneau D'Argent and Mon Coeur Chante, reveal the
        hand of a melodist. See W284e, W321b.

B354   "Amusements of the Week: Mme. Cecile Chaminade." St.
        Louis Daily Globe Democrat, Sunday 22 November 1908,
        part 3 pp. 2-3.

        Announcement of her forthcoming recital in St.
        Louis, at the Odeon, on 24 November. Labeled "one of
        the greatest of the living composers, and an artist
        who has perhaps surpassed in achievement anything
        ever done in music by any other woman in the world's
        history," Chaminade is considered "the most impor-
        tant musical event since the last tour of Rubenstein
        in this country."

B355   Gunn, Glenn Dillard. "Mme. Chaminade Talks of the
        Music of the Present." The Inter Ocean (Chicago),
        Sunday 22 November 1908, 9.

An interview upon her arrival in Chicago on 20 November. Chaminade directs her attention to contemporary music, praising Chausson and lamenting the negative tone many adopt toward Saint-Saëns. This attitude "threatens to make the musical life of Paris, already suffering from the evil effects of overcrowding, as disagreeably contentious as is that of Berlin."

B356   "Music and Musicians." St. Louis Republic, Sunday 22 November 1908, part 5 p. 13.

Notice of Chaminade's recital at the Odeon, under the aegis of the Amphion Club.

B357   "National--Mme. Cecile Chaminade." The Washington Post, Sunday 22 November 1908, "Editorial" section p. 3.

Announcement of Chaminade's upcoming recital in the nation's capital, on 8 December, at the New National Theater. Deemed a composer "in a class by herself," the article states that local interest has been great, with the first box for the concert having been sold in May.

B358   Bennett, James O'Donnell. "Music and the Drama." The Chicago Record-Herald, 23 November 1908, p. 6 col. 6.

Lengthy account of Chaminade's Chicago recital of 22 November: "A perfectly lovely concert--a musical gorge on marshmallow melancholy and soda water graciousness--was the offering of Mme. Cecile Chaminade, composer and pianiste by the grace of God. . . . A few real gems of melody lighted up the vista of names; and on them rather than on this long list of tuneful concoctions will rest the wide fame already Mme. Chaminade's by virtue of the several exquisite miniatures known everywhere." Her pieces are "facile charm and little else." Of the piano works, the reviewer prefers Pastorale, L'Ondine, and the two Contes Bleus; of the songs, Reste, Nuit D'Eté, and Bonne Humeur. Overall, her works "are salon pieces, and as such they are relatively ineffective in the large hall." Yet, "the opportunity of hearing these Lilliputian effects from the one most cognizant of their significance is a treat that comes too seldom in the annals of any city's art. Yesterday's concert was one to be remembered." See W148b, W161b, W169-71a, W326c, W338c, W363b.

B359   Campbell, Evelyn. "Chaminade Captive of American Prune!" Chicago Examiner, 23 November 1908.

A lighthearted piece on Chaminade, with considerable personal interest.

B360   "Chaminade Concert." <u>Chicago Daily Tribune</u>, 23 November 1908, p. 8 cols. 6-7.

Almost half the review is taken up with an allegory about a rosebush and its delicate blooms, which, when transported to foreign lands where larger and more robust blooms grow, is maligned by many for its inferior status. Chaminade's compositions "are delicate, graceful creations, not pretentious, not vastly significant when viewed in the light of the great musical utterances of the world, but they are beautiful, they are neatly formed, they are melodious, and they are fragrant with a certain elegant feminine charm that makes them pleasing and therefore of value in the world of music. They are not the largest nor the rarest blossoms in the tonal garden, but they are exquisite in their own way, and they make the garden all the finer, all the more agreeable, and all the more attractive by their presence."

B361   Katzenberger, Gabriel. "Aus dem Reiche der Töne." <u>Tägliche Illinois Staats-Zeitung</u>, 23 November 1908.

Substantial account of 22 November concert. "She is an imaginative genius, like few of her sex on the face of the earth." Almost everyone knows and enjoys Chaminade's music. "Her creations bear . . . the stamp of incomparable daintiness and playfulness." As a pianist she belongs to the French school. She performed three encores.

B362   Rosenfeld, Maurice. "Chaminade's Music Thrills Big Audience." <u>Chicago Examiner</u>, 23 November 1908.

Review of 22 November concert. Several pieces "rose above the merely pleasing, that is, they had some thematic development and contrapuntal contents; such were the <u>Thème Varié</u> and the <u>Deuxième Gavotte</u>. L'Ondine, <u>Contes Bleus</u>, and <u>Elévation</u> were more in the impromptu genre, while the <u>Caprice Humoristique</u> and the <u>Troisième Valse</u> afford for the pianist some effective and brilliant display of technique." <u>See</u> W99, W108, W124c, W148b, W160, W168, W169-71a.

B363   "Two Interesting Recitals: Mme. Chaminade, French Composer, Sunday--Hans Schroeder Saturday." <u>The Chicago Daily News</u>, 23 November 1908, p. 14 col. 4.

A mostly favorable evaluation of Chaminade's recital of 22 November, in Orchestra Hall. "The compositions of Mme. Chaminade . . . are so closely allied with the formative period of many young musicians that they control a far wider field of interest and really lead the so-called popular music in its highest estate. . . . There was plentiful finesse and charm in these compositions, that have been chiefly designed for the parlor, even in this large auditorium, freighted with the intimate and personal note

from their creator." Among the piano pieces, considered less diversified than the songs, Thème Varié
and Contes Bleus are singled out for praise. The
songs garnering plaudits are Nuit D'Eté, L'Anneau
D'Argent, and Bonne Humeur. See W124c, W169-71a,
W284f, W326c, W363b.

B364   Cole, Ida B. "Mme. Chaminade, Famous French Composer,
        Calls Women Here `Adorable'." St. Louis Star, 25
        November 1908.

        Interview with Chaminade and Yvonne de St. André
        that appeared after their St. Louis recital. Chami-
        nade dubs Les Amazones her favorite composition (see
        W29) and is impressed with American women.

B365   "Chaminade Recital." The Musical Leader and Concert
        Goer 14 (26 November 1908): 14.

        Brief assessment of the Chicago recital of 22 Novem-
        ber: "Her recital was one of popular interest, but
        even interest palls when the program is devoted to
        one composer." No specific pieces are reviewed.

B366   Murphy, W. R. "Philadelphia: Chaminade." The Musical
        Leader and Concert Goer, 26 November 1908, p. 11.

        A review of Chaminade's Philadelphia appearances
        earlier in the month that focuses on her playing
        rather than her compositions. "The chief character-
        istic of Mme. Chaminade's playing is the utter ab-
        sence of affectation. She is also incapable of the
        Amazonian pianism of Theresa Carreno and the psycho-
        logizing interpretation of Fanny Bloomfield Zeisler.
        . . . The general impression left of her powers of
        playing and of composition was that in both she is
        charming and pleasing without being in any sense
        profound."

B367   The Evening Bulletin (Philadelphia), 28 November 1908,
        p. 8.

        Brief announcement of Chaminade's forthcoming reci-
        tal in Philadelphia, at the Academy of Music, on 9
        December.

B368   Chaminade, Cécile. "How to Play My Best Known Pieces."
        The Etude 26 (December 1908): 759-60.

        In conjunction with her American tour, Chaminade
        writes about several piano pieces: Pas Des Echarpes,
        Pas Des Amphores, La Lisonjera, Zingara (transcribed
        from orchestra), Valse Caprice, Air De Ballet, and
        Pierrette. Then a section seems appended, probably
        by the journal, on two later works--Contes Bleus and
        Poème Provençal. A short biography completes the
        article. See W31, W34, W39, W51, W52, W59, W68,
        W169-71, W197-200.

B369   La Perrière, H. de. "Les Femmes Compositeurs en France
        dans ces Dernières Années." Paris Musical et Artis-
        tique 4 [December 1908], 3-4.

        There have been many female performers but few com-
        posers. "For women, it is much better to utilize her
        charm, and it is the totally feminine charm that has
        fashioned the success of Mme. Cécile Chaminade, a
        true French woman; in this case, more than just a
        French woman--a Parisian woman." Is is in the area
        of piano music and song that she is most famous.
        Contrary to Augusta Holmès, a foreigner who made her
        name in France, Chaminade is a French woman who made
        her reputation "in all the countries of the world."
        She just left recently, in October, for a trip to
        the United States.

B370   "Visit of Chaminade." Current Literature 45 (December
        1908): 670-71.

        This article is mostly derivative, quoting exten-
        sively from major reviews in New York and Philadel-
        phia.

B371   "Mme. Chaminade Comes for Concert To-Night." The In-
        dianapolis News, 3 December 1908, p. 7 col. 3.

        Article in anticipation of Chaminade's concert that
        evening. The account is based largely on the com-
        poser's comments published previously in American
        newspapers.

B372   "Chaminade Concert Was Unlike Any Other." The Indiana-
        polis News, 4 December 1908, p. 18 col. 3.

        Flattering evaluation of the concert of 3 December.
        "The Chaminade concert . . . was unique in the his-
        tory of music in this city. . . . The scores of stu-
        dents . . . found new meanings in her musical mes-
        sages, for every one that plays or sings has Chami-
        nade compositions in the repertory. . . . [She]
        makes no pretensions as a pianist, but she was fully
        capable technically of interpreting her program and
        playing it with the spirit and intent from within.
        Her music is always melodious and refined. . . .
        [The concert] was more like an elegant drawing-room
        affair, which the audience quickly recognized and
        appreciated."

B373   "Cécile Chaminade: The Cherished Composer for Her
        Sex." Boston Transcript, 5 December 1908, section 2
        p. 8.

        In ancipation of her forthcoming Boston concert,
        this article provides extensive quotation from the
        earlier interview in the New York Sun (see B304).

B374   Speaks, Oley. "In the World of Music." The Ohio State
        Journal (Columbus), Sunday 6 December 1908, "Socie-
        ty" section, p. 7 col. 5.

        Listing of program of the Women's Music Club reci-
        tal, on 10 December, which includes several works by
        Chaminade.

B375   "Mme. Chaminade's Visit." Ledger (Philadelphia), 6
        December 1908, 6.

        Announcement of Chaminade's activities when she re-
        turns to the city in a few days. The events are
        clustered around her recital, on 9 December.

B376   Philadelphia Press, 6 December 1908, 13.

        Notice of Chaminade's recital on 9 December, with a
        listing of the program.

B377   "Social and Personal." The Washington Post, 8 December
        1908, p. 7 col. 4.

        Society notice of Chaminade's activities in Washing-
        ton on 7 December: "The French ambassador and Mme.
        Jusserand entertained at luncheon in honor of Mme.
        Chaminade. . . . After the luncheon Mme. Jusserand
        took Mme. Chaminade to the White House to be presen-
        ted to President and Mrs. Roosevelt."

B378   "Chaminade Delights Brilliant Audience." The Washing-
        ton Times, 9 December 1908, p. 6 col. 4.

        A flattering review whose first paragraph tells of
        the important figures present in the audience, among
        them Mrs. Roosevelt. "Revelation after revelation
        followed in the bewitching program which Mme. Chami-
        nade had prepared. . . . In her second group [her]
        most delightful performance was her reading of the
        Valse Romantique. . . . One of the greatest of all
        of Mme. Chaminade's attributes, however, must be
        conceded to be her accompaniments." Included on the
        program were Consolation, Pastorale, Ondine, Caprice
        Humoresque ("an exacting number"), Thème Varié, and
        Contes Bleus. See W121d, W124d, 148c, W160c, W161c,
        W162d, W169-71b.

B379   "New Compositions Charm; Mme. Chaminade Presents Pro-
        gram of Unfamiliar Works." The Washington Post, 9
        December 1908, p. 2 col. 4.

        The reviewer is happy to note that Chaminade per-
        formed works that are unknown to the public, con-
        trary to the practice of most pianists. "One of the
        most vivacious and delicate morsels of the afternoon
        was the Pastorale. . . . Another delightful composi-
        tion was the Contes Bleus No. 2, a number which all
        pianists should have in their repertoire. The Valse
        Romantique was every bit as good as Moskowski, and

the Troisième Valse could be substituted with pro-
priety for almost any of the Chopin waltzes commonly
included in today's concert programs." See W108b,
W161c, W162d, W169-71b.

B380   "Social and Personal." The Washington Post, 9 December
        1908, p. 7 col. 3.

        Chaminade's recital of the previous day is the focal
        point for a discussion of who attended and what they
        wore.

B381   "Chaminade at Academy." Philadelphia Press, 10 Decem-
        ber 1908, 8.

        Short review of her recital on 9 December. "She
        plays as she writes, impetuously and frequently with
        a total disregard of conventional standards of
        tempo. But her rubato is always charming and indeed
        necessary in much that she writes. Her fondness for
        melody in the bass, her wandering away from a theme
        only to return to it in phrases of most delicate
        beauty, her rich ornamentations and, above all, her
        light and dainty touch, were exemplified at yester-
        day's concert in such familiar works as The Scarf
        Dance, The Flatterer, Autumn, the popular Fourth
        Waltz, and Elevation, a composition which deserves
        longer life than some of the ones that are better
        known." See W42e, W52d, W68b, W99d, W126b.

B382   "Mme. Chaminade's Recital." Ledger (Philadelphia), 10
        December 1908, 3.

        "Mme. Chaminade's art--as composer more particular-
        ly, of course--commands respect. . . . Her Automne
        especially is one of the perdurably lovely things
        that haunt the memory long after they are played or
        sung or seen." See W42e.

B383   "The Chaminade Recital." Philadelphia Inquirer, 10
        December 1908, 8.

        A review that asserts the recital must be judged on
        its own terms: not as great art, but as a represen-
        tation of the best in parlor music. "It must be said
        in all frankness that Madame Chaminade is not a
        great composer nor a pianist of the first rank. That
        is conceded by herself, as is understood. . . . She
        has a very pretty sentiment and reaches a peculiar
        vein of romanticism that others have not been able
        to touch. . . . It was a pleasing exposition of a
        popular form of music." No specific pieces are dis-
        cussed.

B384   "Honor Mme. Chaminade." Philadelphia Press, 11 Decem-
        ber 1908, 12.

The musical leaders of the city attended a reception in honor of the composer, sponsored by the Chaminade Club and another organization.

B385   "Mme. Chaminade's Reception." Ledger (Philadelphia), 11 December 1908.

Another notice of the reception.

B386   [Hale, Philip.] "Concert by Chaminade." Sunday Herald (Boston), 13 December 1908, p. 14 col. 2.

Moderately favorable assessment of her program of 12 December: "Mme. Chaminade has long been known to the musical world as a composer of songs and piano pieces. Many of them show her indisputable melodic gift and sound musical training. . . . However light her music may be, however slight the expression of true sentiment, her songs and piano pieces have individuality and a certain elegance." The reviewer discerns rhythmic irregularities in her rendition of piano pieces and also notes that the recital was too much of one style: "A little Chaminading goes a long way no matter how gracefully the Chaminading may be done."

B387   [Elson, Louis C.] "The Chaminade Concert." Boston Daily Advertiser, 14 December 1908, p. 5 col. 2.

"We were heartily glad of the great success of the Chaminade concert . . . for we believe in the female composer, and this was a definite endorsement of the work of a female creator in music. The entire programme was made up of works of Mme. Chaminade, a test that few composers of either sex could meet without boring the public. . . . The success of Mme. Chaminade in the field of composition lies largely in the fact that she does not attempt too much. . . . In the songs . . . as compositions, we found the fault of many pianist composers--they were not entirely vocal; they were piano compositions in disguise. . . . The piano works given were all filled with feminine charm. . . ."

B388   "Mme. Chaminade and Candy." Boston Evening Transcript, 14 December 1908, part 2 page 13.

This decidedly negative review begins by mentioning a line from Gilbert's Patience, that "candy in moderation was a capital confection, but that in certain circumstances even candy might become monotonous. Mme. Cécile Chaminade's songs and duets and piano pieces are no less enticing musical confections, but two hours of them, two unbroken and unvaried hours of them, did become a little monotonous. . . . The audience that filled the room had come, however, as much to see as to hear. Almost every one in it knew the music of Mme. Chaminade and the pleasure that in moderation it gives. Many a one had played or sung it. As many more had the peculiar affection for it that is the reward of charm and that power may not often win. . . ."

B389   "Chaminade Meets the President and Mrs. Roosevelt." <u>Musical Courier</u> 57 No. 25 (16 December 1908): 13.

Brief mention of Chaminade being introduced to the first couple; <u>see</u> also B343.

B390   "Mme. Chaminade's Farewell." <u>The Sun</u> (New York), 16 December 1908, 7.

Brief notice of Chaminade's Carnegie Hall recital, the last performance of her American tour, on 15 December. "The most important number on the list was Mme. Chaminade's second <u>Trio</u>." <u>See</u> W40j.

B391   "Mme. Chaminade's Recital." <u>The New York Times</u>, 16 December 1908, p. 6 col. 5.

Short but substantial evaluation of the 15 December recital. " . . . Although the concert was more ambitious in its artistic scope . . . there could not be said to be a new view of Mme. Chaminade's art presented in it. . . . [Her music] gives pleasure in not too copious draughts, but it has hardly sufficient substance and variety to fill out a whole concert programme without monotony. . . . [Though] her individuality has gained a prominence something out of its due proportion from the fact that she is a woman, she has a substantial endowment of talent and skill that have given her music a place of its own."

B392   "Notes." <u>The Evening Post</u> (New York), 16 December 1908, 9.

Brief notice of Carnegie Hall recital. "At the close there were loud calls for her <u>Scarf Dance</u>. Before playing it, she addressed a few words to the audience explaining that this piece was not so popular abroad as it seemed to be here, for which reason she had not thought of including it in her programmes." <u>See</u> W52e.

B393   "Chaminade's `Tolerance'." <u>The Musical Leader and Concert Goer</u> 14 (17 December 1908): 5.

An article that takes a journalist's statment that Chaminade is tolerant in judging her musical contemporaries (e.g. Debussy, Ravel, and Strauss), and then quotes extensively from her published statements, which seem to belie the epithet "tolerant."

B394   "French Composer Mme. CLS Chaminade Honored at Club Reception." <u>The New York Times</u>, 21 December 1908, p. 9 col. 3.

Report of reception given in the composer's honor by the Chaminade Ladies' Glee Club of Brooklyn.

B395   "Chaminade's Farewell Concert." Musical Courier 57 No. 26 (23 December 1908): 8.

A farewell to Chaminade's entire tour as well as a report on her final concert.

1909 TO 1918

B396   "Chaminade-Carbonel (Mme. Cécile)." Les Hommes et Les Oeuvres. [early 1909].

Entry in a biographical dictionary. A factual, substantial account, which lists as its sources Chapotot's article in La Chanson (see B294), the article in Le Petit Poucet (see B272), and miscellaneous items in The Etude (see, e.g., B368). The publication can be dated by its statement that Chaminade is returning from her American trip.

B397   Putnam's Magazine 5 (January 1909): 510.

A paragraph expressing gratitude to the John Church Company for having made Chaminade's American visit a reality. The writer hopes she will return.

B398   "What Mme. Chaminade Says of Art." Philadelphia Inquirer, 2 February 1909, 5.

The composer speaks of women and the art of music. "There is no sex in art. . . . The woman of the future, with her broader outlook, her greater opportunities, will go far, I believe, in creative work of every description."

B399   Musette. "Musique: Récital de Mme. Cécile Chaminade à la Grande Salle Franklin." [source unknown] (Bordeaux), November [1909].

A recital devoted exclusively to her works, featuring the Concertino. "M. Hennebains, soloist of the Opéra, and professor at the Conservatoire, came specially from Paris to perform with Mme. Chaminade her Concertino for flute. What an interpretor of this exquisitely original work. Those who heard it will never forget it." Except for the Trio No. 2, all the pieces were for piano. See W40, W154c.

B400   "Perfiles de Mujeres: Cecile Chaminade." [El Mundo] (Havana), [1909].

Article declares that in the past twenty years Chaminade has been one of the three most important female composers. "Her popularity is such that not only are her compositions heard in concerts through-

out the world, but her music has also infiltrated
all households; there are few respectable afficiona-
dos who have no works of Chaminade in their repertoire."

B401   Le Cigalier. "Nos Biographies: Cécile Carbonel-Chami-
        nade." La Cigale Littéraire et Artistique (Organe
        Officiel de l'Académie Provençale de Cigaliers et de
        Cigalières) 15 [1910]: 1-2.

        Substantial biography, including very favorable as-
        sessment of her works, taken largely from Chapotot
        (see B294).

B402   "La Musique: Le Récital Chaminade." Figaro Illustré,
        [April] 1910.

        Notice of a forthcoming recital in which Chaminade
        will collaborate with a Pianola in performing two of
        her pieces for two pianos. "The 20th of May 1910
        will be a memorable date in the annals of the Aeol-
        ian Company. It is the first time that a musical
        celebrity, both a highly appreciated composer and
        noted pianist, will participate in a recital of the
        Pianola." She was one of the first to champion the
        mechanism. The works on this program will be Callir-
        hoë and Valse Carnavalesque. See W53a, W95b.

B403   Lowe, George. "The Pianoforte Works of Mlle. Chami-
        nade." The Musical Standard (Great Britain) 36 No.
        932, Illustrated Series (11 November 1911): 307.

        A wide-ranging, mostly intelligent survey of her
        piano music, revealing broad acquaintance with her
        works in this medium. "Her solo works for pianoforte
        now number over one hundred. . . . Mlle. Chaminade
        belongs essentially to the French school, but to the
        school of Godard, Massenet and Delibes rather than
        to that of Debussy and Ravel . . . . Her music also
        shows traces of the influence of Chopin. . . . But
        Mlle. Chaminade has not the genius of Chopin. . . .
        It is just 'salon' music, but salon music of the
        most refined and pleasing kind. There is also a par-
        ticularly feminine element about it just as there
        was about the music of Chopin." Specific traits dis-
        cussed are her melodic gifts, her reliance on ter-
        nary form, and her imitation of old styles in some
        pieces, e.g. Toccata, Passepied, or Pièce Dans Le
        Style Ancien. Among her best pieces are several of
        the Six Etudes de Concert, Op. 35, and the Etude
        Mélodique. "It would be foolish to contend that
        Mlle. Chaminade ranks with the really great compo-
        sers, for her style is too limited for her to do so.
        But she does supply a want, and her music contains
        much individuality." See W41-46, W57, W96, W130,
        W165.

B404   Chaminade, Cécile. "Recollections of My Musical Child-
        hood." The Etude 29 (December 1911): 805-06.

Lengthy article on various subjects, including her teachers, her musical influences, her views on contemporary composers and favorites now deceased, and her methods of composing. She pinpoints the start of her public career to her success in 1889 in performing the Concertstück at the Lamoureux concerts (see W58b). Although the essay contains a great deal of useful insight, still one should apply caution in accepting at face value many of the romanticized statements, especially so many years later, in a popular magazine, and in a translation, where the translator's name is not given.

B405   Barillon-Bauché, Paula. Augusta Holmès et La Femme Compositeur. Librairie Fischbacher, 1912, 76-77.

Chaminade is one of two composers featured in the chapter "'Au Pays Bleu': Deux Contemporains d'Holmès." The author lists her most important pieces and asserts that Chaminade enjoyed great vogue. Most interesting is the comparison to Holmès. Chaminade did not aim as high in the sense of cultivating mainly the larger forms (orchestral music). On the other hand, her fame has been more long-lived, because of the immediate appeal of her pieces.

B406   "Promotions in the Legion of Honour." The Times (London), 11 August 1913, p. 7 col. 3.

The newest promotions to the Legion of Honor are announced in Paris on 10 August. Chaminade is one of several notables who are awarded the status of Officer.

B407   "Chaminade Member of Legion of Honor." Musical America 18 No. 15 (16 August 1913): 32.

Among the 374 persons decorated this year, three, including Chaminade, are women.

B408   "Decoration of Chaminade." Musical Leader 26 No. 9 (28 August 1913): 248.

Another announcement of Chaminade being awarded the Legion of Honor. This account goes on to discuss the issue of women's creativity and asserts that in this regard men are superior to women. Chaminade is compared to a few other female composers, and her pieces are deemed of lesser quality than those of Mrs. Beach.

B409   "Chaminade's Career: First Woman to be Given Membership in Legion of Honor in Recognition of Ability as Musician and Composer." Musical Leader 26 No. 10 (4 September 1913): 255.

Of the 100-plus women who have been awarded the Legion of Honor, Chaminade is the first who is a composer.

B410   Monsigny. "Mlle. Cécile Chaminade Reçoit Le Ruban Rouge." L'Excelsior (Paris), 28 October 1913, 2.

Article and photo published the day after Chaminade received the Legion of Honor award. The photo shows her receiving the ribbon, from Poilpot, the painter, at the Orphélinat des Arts. The following is from his tribute: "You are universally famous. In France you are adored, and, beyond the seas, you are also adored, for your poetry, for the charm of your music, for your considerable musical output. . . ."

B411   Musica 12 (October 1913): 208.

Portrait of Chaminade, under which the caption reads, "Mme. Cécile Chaminade, the charming musician who has composed so many celebrated songs, has been named knight ['chevalier'] of the Legion of Honor."

B412   "Le Trio Livon." Les Coulisses (Draguignon), 18-25 October 1913.

Review of the Trio No. 2, "which deserves special mention for the fine construction of its first movement, the charm of the andante, and the sparkling spirit of the finale. See W40.

B413   "Le Concert Livon." La République de L'Isère (Grenoble), 24 October 1913.

Another review of the Trio No. 2: "I truly appreciated the second Trio of Chaminade. Like the majority of works of this author, it is a succession of very charming themes, supported by harmonies that willingly separate themselves from the basic tonality, and impart to the whole a strongly romantic character. A genuine impression of power is released in the finale." See W40.

B414   Petit Annonéen (Annonay), 25 October 1913.

Additional review of the Livon tour and the Trio: "Who doesn't know M. [sic for 'Monsieur'] Chaminade . . . ? His all-too-short composition that we heard on Thursday has convinced us again that Chaminade's talents are spread equally among all genres, and he can be compared to the most skillful and the most knowledgeable [composers]. . . ." See W40.

B415   "Le Concert Du Célèbre Trio Livon." Le Petit Briançonnais, 26 October 1913.

"We owe special mention to the superb Trio in a minor by Chaminade, which, from one end to the

other, contains great musical interest. . . ." <u>See</u>
W40.

B416   Guichard, Arthur de. "Cécile Chaminade." <u>The Musician</u>
(Boston) 19 (March 1914): 165.

The Legion of Honor award prompts this article,
which assesses Chaminade's worldwide fame. "This is
the first time in the history of the Order that a
woman composer has been admitted to its ranks and
granted so great a distinction. . . . Mme. Chaminade has fully won the ribbon . . . by being the
most popular woman composer of the time." Statistics
showing her popularity are the more than 250 Chaminade Clubs in the United States, and the fact that
"one little piece alone, <u>Automne</u>, . . . published
some twenty-five years ago, had a sale of over eight
thousand copies last year" (<u>see</u> W42).

B417   Huré, Jean. "Filles d'Euterpe." <u>Musique et Théâtre</u>
[1916]: 3-4.

Interesting article, authored by a man who thinks
very highly of women's cultural level and artistic
abilities. He recounts how he arrived at this appreciation, in earlier years (1895). Chaminade,
whose compositions he had already liked but whom he
believed was a man, was responsible for changing his
mind about women's creative powers.

B418   <u>Le Parthénon</u> (Revue Indépendante, Politique, Litté-
raire et Scientifique) 7 ([January] 1916).

Chaminade will participate with others, including
the soprano Marie Capoy, in a recital on 31 January
that will include one or more of her works.

B419   "Famous Women Composers." <u>The Etude</u> 35 (April 1917):
237-38.

In this article that first generalizes about women
as composers and then proceeds to discuss indivi-
dually several contemporary exponents, Chaminade is
accorded a substantial biographical description. No
new information is presented here; rather, much is
drawn from the 1911 article that the composer wrote
for the same magazine (<u>see</u> B404).

B420   "A List of Well-Known Women Composers." <u>The Etude</u> 36
(November 1918): 699-700.

A directory of approximately 200 women composers,
most of them contemporary or near contemporary, but
also a few long deceased. The entry for Chaminade is
relatively long. "At present she is devoting her
whole time to work for the convalescent soldiers in
France."

1919 TO 12 APRIL 1944

B421   "15-Year-Old Pianist Creates Sensation in Debut in
        This City." Philadelphia Public Ledger, 8 December
        1919, 3.

        Review of Israel Vichnin's performance of the Con-
        certstück, on 7 December: "He played [it] with all
        the assurance and facility of a mature musician. . .
        . [His exquisite musical taste] enabled him to make
        a thing of great beauty out of the charming, pas-
        torally written piano part of the concerto." See
        W58L.

B422   "Philharmonic Concert." Philadelphia Bulletin, 8 De-
        cember 1919, 12.

        "His playing of the Concertpiece for Piano and Or-
        chestra by Chaminade was remarkable. . . ." See
        W58L.

B423   "Two Soloists on Program." The Philadelphia Record, 8
        December 1919, 15.

        Another assessment of the Concertstück: "The Chami-
        nade concert piece, with orchestra, was a good med-
        ium for the display of a fluent technique and excel-
        lent interpretative ability." See W58L.

B424   "Selects 25 Women as Greatest in History." The Wash-
        ington Post, 5 July 1922, p. 2 col. 4.

        "Mrs. James R. Mann, wife of one of the Republican
        leaders in Congress, has submitted a list of ent-
        ries" for the 25 greatest women, of the past. She
        includes Chaminade in the group, not realizing that
        the composer is still living.

B425   "Mme. Chaminade at the Central Hall." The Times (Lon-
        don), 2 October 1922, p. 18 col. 2.

        Brief review of concert of 30 September. "Among the
        nine piano solos which she played were three new
        ones, the Berceuse du Petit Soldat Blessé, Ecrin,
        and Chanson Nègre. Mme. Chaminade was joined by M.
        Louis Fleury in her Concertino for flute and piano.
        . . ." See W154, W229a, W234a, W359b.

B426   Brancour, René. "Les Femmes et La Musique." Rivista
        Musicale Italiana 32 (1925): 363-80.

        In this wide-ranging treatment of women as creators,
        Chaminade is assigned a short paragraph and consi-
        dered alongside her compatriot, Augusta Holmès.
        "Chaminade has written very lovely compositions. . .
        . Perhaps she has written too many. . . . But one
        would not deny her grace, nor a highly personal
        charm combined with a striking stylistic elegance."

B427   "Cecile Chaminade." Duo-Art Piano Music. New York: The
        Aeolian Company, 1927, p. 248.

        In this one-page feature there appears a biographi-
        cal sketch and a paragraph on Chaminade's associa-
        tion with Duo-Art piano rolls. Guitare, Op. 32, is
        mentioned as the first of her works issued in this
        form (see W38, D220).

B428   M. Hs. "Moderne Komponisten." Der Artist--Düsseldorf
        No. 261 ([after March] 1927).

        Interesting piece on Chaminade. The author begins by
        declaring that although Hans von Bülow said that he
        did not know any women with compositional talent, he
        would have changed his mind had he known the works
        of Chaminade. As proof of her popularity, an anec-
        dote is presented about La Lisonjera being offered
        as an encore by Teresa Carreño and then having to be
        repeated (see W68). The ensuing biography relates
        that Chaminade's Prelude for Organ, Op. 78, was per-
        formed at Queen Victoria's burial (see W105). Her
        pieces possess "an original, tender charm." Chami-
        nade is quoted as saying, "I don't deny that some of
        my music is considered light, but I prefer my pre-
        ludes, concert-pieces, sonatas, trios, and religious
        poems ['Evangelische Dichtungen'], whose character
        is much more serious, and to which I actually at-
        tribute my reputation among artists and conservato-
        ries. Today there is a new style in music, and it is
        very easy to forget those artists whom one had re-
        spected and acknowledged in the past."

B429   "Audition Musicale: Festival Chaminade." Journal de
        Rouen, 9 February 1928.

        Report on the event of 5 February, organized by
        Marie Capoy, with the assistance of E. Dubruille,
        famous local cellist. Pieces performed are Viatique,
        orchestral excerpts from Callirhoë, orchestral ver-
        sion of Le Matin, as well as Pavane et Courante, O
        Salutaris and Gloria (from the Mass), Le Thrône Du
        Vieux Roi, and Ma Première Lettre. In addition,
        there was a lecture on Chaminade's life and works by
        Capoy. The reviewer declares: "Mme. Chaminade has
        not needed to dispense with polytonality to be a
        great artist, to communicate her feelings to an au-
        dience of connaisseurs. . . . Brilliant success for
        Mme. Chaminade, for her performers, and especially
        for Mme. Marie Capoy, fervent and tireless proponent
        of Chaminade's art." See W106c, W131a, W132b, W241a,
        W243a, W293a, W313e, W389a.

B430   R. P. "Concerts Divers: Concerts Dubruille." Le Ménes-
        trel 90 No. 6 (10 February 1928): 62-63.

        On 5 February there was a festival of Chaminade
        works, very well received. Among the numerous com-

positions on the program were excerpts from <u>Callir-hoë</u>, <u>Sommeil D'Enfant</u>, <u>La Chaise à Porteurs</u>, and <u>Sérénade Espagnole</u> (violin and piano). <u>See</u> W50, W74c, W223a, W362a.

B431   "Nos Concerts Classiques: Le Festival Chaminade." <u>Le Petit Var</u> (Toulon), 29 March 1928.

A concert devoted to the works of Chaminade. The reviewer notes the Frenchness of the style and the familiarity that most audience members already had with the compositions. The <u>Concertstück</u> was rendered by Excoffier, professor at the Conservatoire. <u>See</u> W58m.

B432   "Les Concerts du Conservatoire; Le Festival Chaminade" [source unknown] (Toulon), [30 March 1928].

Review of the concert in homage to Chaminade. On the program were the <u>Concertstück</u>, <u>Suite D'Orchestre</u>, <u>Prélude</u> for organ, and several choruses for girls. "These pieces of Mme. Chaminade are already old. One can say that they will remain, whereas many of the empty modern works will disappear. For, what Mme. Chaminade has written, and especially what we heard yesterday, possesses the typically French qualities of clarity, freshness, tenderness, sensitivity, as well as originality, which means that they will never cease to be played, because there will always be a public of refined taste to appreciate them." <u>See</u> W19-22, W58, W105a.

B433   H. H. "Conférence Musicale et Concert: Mme. Marie Capoy--Cécile Chaminade et Son Oeuvre." <u>Journal de Rouen</u>, 6 July [1928].

Review of Capoy's lecture-performance of Chaminade's works. The first part included the first movement of the <u>Trio No. 2</u>, <u>Retour</u>, <u>Concertino</u>, <u>Sérénade Espagnole</u>, and several songs. <u>See</u> W154e, W207a, W232b.

B434   H. F. [Helen Fetter]. "Chaminade's Washington Visit in 1908 Recalled." <u>Sunday Star</u> (Washington), 4 August 1929, part 4, p. 3, cols. 4-6.

Article includes a short biography, reminiscences about her meeting with President Theodore Roosevelt, and a conclusion that her pieces are still in great demand. "There is no woman composer who has won higher honor and recognition than Mme. Cecile Carbonel Chaminade of France."

B435   <u>Musical Leader</u> (Chicago) 57 No. 8 (22 August 1929): 10.

A paragraph marking her 61st [sic] birthday. "It will be remembered that John McCormack included 'The Little Silver Ring' on his programs within the past two seasons." <u>See</u> W284.

B436   Elson, Arthur and E. E. Truette. Woman's Work in
       Music. Rev. ed. Boston: L. C. Page and Co., [1931].

       The information provided in the section on Chami-
       nade, in the "France" chapter, is not current as of
       1931 but seems to go through c. 1901, which would be
       the approximate cutoff point for the first edition
       (1903). In any case, the information is the standard
       Chaminade biography. Elson considers her songs the
       main reason for her fame.

B437   Lee, Markham. "The Student-Interpreter: A Short Reci-
       tal of Light Pianoforte Pieces." Musical Opinion
       (Great Britain) 55 (February 1932): 413-14.

       Chaminade's Thème Varié is one of five piano works
       discussed in detail for the benefit of potential
       students. "[It] is . . . feminine and delicate. Mad-
       ame Chaminade is not performed as she was in the
       days of my pupilage; . . . . This is not a theme
       with variations, but a kind of rondo . . . . This
       will not be acceptable to patrons of a contemporary
       musical society . . . but it will please those who
       like tune and simplicity and a non-disturbing at-
       mosphere . . . . Besides being graceful, there is
       opportunity for brilliance now and again, especially
       when the theme occurs in the minor. It is good prac-
       tice for scales in double notes." See W124.

B438   Johnson, Thomas Arnold. "The Pianoforte Music of Cham-
       inade." Musical Opinion 59 (May 1936): 678-79.

       The most thorough and detailed discussion of her
       piano works. "Although she has produced practically
       nothing of great importance, her name and her work
       are known and admired the whole world over. Her
       solos for the piano are mostly of the light salon
       type, and are characterised by graceful and dainty
       writing. . . Her music is very pianistic. . . . The
       real Chaminade appears in the Air de Ballet, Scher-
       zos, Valses, etc. . . . Chaminade has a happy knack
       of being able to write interesting music in the an-
       cient style. . . ." In her Prélude, Op. 84 No. 1,
       she is faulted for writing in the style of others,
       namely Rachmaninoff, Brahms, Chopin, and Franck (see
       W112-14). "Since the war, Chaminade's music has not
       been quite as good, and it now seems that she has
       ceased to write altogether. There are some, no
       doubt, who consider this a pity; but it must be rea-
       lised that she has produced quite enough for us to
       enjoy intelligently. . . . Far better for her to
       cease writing than to try to alter her style to suit
       modern tastes."

B439   Gilman, Lawrence. "Notes on the Program." New York
       Philharmonic-Society Notes, for concerts of 2-3 Jan-
       uary 1937, n. p.

The Concertino is performed on these concerts. "A remarkable feature of the work is its use of the orchestra's heaviest artillery in the accompaniment, for which three trombones and tuba are requisitioned (the trumpets take a holiday)." See W154f.

B440   N. S. "Music in Review." The New York Times, Sunday 3 January 1937, section II, p. 5 col. 2.

Review of New York Philharmonic-Society program. The Concertino "was a nicely orchestrated confection, a one-movement affair in rondo form, which gave the flautist plenty of opportunity for fancy fireworks of which he took the utmost advantage, in a brilliant encompassment of its many difficulties." See W154f.

B441   "Anniversaire Qui Créa de L'Intérêt." L'Etoile (Lowell, Mass.), September 1938.

In honor of the recent 77th [sic] birthday of Chaminade, patroness of the Académie Guilbault in Lowell, the director, Louis Guilbault, wrote to the composer.

B442   "You Are Invited to Take Part in a World-Wide Birthday Surprise Party." The Etude 57 (June 1939): 362.

Announcement encouraging readers to send birthday greetings to Chaminade, who is bed-ridden, at her home in Monte Carlo.

B443   "Programme de Chaminade à La Radio Mardi Soir." L'Etoile (Lowell, Mass.), 5 August 1939.

In celebration of Chaminade's 78th [sic] birthday, Guilbault will perform four Chaminade works on a radio broadcast: Scherzo Valse, Op. 126 No. 6; Pas des Echarpes; Novelette, Op. 126 No. 8; and La Lisonjera. There is a brief mention of Etude magazine's recent project to have as many greetings as possible sent to the composer (see B442). See W52f, W68c, W190a, W192a.

B444   "Chaminade Sends a Birthday Message to Her American Friends in Wartime." Musical Courier 120 No. 10 (15 November 1939): 7.

English translation of Chaminade's expression of gratitude to her American admirers who had sent birthday wishes. The letter is dated "Wednesday, September 20. Hardelot Plage, Pas de Calais," where she went to escape the heat of Monte Carlo. It is actually addressed to her old friend, Irving Schwerké, "Paris representative of the Musical Courier."

B445   "M. Mussolini Emeut Un Violiniste Hongrois Par Sa Mu-
          sicalité de Grande Classe." L'Echo de Paris, [1940].
          (Reprinted from La Transalpine.)

          The violinist Szekeley recounts his meeting with
          Mussolini, himself an accomplished violinist, and of
          the Italian leader speaking to him about certain
          violin pieces, among which he lists some by Chami-
          nade. No specific titles are given.

OBITUARIES

B446   Typescript (copy in possession of Family): "Société
          Radio Monte-Carlo, Mort de Mme. Cécile Chaminade,
          Oraison Funèbre Prononcée par Théodore Mathieu."
          Broadcast Monte Carlo, 14 April 1944.

          A one-page tribute. "It is a gentle comfort to me to
          think that, this winter, Radio Monte Carlo organized
          an important concert of the works of Cécile Chami-
          nade; that I had the opportunity, furthermore, after
          having recalled her life, to discuss her level of
          activity and her keen intelligence. . . . Farewell,
          Cécile Chaminade, your name will become the symbol
          of talent, of duty, of kindness; and know that your
          works will sing forever in our hearts." In conclu-
          sion, L'Anneau D'Argent and the finale of the Con-
          certstück were aired; see W58, W284h.

B447   "Mort de Cécile Chaminade." L'Eclaireur (Nice), 18
          April 1944.

          "We learn of the death, in Monte Carlo, of Mme. Cé-
          cile Chaminade. Pianist of great talent and prolific
          composer of charm and melodic invention, she knew
          fame at a very early age thanks to her dual gifts of
          inspiration and musical craft. Despite her advanced
          age--83 [sic]--Cécile Chaminade was still working.
          She leaves numerous works, among which many songs,
          such as L'Anneau D'Argent, Viens Mon Bien-Aimé, and
          Le Jardinier D'Amour, were extremely popular." See
          W284, W290, W296.

B448   Aujourd'Hui, 19 April 1944, p. 2.

          Brief statement: "We learn of the death of Mme. Cé-
          cile Chaminade, composer-pianist, dead at the age of
          83 years [sic] in Monte Carlo."

B449   "Cecile Chaminade Dies at 82, Composer of 200 Piano
          Pieces." New York Herald Tribune, 19 April 1944, 20.

          The notice begins with a simple statement of her
          death, listing her age at 82 [sic]. "During the clo-
          sing years of the nineteenth century [she] was im-
          mensely popular in Paris. The songs and piano pieces
          she composed were clever, pretty and light. She was

one of the few successful woman composers of her
era. Melba was among the singers who charmed Parisi-
ennes of that day with her songs. . . The critics
found her compositions tuneful and agreeable salon
music containing little of deep significance. . .
Almost any one who ever took piano lessons played
some Chaminade composition."

B450   The New York Times, 19 April 1944, p. 23 col. 1.

In this factually correct and comprehensive account
we learn her real age, 86, and therefore her correct
year of birth (1857). "Cécile Chaminade was one of
the few women to achieve distinction in musical composition. . . . Her songs and piano pieces, written
in salon style, were popular a third of a century
ago." Her decorations, her American tour in 1908,
her brief marriage, and the vogue of Chaminade clubs
are mentioned.

B451   Paris-Soir, 19 April 1944, p. 2.

"From Monte Carlo we learn of the death of Mme. Cécile Chaminade, at the age of 83 [sic], a pianist of
great talent as well as a composer of charming
songs. Some of her works were extremely popular,
such as L'Anneau D'Argent, Viens, Mon Bien-Aimé, and
Le Jardinier D'Amour." See W284, W290, W296.

B452   Musical America (25 April 1944): 24.

A fairly complete, reliable account of her life,
including her correct year of birth. "In spite of
her great popularity, Mme. Chaminade's works never
reached the highest standard." The article mentions
her important pieces, her decorations, and her marriage.

B453   Chabanne, Denise. "La Musique en Deuil: à Cécile Chaminade." Le Petit Niçois, 27 April 1944.

"Cécile Chaminade passed away 13 April, placing,
through her death, French music in mourning. . . .
Cécile Chaminade was the greatest woman composer in
the history of music. . . . She enjoyed enormous
success. . . . She had not been composing for a
while, did not go out, was content to receive her
friends with touching good grace. . . . She died at
age 87. . . . Cécile Chaminade rests permanently in
Monaco, in that cemetery that overlooks the blue
sea. . . ."

B454   Concordia, 29 April 1944.

"Mme. Cécile Chaminade just died in Monte Carlo at
the age of 83 [sic]. She was born in Paris in 1861
[sic]. When young she became famous as both pianist
and composer. Despite her [advanced] age she did not
retire from work. She leaves a large number of

compositions, and some of her songs, notably L'Anneau d'Argent, Viens Mon Bien-Aimé, and Le Jardinier
d'Amour, have gained considerable favor with the
public." See W284, W290, W296.

B455   "Exit Chaminade." Time 43 (1 May 1944): 54.

Very interesting obituary, which provides additional
information. For example, Chaminade did not receive
any royalties during World War II because her publishers, who were Jewish [Enoch], had been liquidated.
Scarf Dance sold over five million copies (see W52).
Among the avid performers of her works were Nellie
Melba and John Philip Sousa. As a composer she is
judged a facile melodist; her pieces "stand in the
same relation to Frédéric Chopin as strawberry soda
does to cognac."

B456   "Vale Chaminade." The Etude 62 (June 1944): 332.

A shorter account, which provides her correct year
of birth. Always a champion of Chaminade's music,
the magazine praises her as a composer: "Her melodic
gifts were fresh, original, and endowed with rare
charm. She might be called a master musical lapidary
whose tonal jewels have become a permanent part of
the literature of music. She knew her limitations
and never tried to waste her ability upon works of
large dimentions"--a curious statement in light of
the article having previously cited titles of large
works such as Callirhoë and Les Amazones (see W29).
Scarf Dance sold "over a million copies," in contrast to the much larger figure in the Time account
(see W52).

SINCE HER DEATH

B457   Pontalba. "Cécile Chaminade." Le Canada Français 32
        (November 1944): 182-88.

An interesting and substantial account of Chaminade's life and reputation, although the author seems
unaware that she has died. She is considered a
"petit maître." The article assesses both positive
and negative evaluations from several reviews. The
issue of changing taste is brought to the fore: "We
are well aware that the younger generation almost
always makes fun of the things highly respected by
the previous generation." Furthermore, one has to
ask whether critics or the public at large is better
qualified to pass judgment: for whom were her pieces
intended? We also learn about Chaminade's views
concerning fellow French composers, especially
Saint-Saëns and Debussy.

B458   Delhaise, M.-L. "Anniversaire: Cécile Chaminade Auteur
       des 'Deux Ménétriers' Fut L'Ambassadrice de La Mu-
       sique Française." L'Espoir (Nice), 1 April 1945.

       The author recalls an afternoon spent with Chaminade
       one month before she died, in which she had spoken
       of her life. She singled out a private meeting with
       Queen Victoria, in 1898, in which the British mon-
       arch had her notate some music in a book reserved
       for that purpose; others in it were Berlioz, Chopin,
       Mendelssohn, and Paderewski.

B459   Savelli, Laurent. "Un Festival Chaminade à Monte
       Carlo," [source unknown, probably Nice] [25] April
       1946.

       Report on the artistic gathering devoted to the
       works of Chaminade at the home of Lily de Mourgues,
       on 23 April.

B460   Ariste. "Le 'Festival Chaminade' Dans L'Intimité."
       [source unknown, probably Nice] [25 April 1946].

       Another notice of the private performance of Chami-
       nade works in the salons of Lily de Mourgues.

B461   De Lange, Daniël. "Cécile Chaminade Schiep Muziek."
       Iris: Tijdscrift Voor de Vruow en Haar Levenskunst 1
       (April 1947): 12-13, 20.

       Substantial biographical account. The most valuable
       component may be the information about her Central
       European tour in 1900, to the Balkans, Greece, and
       Turkey. The preface speaks of the assistance of An-
       toinette Chaminade-Lorel, the composer's niece, who
       has written a biography of Chaminade soon to be pub-
       lished and who is attempting to have a film made
       about her life. See, for example, p. 26 in the "Bio-
       graphy," as well as "Appendix III."

B462   Kerr, Laura (Nowak). Scarf Dance; The Story of Cecile
       Chaminade. New York: Abelard Press, 1953.

       The only full-length account of Chaminade, but a
       highly fictionalized, romanticized view, authored by
       a writer of popular biographies. Specific dates for
       events rarely appear. Excerpts from reviews only
       occasionally provide the name of the source and
       rarely the date. Because of the lack of scholarly
       method, many errors appear, such as the statement
       that Chaminade studied at the Conservatoire, or that
       Les Amazones was performed in March 1888 in
       Marseille, or that her husband died a year after
       they were married, or that it was in 1918 that she
       was awarded the Legion of Honor.

B463   "Concours de Piano Cécile Chaminade à Monte Carlo."
       Nice-Matin, 1 March 1957, 2.

Announcement of a piano competition bearing Chaminade's name, to take place in Monte Carlo on 24
April, at 2 PM.

B464   "Un Prix de Piano Cécile-Chaminade." L'Espoir (Nice),
1 March 1957, 4.

The same as the preceding.

B465   "Some Composers We Had Almost Forgotten--And The Reason We Ought to Remember Them." The Times (London),
8 March 1957, p. 3 cols. 4-6.

This year is the centenary of the birth of three
composers: Alfred Bruneau, Edward Elgar, and Cécile
Chaminade. The last is an example of a forgotten
composer. Her creative talent is not very strong,
for her pieces have not stood the test of time. "It
was her achievement to be the first professional
woman composer. It is true that Fanny Mendelssohn
and Clara Schumann of an earlier generation both
have something to their credit, but their compositions were by-products of their musical lives. . . .
[Her] short salon pieces, . . . disarming in their
superficiality, were a distinctive achievement. If
they no longer have a vogue it is because salons are
no longer a form of musical entertainment and draw-
ing-room pianos now have their lids shut, both ex-
tinguished by radio and gramophone. If musicians
will not celebrate her centenary perhaps feminists
will discharge their debt."

B466   Deila, Paul. "Une Agréable Réunion Artistique Pour
Commémorer Le Centenaire de La Naissance de Cécile
Chaminade." Nice-Matin, 24 October 1957, "Monaco"
section p. 1.

Report of a lecture/performance at Antoinette Lorel's home in honor of Chaminade. Laurent Savelli, of
the Society of French Poets, recounted her life and
summarized her musical works. He asserts that Chaminade sacrificed her fame to her strong commitment to
orphans, widows, and the wounded during World War I.
Chaminade had set a few of Savelli's poems, such as
Eglogue and Méditation; see W101, W103.

B467   Pouzin, C. "Chaminade (Mme. Cécile)." Dictionnaire de
Biographie Universelle, Vol. 8. Librairie Letouzey
et Ané, 1959, col. 286.

A two-paragraph biographical account. The birth date
is correct, but the death date is not (17 April);
the year given for her marriage to Carbonel, 1903,
is also erroneous.

B468   "Echos Du Passé: Cécile Chaminade." Revue Municipale
du Vésinet No. 38 (April 1977): 43.

A brief article, under the section "Echos du Passé."
It furnishes the usual biographical details and some
pertinent information on piano rolls. "She was considered the most talented female composer, as well
as a virtuosa on the piano. Because she signed a
contract giving Aeolian exclusive recording rights,
with their Duo-Art system, it is thus possible for
us today to listen to her perform her works herself
on a real piano. For this one needs to place one of
her rolls in a piano equipped with the Duo-Art reproducing system."

B469   Stern, Susan. Women Composers: A Handbook. Metuchen:
Scarecrow Press, 1978, 57.

Presents the best list of sources (twelve) pertain-
ing to Chaminade. Especially informative regarding
Etude articles.

B470   Urtin, Albane. "Le Récital Wilfrid Maggiar." Le Courrier D'Aix (en Provence), 23 December 1978.

Very favorable assessment of this recital, devoted
exclusively to piano works of Chaminade. The reviewer is impressed with the pieces and the interpretation. The event is deemed a "memorable concert, . .
. a revelation for those who were unacquainted with
Cécile Chaminade, who could not have received a
better performance than by Wilfrid Maggiar, one of
the few pianists with the gift of sentiment!" See
W32a, W33e, W42f, W46b, W57d, W59e, W68d, W83c,
W99e, W108c, W112-14b, W148d, W151a, W167a, W168b,
W205a, W210a, W212a, W219a, W221a.

B471   Condé, Gérard. Liner Notes to Record, "Pièces Pour
Piano--Cécile Chaminade," [1980]. See D205.

The most factually detailed account of her life.
Although a few inaccuracies appear (she never married, she met Franklin Roosevelt), still this is an
excellent, informative essay, and constitutes the
first published narrative to be based on the family's documents.

B472   Ferrari, Gustave and Jean Mongrédien. "Cécile Chaminade." The New Grove's Dictionary of Music and Musicians. 20 Vols., ed. Stanley Sadie. London: Macmil-
lan and Co., 1980; IV: 125.

An abridged version of the Ferrari entry that has
appeared in all editions of Grove since 1904. The
only updating involves the listing of three articles
for the "Bibliography," and a very brief summary
list of her music and their publication.

B473   Condé, Gérard. "Découverte: Le Mystère Chaminade." Le
Monde de la Musique 1 (April 1980).

Commencing with a narration of the writer's chance acquaintance with Chaminade, the article mentions the recently-released EMI recording of her piano works (see D205 and B471) and then outlines her life.

B474   Weissweiler, Eva. Komponistinnen aus 500 Jahren. Frankfurt: Fischer Taschenbuch Verlag, 1981, p. 327.

A brief but provocative treatment of Chaminade, in which the author declares that her music has been categorized as salon music without any basis in systematic musical analysis. The Concertino is still in the standard repertoire (see W154), but pieces like Les Amazones have totally disappeared (see W29), as have favorable contemporary assessments of her works.

B475   Labhard, Walter. "Die Frau als Komponistin: Anmerkungen zu einem Seitenthema der Musikgeschichte des 19. und 20. Jahrhunderts." Med. Schweizer Magazin für Artzliche Okonomie, [1982]: 59-69.

A discussion of several female composers of these two centuries, mostly in relation to recent recordings of their works. The EMI anthology of piano pieces (see D205) occupies center stage in the Chaminade section. The author judges it a fine performance of fine works and asserts that the question of whether written by a woman or a man should always be irrelevant.

B476   Foy, Alain-Marie. "Qui Etait Cécile Chaminade?" Revue Municipale du Vésinet No. 58 (March 1982): 73.

A fairly substantial, detailed biographical account, with special attention paid to her childhood activities in Le Vésinet. It is based on Condé's record liner notes (see B471 and D205), as well as documentary material supplied by a second cousin of the composer who, as of 1982, was living in Le Vésinet (she has since died).

B477   Peyregne, André. "Cécile Chaminade, La Vieille Dame de Monaco Qui Aurait Pu Etre L'Un des Grands Compositeurs de L'Autre Siècle." Nice-Matin, 8 March 1982, [1023].

Background article for the scheduled recital that day of Danielle Laval, performing piano works of Chaminade. A substantial section focuses on the composer's last, solitary years in Monte Carlo, although earlier biography is also furnished.

B478   Jerrould, John. "Piano Music of Cécile Chaminade." American Music Teacher 37 No. 3 (January 1988): 22-23, 46.

Prompted by Kalmus's recent reissue of Schirmer's
two-volume collection of piano music from 1899, this
article provides some interesting assessments of
Chaminade's place in music (she is judged a successful saloniste). It then discusses the works included
in the collection. Many of the pieces fall under one
of the broad categories of Spanish-influenced, char-
acteristically French, or dance-derived, and display
affinities with other French composers. Marring this
otherwise helpful and perceptive essay, however, are
a few inaccuracies: the dubbing of Chaminade a spin-
ster, and the claim that she studied with Saint-
Saëns and Bizet.

WRITINGS BY CHAMINADE

B479   "Georges Bizet." The Century Library of Music, 20
vols., ed. Paderewski. New York: The Century Co.,
1900; VI: 165-80.

A sympathetic account of the life and principal
works of Bizet, especially of his operas. "Little
has been written concerning Bizet," with the exception of Charles Pigot's fine book (Bizet and His
Work, 1886). But although a close friend and neighbor (in Le Vésinet), Chaminade refrains from inserting herself directly into the narrative. She does,
however, lament the fickle taste of the Parisian
public in first spurning Carmen (1875), leading in
large part to the composer's premature death, and
then enthusing over it only eight years later. Chaminade claims that "from an esthetic standpoint,
'L'Arlésienne' impresses one as Georges Bizet's most
complete masterpiece."

"How to Sing and Play My Compositions"; see B287.

"How to Play My Compositions"; see B299.

"How to Play My Best Known Pieces"; see B368.

"Recollections of My Musical Childhood"; see B404.

Appendix I:
Alphabetical List of Works

The mnemonics "W," "WU," and "WU" refer to listings in the "Works and Performances" chapter.

A L'Inconnue, W288
A Travers Bois, Op. 63, W86
L'Absente, W271
Agitato, Op. 108, W155
Air à Danser, Op. 164, W237
Air De Ballet, Op. 30, W34
   No. 11 of Album Des Enfants, Op. 123, W182
Air Italien, Op. 170, W247
Album Des Enfants, 1st series, Op. 123, W172-83
Album Des Enfants, 2nd series, Op. 126, W185-96
L'Allée D'Eméraude Et D'Or, W346
Alleluia, W357
Les Amazones, W29, WU1
Amertume, W333
Amoroso, W283
L'Amour Captif, W292
Amour D'Automne, W276
Amour Invisible, W376
Andante, WU2
Andante et Scherzettino, Op. 59, W82
Andante Tranquillo, WU3
Andantino, No. 1 of Trois Morceaux, Op. 31, W35
L'Angélus, Op. 69, W92
L'Anneau D'Argent, W284
L'Anneau Du Soldat, W392
Appassionato, No. 4 of Six Etudes De Concert, Op. 35, W44
Arabesque, Op. 61, W84
Deuxième Arabesque, Op. 92, W127
Arléquine, Op. 53, W71
Attente, W387
Au Clair De La Lune, WU4
Au Firmament, W352
Au Pays Bleu, W332
Au Pays Dévasté, Op. 155, W228
Aubade, Op. 140, W213
   No. 2 of Album Des Enfants, Op. 126, W186
Aubade, W309
Auprès De Ma Vie, W268
Automne, No. 2 of Six Etudes De Concert, Op. 35, W42
Autrefois, No. 4 of Six Pièces Humoristiques, Op. 87, W120

Aux Dieux Sylvains, Op. 100, W147
Avenir, W375
Avril S'Eveille, W323

Ballade, Op. 86, W116
    No. 5 of Album Des Enfants, Op. 126, W189
Ballade A La Lune, W304
Balle A La Terre, WU5
Barcarolle, Op. 7, W9
    No. 8 of Album Des Enfants, Op. 123, W179
Barcarolle, Op. 62, W85
La Barque D'Amour, Op. 135, W208
Le Beau Chanteur, W342
Berceuse, Op. 6, W8
Berceuse, W287
Berceuse Arabe, Op. 166, W239
Berceuse Du Petit Soldat Blessé, Op. 156, W229
Bleus, W328
Bohémienne, No. 3 of Trois Morceaux, Op. 31, W37
Les Bohémiens, Op. 147, W220
Bonne Humeur, W363

Callirhoë, Op. 37, W49, W53, WU6
Callirhoë, Quatrième Air De Ballet, from Op. 37, W53
Callirhoë, Suite D'Orchestre, [Op. 37], W50
Canzonetta, No. 3 of Album Des Enfants, Op. 123, W174
Capriccio, Op. 18, W17
Capriccio Appassionato, Op. 52, W70
Caprice Espagnole, Op. 67, W90
Caprice-Etude, Op. 4, W6
Caprice Humoristique, Op. 113, W160
Caprice-Impromptu, Op. 153, W226
Capricietto, Op. 136, W209
La Capricieuse, WU7
C'Etait En Avril, W345
Chaconne, Op. 8, W10
La Chaise A Porteurs, No. 2 of Six Pièces Romantiques, Op.
    55, W75, WU8
Chanson Bretonne, No. 5 of Romances Sans Paroles, Op. 76,
    W102
Chanson De Mer, W388
Chanson De Neige, W380
Chanson D'Orient, Op. 157, W230
La Chanson Du Fou, W335
Chanson Espagnole, W315
Chanson Forestière, W367
Chanson Groënlandaise, W300
Chanson Naive, W381
Chanson Napolitaine, Op. 82, W110
Chanson Nègre, Op. 161, W234
Chanson Russe, No. 5 of Six Feuillets D'Album, Op. 98, W139
Chanson Slave, W262
Chanson Triste, W329
Chant D'Amour, W305
Chant Du Nord, Op. 96, W133
Le Charme D'Amour, W351
Choeurs, W62-67
Choral, No. 4 of Suite D'Orchestre, Op. 20, W22
Le Ciel Est Bleu, W320

Colette, W285
Comme Autrefois--Le Bon Vieux Temps, WU9
Concertino, Op. 107, W154
Concerto-Légende, WU10
Concertstück, Op. 40, W58
Consolation, No. 5 of Six Pièces Humoristiques, Op. 87, W121
Console-Moi, W348
Conte De Fées, W349
   No. 11 of Album Des Enfants, Op. 126, W195
Contes Bleus, Op. 122, W169-71
Cortège, Op. 143, W216
Couplets Bachiques, W325
Courante, No. 3 of Trois Danses Anciennes, Op. 95, W132

La Damoiselle, W350
Dans La Lande, No. 1 of Poème Provençal, Op. 127, W197
Dans L'Arène, Op. 168, W245
Danse Ancienne, Op. 75, W97
Danse Créole, Op. 94, W129
Danse Hindoue, No. 5 of Six Pièces Romantiques, Op. 55, W78
Danse Orientale, from Op. 37, W55
Danse Paienne, Op. 158, W231
Danse Pastorale, from Op. 37, W54
Trois Danses Anciennes, Op. 95, W130-32
Départ, W369
Les Deux Coeurs, W295
Les Deux Ménétriers, W277, WU11
Dites-Lui, W372
Divertissement, Op. 105, W152
Duetto, No. 1 of Deux Morceaux, Op. 27, W30
Duo D'Etoiles, Op. 71, W94
Duo Symphonique, Op. 117, W164
Duos, Op. 62-65, Op. 68-71, W85-88, W91-94

Ecossaise, Op. 151, W224
Ecrin, W359
Eglogue, No. 4 of Romances Sans Paroles, Op. 76, W101
   No. 4 of Album Des Enfants, Op. 126, W188
Egmont, WU13
Elégie, No. 3 of Six Feuillets D'Album, Op. 98, W137
   No. 7 of Album Des Enfants, Op. 126, W191
Elévation, No. 2 of Romances Sans Paroles, Op. 76, W99
Les Elfes Des Bois, Op. 159, W232
Espoir, W317
L'Eté, W303, WU14
L'Etoile, No. 1 of Poèmes Evangéliques, Op. 99, W141
Etude, [Op. 1], W3
Etude Humoristique, Op. 138, W211
Etude Mélodique, Op. 118, W165
Etude Pathétique, Op. 124, W184
Etude Romantique, Op. 132, W205
Etude Scolastique, Op. 139, W212
Etude Symphonique, Op. 28, W32
Six Etudes De Concert, Op. 35, W41-46
Exil, W365
Expansion, Op. 106, W153
L'Extase, W343

Feuilles D'Automne, Op. 146, W219
Six Feuillets D'Album, Op. 98, W135-40
Les Feux De St. Jean, Op. 44, W62
La Fiancée Du Soldat, W267
Les Fiancés, Op. 68, W91
Fileuse, No. 3 of Six Etudes De Concert, Op. 35, W43
Les Filles D'Arles, Op. 49, W67
Fleur Du Matin, W322
Fleur Jetée, W275
Fragilité, W274

Gavotte, Op. 9 No. 2, W12
Deuxième Gavotte, Op. 121, W168
Troisième Gavotte, Op. 144, W217
Quatrième Gavotte, Op. 149, W222
Cinquième Gavotte, Op. 162, W235
Gigue, Op. 43, W61
   No. 6 of Album Des Enfants, Op. 123, W176
Le Gladiateur, WU15
Guitare, Op. 32, W38

Havanaise, Op. 57, W80
L'Heure Du Mystère, W257
Les Heureuses, W382
Les Humbles, No. 2 of Poèmes Evangéliques, Op. 99, W142
Humoresque, No. 2 of Deux Morceaux, Op. 25, W28
Hymne, WU16

L'Idéal, W269
Idylle, No. 3 of Romances Sans Paroles, Op. 76, W100
   No. 1 of Album Des Enfants, Op. 126, W185
Idylle Arabe, No. 3 of Six Pièces Romantiques, Op. 55, W76,
   WU17
Immortalité, W336
Impromptu, No. 5 of Six Etudes De Concert, Op. 35, W45
Infini, W360
Inquiétude, No. 3 of Six Pièces Humoristiques, Op. 87, W119
Interlude, Op. 152, W225
Intermède, Op. 36 No. 1, W47
Intermezzo, No. 2 of Suite D'Orchestre, Op. 20, W20
   No. 2 of Album Des Enfants, Op. 123, W173
Invocation, W291

Jadis, W337
Je Voudrais, W386
La Jeune Fille, No. 4 of Poèmes Evangéliques, Op. 99, W144
Joie D'Aimer, Op. 102, W149

Légende, Op. 90, W125
Légende Du Vieux Manoir, WU18
Lettres D'Amour, W383
Libellules, Op. 24, W26
La Lisonjera, Op. 50, W68
La Livry, Op. 51, W69
Lolita, Op. 54, W72
La Lune Paresseuse, W377

Ma Première Lettre, W293
Madeleine, W263

Madrigal, W266
Malgré Nous, W294
Mandoline, W319
Marche, No. 1 of Suite D'Orchestre, Op. 20, W19
Marche Américaine, Op. 131, W204
Marche Hongroise, WU19
Marche Russe, No. 12 of Album Des Enfants, Op. 123, W183
Marine, Op. 38, W56
Marthe et Marie, Op. 64, W87
Le Matin, No. 1 of Deux Pièces, Op. 79, W106
Mazurk' Suédoise, Op. 58, W81
Deux Mazurkas, [Op. 1], W1-2
Méditation, No. 6 of Romances Sans Paroles, Op. 76, W103
Mélancholie, No. 1 of Deux Morceaux, Op. 25, W27
Menuet, Op. 5, W7, WU20
Menuet, W368
Menuet Galant, Op. 129, W202
Messe, Op. 167, W240-44
Mignonne, W302
Minuetto, Op. 23, W25
Mirage, W358
Moment Musical, Op. 103, W150
Mon Coeur Chante, W321
Deux Morceaux, Op. 25, W27-28
Deux Morceaux, Op. 27, W30-31
Trois Morceaux, Op. 31, W35-37
Mots D'Amour, W331

N'Est-Ce Pas, W370
Ne Nos Inducas In Tentationem, WU21
La Nef Sacrée, Op. 171, W248
Nice La Belle, W273
Ninette, W258
Noce Hongroise, Op. 47, W65
Les Noces D'Argent, Op. 12, W15
Nocturne, Op. 165, W238
Nocturne Pyrénéen, Op. 65, W88
Noël Des Marins, Op. 48, W66
Le Noël Des Oiseaux, W297
Norwégienne, No. 6 of Six Pièces Humoristiques, Op. 87, W122
Nous Nous Aimions, W344
Novelette, Op. 110, W157
    No. 8 of Album Des Enfants, Op. 126, W192
Nuit D'Eté, W326
Nuit Etoilée, W341

O Salutaris, WU22
L'Ondine, Op. 101, W148
L'Ondine Du Léman, W384
L'Orgue, W355
Orientale, Op. 22, W24, WU23
    No. 9 of Album Des Enfants, Op. 123, W180
Ouverture (to La Sévillane), Op. 19, W18

Les Papillons, W259
Pardon Breton, Op. 46, W64
Partout, W316
Pas Des Amphores, from Op. 37, W51
Pas Des Cymbales, Op. 36 No. 2, W48

Pas Des Echarpes, from Op. 37, W52
Passacaille, Op. 130, W203
Le Passé, No. 3 of Poème Provençal, Op. 127, W199
Passepied, No. 1 of Trois Danses Anciennes, Op. 95, W130
Pastel, Op. 128, W201
Pastorale, Op. 114, W161
Pastorale Enfantine, Op. 12, W16
Patrouille, No. 9 of Album Des Enfants, Op. 126, W193
Pavane, No. 2 of Trois Danses Anciennes, Op. 95, W131
Le Pêcheur Et L'Ondine, Op. 70, W93
Les Pêcheurs, No. 3 of Poèmes Evangéliques, Op. 99, W143
Les Pêcheurs De Nuit, No. 4 of Poème Provençal, Op. 127,
    W200
Petits Coeurs, W347
Les Petits Enfants, No. 5 of Poèmes Evangéliques, Op. 99,
    W145
Pièce Dans Le Style Ancien, Op. 74, W96
Pièce Romantique, Op. 9 No. 1, W11
Pièce Romantique, W327
Deux Pièces, Op. 79, W106-07, WU12
Six Pièces Humoristiques, Op. 87, W117-22
Six Pièces Romantiques, Op. 55, W73-78
Pierrette, Op. 41, W59
Plaintes D'Amour, W281
La Plus Jolie, W354
Poème Provençal, Op. 127, W197-200
Poèmes Evangéliques, Op. 99, W141-46
Portrait, W366
Pourquoi, W356
Prélude, Op. 78, W105
    No. 1 of Album Des Enfants, Op. 123, W172
Trois Préludes Mélodiques, Op. 84, W112-14
Les Présents, W330
Presto, Op. 2, W4
Primavera, No. 1 of Six Pièces Romantiques, Op. 55, W75
Promenade, No. 1 of Six Feuillets D'Album, Op. 98, W135

Râvana, W312
Refrain De Novembre, W364
La Reine De Mon Coeur, W378
Le Rendez-Vous, W289
Ressemblance, W310
Reste, W338
Le Retour, Op. 134, W207
Rêve D'Un Soir, W278
Réveil, No. 1 of Six Pièces Humoristiques, Op. 87, W117
Les Rêves, W280
Rêves Défunts, W340
Rigaudon, No. 6 of Six Pièces Romantiques, Op. 55, W79
    No. 3 of Album Des Enfants, Op. 126, W187
Rimembranza, Op. 88, W123
Ritournelle, W265
Ritournelle, Op. 83, W111
Romance, No. 7 of Album Des Enfants, Op. 123, W178
Romance En Ré, Op. 137, W210
Romances Sans Paroles, Op. 76, W98-103
Romanesca, Op. 163, W236
Romanza Appassionata, No. 2 of Trois Morceaux, Op. 31, W36
Ronde D'Amour, W311

Ronde Du Crépuscule, Op. 133, W206
Rondeau, Op. 97, W134
    No. 4 of Album Des Enfants, Op. 123, W175
Rondo Allègre, No. 6 of Six Feuillets D'Album, Op. 98, W140
Rosemonde, W298
Roulis Des Grèves, W361

Sainte-Magdeleine, No. 6 of Poèmes Evangéliques, Op. 99,
    W146
Sans Amour, W318
Scaramouche, Op. 56, W79
Scherzando, Op. 10, W13
Scherzetto, No. 2 of Six Feuillets D'Album, Op. 98, W136
Scherzo, No. 1 of Six Etudes De Concert, Op. 35, W41
Scherzo, No. 3 of Suite D'Orchestre, Op. 20, W21
Scherzo-Caprice, Op. 145, W218
Scherzo-Etude, Op. 3, W5
Scherzo-Valse, Op. 148, W221
    No. 6 of Album Des Enfants, Op. 126, W190
Sérénade, Op. 29, W33, WU24
Sérénade Aux Etoiles, Op. 142, W215
Sérénade D'Automne, No. 4 of Six Pièces Romantiques, Op. 55,
    W77, WU25
Sérénade Espagnole, Op. 150, W223
Sérénade Sévillane, W299
Sérénade Vénitienne, Op. 154
Serenata, W272
Ses Yeux, W374
La Sévillane, W18, WU26
Si J'Etais Jardinier, W296
Les Sirènes, Op. 160, W233
Le Soir, No. 2 of Deux Pièces, Op. 79, W107
Solitude, No. 2 of Poème Provençal, Op. 127, W198
Sombrero, W301
Sommeil D'Enfant, W362
Son Nom, W371
Sonata, Op. 21, W23
Sonne, Clairon, W391
Un Souffle A Passé, W379
Souhait, W264
Sous Bois, No. 2 of Six Pièces Humoristiques, Op. 87, W118
Sous L'Aile Blanche Des Voiles, Op. 45, W63
Sous Le Masque, Op. 116, W163
Sous Ta Fenêtre, W260
Souvenance, No. 1 of Romances Sans Paroles, Op. 76, W98
Souvenirs D'Enfance, WU27
Souvenirs Lointains, Op. 111, W158
Studio, Op. 66, W89
Suédoise, Op. 141, W214
Suite D'Orchestre, Op. 20, W19-22
Sur La Plage, W286
Les Sylvains, Op. 60, W83

Les Tambourinaires, Danse Provençale, WU28
Tarentelle, No. 6 of Six Etudes De Concert, Op. 35, W46,
    WU29
    No. 10 of Album Des Enfants, Op. 123, W181
Te Souviens-Tu, W261
Terpsichore, Op. 81, W109

Thème Varié, Op. 89, W124
Le Thrône Du Vieux Roi, W389
Toccata, Op. 39, W57
Toi, W314
Ton Sourire, W353
Trahison, W308
Trio, Op. 11, W14
Trio, Op. 34, W40
Tristesse, Op. 104, W151
Les Trois Baisers, W339
Tu Me Dirais, W282

Deuxième Valse, Op. 77, W104
Troisième Valse Brillante, Op. 80, W108
Quatrième Valse, Op. 91, W126
Cinquième Valse, Op. 109, W156
Valse Arabesque, No. 4 of Six Feuillets D'Album, Op. 98,
    W138
Valse-Ballet, Op. 112, W159
Valse Caprice, Op. 33, W39
Valse Carnavalesque, Op. 73, W95
Valse D'Automne, Op. 169, W246
Valse Humoristique, Op. 93, W128
Valse Mignonne, No. 12 of Album Des Enfants, Op. 126, W196
Valse Romantique, Op. 115, W162
Valse Tendre, Op. 119, W166
Variations Sur Un Thème Original, Op. 120, W167
Vert-Galant, Op. 85, W115
Veux-Tu, W324
Viatique, W313
Vieille Chanson, W307
Viens, Mon Bien-Aimé, W290
Vieux Portrait, W279
Le Village, W390
Villanelle, W306
    No. 10 of Album Des Enfants, Op. 126, W194
Voeu Suprême, W385
Voisinage, W270
Voix Du Large, W373
Vous Souvient-Il, W334

Les Willis, Op. 42, W60

Zingara, No. 2 of Deux Morceaux, Op. 27, W31, WU30

Appendix II:
Classified List of Works

The mnemonics "W," "WC," and "WU" refer to listings in the "Works and Performances" chapter.

SOLO KEYBOARD

All works are for piano, unless otherwise indicated.

Agitato, Op. 108, W155
Air A Danser, Op. 164, W237
Air De Ballet, Op. 30, W34
Air Italien, Op. 170, W247
Album Des Enfants, Op. 123, W172-83
Album Des Enfants, Op. 126, W185-96
Appassionato, Op. 35 No. 4, W44
Arabesque, Op. 61, W84
Deuxième Arabesque, Op. 92, W127
Arlequine, Op. 53, W71
Au Pays Bleu, Op. 170, W247
Au Pays Dévasté, Op. 155, W228
Aubade, Op. 140, W213
Automne, Op. 35 No. 2, W42
Autrefois, Op. 87 No. 4, W120

Ballade, Op. 86, W116
Barcarolle, Op. 7, W9
La Barque D'Amour, W208
Berceuse Arabe, Op. 166, W239
Berceuse, Op. 6, W8
Berceuse Du Petit Soldat Blessé, Op. 156, W229
Bohémiens, Les, Op. 147, W220

Callirhoë, Air De Ballet, from Op. 37, W53
Canzonetta, Op. 123 No. 3, W174
Capriccio Appassionato, Op. 52, W70
Caprice Espagnole, Op. 67, W90
Caprice-Etude, Op. 4, W6
Caprice Humoristique, Op. 113, W160
Caprice-Impromptu, Op. 153, W226
Capricietto, Op. 136, W209
La Capricieuse, WU7
Chaconne, Op. 8, W10
Chanson Bretonne, Op. 76 No. 5, W102

Chanson D'Orient, Op. 157, W230
Chanson Espagnole, Op. 150, W223
Chanson Napolitaine, Op. 82, W110
Chanson Nègre, Op. 161, W234
Chanson Russe, Op. 90 No. 5, W139
Chant Du Nord, Op. 96, W133
Comme Autrefois--Le Bon Vieux Temps, WU9
Consolation, Op. 87 No. 5, W121
Conte de Fées, Op. 126 No. 11, W195
Contes Bleus, Op. 122, W169-71
Cortège, Op. 143, W216
Courante, Op. 95 No. 3, W132

Dans L'Arène, Op. 168
Dans La Lande, Op. 127 No. 1, W197
Danse Ancienne, Op. 75, W97
Danse Créole, Op. 94, W129
Danse Orientale, from Op. 37, W55
Danse Paienne, Op. 158, W231
Danse Pastorale, from Op. 37, W54
Trois Danses Anciennes, Op. 95, W130-32
Divertissement, Op. 105, W152
Duetto, Op. 27 No. 1, W30

Ecossaise, Op. 151, W224
Eglogue, Op. 76 No. 4, W101
Elégie, Op. 90 No. 3, W137
Elévation, Op. 76 No. 2, W99
Etude, [Op. 1], W3
Etude Humoristique, Op. 138, W211
Etude Mélodique, Op. 118, W165
Etude Pathétique, Op. 124, W184
Etude Romantique, Op. 132, W205
Etude Scolastique, Op. 139, W212
Etude Symphonique, Op. 28, W32
Six Etudes De Concert, Op. 35, W41-46
Expansion, Op. 106, W153

Feuilles D'Automne, Op. 146, W219
Six Feuillets D'Album, Op. 90, W135-40
Fileuse, Op. 35 No. 3, W43

Gavotte, Op. 9 No. 2, W12
Deuxième Gavotte, Op. 121, W168
Troisième Gavotte, Op. 144, W217
Quatrième Gavotte, Op. 149, W222
Cinquième Gavotte, Op. 162, W235
Gigue, Op. 43, W61
Le Gladiateur, WU15
Guitare, Op. 32, W38

Havanaise, Op. 57, W80
Humoresque, Op. 25 No. 2, W28

Idylle, Op. 76 No. 3, W100
Impromptu, Op. 35 No. 5, W45
Inquiétude, Op. 87 No. 3, W119
Interlude, Op. 152, W225

Légende, Op. 90, W125
Légende Du Vieux Manoir, WU18
Lisonjera, La, Op. 50, W68
La Livry, Op. 51, W69
Lolita, Op. 54, W72

Marche Américaine, Op. 131, W204
Marine, Op. 38, W56
Mazurk'Suédoise, Op. 58, W81
Deux Mazurkas, [Op. 1], W1-2
Méditation, Op. 76 No. 6, W103
Mélancholie, Op. 25 No. 1, W27
Menuet, Op. 5, W7
Menuet Galant, Op. 129, W202
Minuetto, Op. 23, W25
Moment Musical, Op. 103, W150
Deux Morceaux, Op. 25, W27-28
Deux Morceaux, Op. 27, W30-31

La Nef Sacrée, Op. 171, W248-56 (for organ or harmonium)
Nocturne, Op. 165, W238
Norwégienne, Op. 87 No. 6, W122
Novelette, Op. 110, W157

L'Ondine, Op. 101, W148
Orientale, Op. 22, W24

Pas Des Amphores, from Op. 37, W51
Pas Des Echarpes, from Op. 37, W52
Pasacaille, Op. 130, W203
Le Passé, Op. 127 No. 3, W199
Passepied, Op. 95 No. 1, W130
Pastel, Op. 128, W201
Pastorale, Op. 114, W161
Pastorale Enfantine, Op. 12, W16
Patrouille, Op. 126 No. 9, W193
Pavane, Op. 95 No. 2, W131
Les Pêcheurs De Nuit, Op. 127 No. 4, W200
Pièce Dans Le Style Ancien, Op. 74, W96
Pièce Romantique, Op. 9 No. 1, W11
Six Pièces Humoristiques, Op. 87, W117-22
Pierrette, Op. 41, W59
Poème Provençal, Op. 127, W197-200
Prélude, Op. 78, W105 (for piano or organ)
Trois Préludes Mélodiques, Op. 84, W112-14
Presto, Op. 2, W4
Promenade, Op. 90 No. 1, W135

Le Retour, Op. 134, W207
Réveil, Op. 87 No. 1, W117
Rimembranza, Op. 88, W123
Ritournelle, Op. 83, W111
Romance, Op. 123 No. 7, W178
Romance En Ré, Op. 137, W210
Romances Sans Paroles, Op. 76, W98-103
Romanesca, Op. 163, W236
Rondo Allègre, Op. 90 No. 6, W140

Scaramouche, Op. 56, W79
Scherzando, Op. 10, W13
Scherzetto, Op. 90 No. 2, W136
Scherzo, Op. 35 No. 1, W41
Scherzo-Caprice, Op. 145, W218
Scherzo-Etude, Op. 3, W5
Scherzo-Valse, Op. 148, W221
Sérénade, Op. 29, W33
Sérénade Vénitienne, Op. 154, W227
Solitude, Op. 127 No. 2, W198
Sonata, Op. 21, W23
Sous Bois, Op. 87 No. 2, W118
Sous Le Masque, Op. 116, W163
Souvenance, Op. 76 No. 1, W98
Souvenirs D'Enfance, WU27
Souvenirs Lointains, Op. 111, W158
Studio, Op. 66, W89
Suédoise, Op. 141, W214
Les Sylvains, Op. 60, W83

Les Tambourinaires, WU28
Tarentelle, Op. 35 No. 6, W46
Terpsichore, Op. 81, W109
Thème Varié, Op. 89, W124
Toccata, Op. 39, W57
Tristesse, Op. 104, W151

Valse Arabesque, Op. 90 No. 4, W138
Deuxième Valse, Op. 77, W104
Troisième Valse Brillante, Op. 80, W108
Quatrième Valse, Op. 91, W126
Cinquième Valse, Op. 109, W156
Valse-Ballet, Op. 112, W159
Valse-Caprice, Op. 33, W39
Valse D'Automne, Op. 169, W246
Valse Humoristique, Op. 93, W128
Valse Mignonne, Op. 126 No. 12, W196
Valse Romantique, Op. 115, W162
Valse Tendre, Op. 119, W166
Variations Sur Un Thème Original, Op. 120, W167
Vert-Galant, Op. 85, W115

Les Willis, Op. 42, W60

Zingara, Op. 27 No. 2, W31

PIANO DUET AND TWO PIANO

Andante Et Scherzettino, Op. 59, W82
La Chaise A Porteurs, Op. 55 No. 2, W74
Danse Hindoue, Op. 55 No. 5, W77
Duo Symphonique, Op. 117, W164
Idylle Arabe, Op. 55 No. 3, W75
Intermède, Op. 36 No. 1, W47
Marche Hongroise, WU19
Le Matin, Op. 79 No. 1, W106
Les Noces D'Argent, Op. 12, W15

Pas Des Cymbales, Op. 36 No. 2, W48
Deux Pièces, Op. 79, W106-07
Six Pièces Romantiques, Op. 55, W73-78
Primavera, Op. 55 No. 1, W73
Rigaudon, Op. 55 No. 6, W78
Sérénade D'Automne, Op. 55 No. 4, W76
Le Soir, Op. 79 No. 2, W107
Valse Carnavalesque, Op. 73, W95

CHAMBER WORKS

Andante, WU2
Andantino, Op. 31 No. 1, W35
Bohémienne, Op. 31 No. 3, W37
Capriccio, Op. 18, W17
Concerto-Légende Pour Violon, WU10
Trois Morceaux, Op. 31, W35-37
Romanza Appassionata, Op. 31 No. 2, W36
Rondeau, Op. 97, W134
Sérénade Aux Etoiles, Op. 142, W215
Sérénade Espagnole, Op. 150, W223
Trio, Op. 11, W14
Deuxième Trio, Op. 34, W40

ORCHESTRAL WORKS

Les Amazones, Op. 26, W29
Callirhoë, Op. 37, W49
Callirhoë, Suite D'Orchestre, [Op. 37], W50
Concertino, Op. 107, W154
Concertstück, Op. 40, W58
Egmont, WU13
Hymne, WU16
Le Matin, Op. 79 No. 1, W106
Menuet, WU20
Orientale, WU23
Ouverture [to La Sévillane], Op. 19, W18
Deux Pièces, Op. 79, W106-07
Sérénade, WU24
Sérénade D'Automne, WU25
Le Soir, Op. 79 No. 2, W107
Suite D'Orchestre, Op. 20, W19-22
Tarentelle, WU29
Zingara, WU30

SOLO VOICE WITH PIANO

A L'Inconnue, W288
L'Absente, W271
L'Allée D'Eméraude Et D'Or, W346
Alleluia, W357
Amertume, W333
Amoroso, W283
L'Amour Captif, W292

Amour D'Automne, W276
Amour Invisible, W376
L'Anneau Du Soldat, W392
Attente, W387
Au Clair De La Lune, WU4
Au Firmament, W352
Au Pays Bleu, W332
Aubade, W309
Auprès De Ma Vie, W268
Avril S'Eveille, W323
Avenir, W375

Ballade A La Lune, W304
Ballade A La Terre, WU5
Le Beau Chanteur, W342
Berceuse, W287
Bleus, W328
Bonne Humeur, W363

C'Etait En Avril, W345
Chanson De Mer, W388
Chanson De Neige, W380
La Chanson Du Fou, W335
Chanson Espagnole, W315
Chanson Forestière, W367
Chanson Groënlandaise, W300
Chanson Naive, W381
Chanson Slave, W262
Chanson Triste, W329
Chant D'Mour, W305
Le Charme D'Amour, W351
Le Ciel Est Bleu, W320
Colette, W285
Console-Moi, W348
Conte de Fées, W349
Couplets Bachiques, W325

La Damoiselle, W350
Départ, W369
Les Deux Coeurs, W295
Les Deux Ménétriers, W277
Dites-Lui, W372

Ecrin, W359
Espoir, W317
L'Eté, W303
Exil, W365
L'Extase, W343

La Fiancée Du Soldat, W267
Fleur Du Matin, W322
Fleur Jetée, W275
Fragilité, W274

L'Heure Du Mystère, W247
Les Heureuses, W382

L'Idéal, W269
Immortalité, W336

Sombrero, W301
Sommeil D'Enfant, W363
Son Nom, W371
Sonne, Clairon, W391
Un Souffle A Passé, W379
Souhait, W264
Sous Ta Fenêtre, W260
Sur La Plage, W286

Te Souviens-Tu, W261
Le Thrône Du Vieux Roi, W389
Toi, W314
Ton Sourire, W353
Trahison, W308
Les Trois Baisers, W339
Tu Me Dirais, W282

Veux-Tu, W324
Viatique, W313
Vieille Chanson, W307
Viens, Mon Bien-Aimé, W290
Vieux Portrait, W279
Le Village, W390
Villanelle, W306
Voeu Suprême, W385
Voisinage, W260
Voix Du Large, W373
Vous Souvient-Il, W334

OTHER VOCAL WITH PIANO

A Travers Bois, Op. 63, W86
L'Angélus, Op. 69, W92
Aux Dieux Sylvains, Op. 100, W147
Barcarolle, Op. 62, W85
Choeurs, Opp. 44-49, W62-67
Duo D'Etoiles, Op. 71, W94
Duos Avec Accompagnement De Piano, Op. 62-65, Op. 68-71, W85-
    88, W91-94
Les Elfes Du Bois, Op. 159, W232
L'Etoile, Op. 99 No. 1, W141
Les Feux De St. Jean, Op. 44, W62
Les Fiancées, Op. 68, W91
Les Filles D'Arles, Op. 49, W67
Les Humbles, Op. 99 No. 2, W142
La Jeune Fille, Op. 99 No. 4, W144
Joie D'Aimer, Op. 102, W149
Marthe Et Marie, Op. 64, W87
Messe, Op. 167, W240-44
Noce Hongroise, Op. 47, W65
Nocturne Pyrénéen, Op. 65, W88
Noël Des Marins, Op. 48, W66
O Salutaris, WU22
Pardon Breton, Op. 46, W64
Le Pêcheur Et L'Ondine, Op. 70, W93
Les Pêcheurs, Op. 99 No. 3, W143
Les Petits Enfants, Op. 99 No. 5, W145

Poèmes Evangéliques, Op. 99, W141-46
Ronde Du Crépuscule, Op. 133, W206
Sainte-Magdeleine, Op. 99 No. 6, W146
Les Sirènes, Op. 160, W233
Sous L'Aile Blanche Des Voiles, Op. 45, W63

Appendix III:
Summary of Archival Resources

I. **FAMILY** (Private Collection, Paris)

   A. Music: autographs in composer's hand of approximately ninety compositions; <u>see</u> "Works and Performances" chapter.

   B. Photographs: approximately forty of the composer. Most are undated but appear to span the period from her early adult years to perhaps as late as the 1920s. Many are identical to the Chaminade photographs published in the literature. See frontispiece for an example from the collection.

   C. Clippings: perhaps as many as 250, mostly from newspapers. Those from the period 1875 to c. 1890 were bound by Chaminade's mother in a 100-page book covered in maroon cloth with leather trim. Many of the items are dated and given source attribution, although the system of dating is inconsistent (sometimes it is of the event, sometimes of the review) and a few sources are misattributed. After c. 1890 clippings are loose and most are without date or source. Often one can identify the city or the approximate time period from internal evidence, but at other times neither is obtainable.

   D. Correspondence: relatively few letters by Chaminade, and most are to Enoch, from the 1920s onward, regarding details of availability, location of manuscript materials, and matters of finance. There is also a fair number of letters from miscellaneous individuals, including members of Chaminade clubs in America. Many letters to and from Chaminade's niece, Antoinette Lorel, exist, most from Chaminade's death (1944) to ca. 1957. They document Lorel's efforts to have her aunt's reputation and music brought to the forefront again.

   E. Programs: mostly of London recitals of the 1890s.

   F. Biographies: there are three. Lorel's extremely valuable biography, "Viatique," is in typescript, almost 200 pages, written c. 1948. She attempted unsuccessfully to have it published, in England. The second is another account in typescript, by an unknown author ("an Englishwoman," on the cover) and one Monsieur Ferti, apparently a family friend. It was written c. 1930, and Chaminade wrote on the title page that she did not like it at all. The third is a prose scenario for a projected Hollywood film on Chaminade, by one Elza Schallert, probably in the early 1950s.

G. Other: miscellaneous materials, such as lists of orchestral compositions, poems, items sent from the Chaminade clubs, etc.

II. DEPARTEMENT DE LA MUSIQUE, BIBLIOTHEQUE NATIONALE (Paris)

A. Music: autographs in the composer's hand of four compositions: *Alleluia*, *Les Papillons*, *Ritournelle*, and *Marche Hongroise*. There is also a melodic fragment in Chaminade's hand.

B. Letters: eight letters in Chaminade's hand, to diverse people. Four come from the Conservatoire's collection, only one of which is dated (3 September 1889). Of the other four, there is one each to Gabriel Astruc, Gustave Marie, Marc Pincherle (postcard), and a publisher (probably Enoch).

C. Other: approximately ten miscellaneous items in the Fonds Montpensier. These consist of two recital programs (25 April 1878 and 12 March 1893), three obituary notices, a photo of Chaminade (1898-99?), two newspaper notices regarding a Brussels concert of 1 December 1895, and two invitations to Chaminade concerts sponsored by Enoch (Paris, 22 October [no year]; London, 2 October 1922). In addition, the library has a glossy photo of Chaminade in its general collection of photos of famous musicians.

III. LIBRARY OF CONGRESS (Washington, D. C.)

A. Music: autographs in the composer's hand of three songs: *L'Absente*, *L'Amour Captif*, and *Madrigal*.

B. Letters: approximately eight autograph letters. Five are in the Schwerké collection and are addressed to Irving Schwerké, in the 1930s. Two, undated, are to an unspecificied individual. In addition, there is at least one letter in the Hammerstein collection.

IV. PIERPONT MORGAN LIBRARY (New York)

A. Music: album leaf with first four measures of *Fleur Du Matin* and an ink portrait of Chaminade.

B. Letters: four autograph letters to various people. One, concerning the *Trio*, Op. 34, is intended for Joseph Bennett.

V. NEW YORK PUBLIC LIBRARY

A. Clippings: a substantial file, containing perhaps 75 articles, drawn mostly from New York newspapers and from music magazines, e.g. *Musical America* and *Musical Courier*.

B. Programs: of Carnegie Hall concerts of 24 October and 15 December 1908.

VI. **UNIVERSITY OF MICHIGAN** (Women's Music Collection, Ann Arbor)

A. Music: autograph in composer's hand of Op. 25 Nos. 1 and 2 (*Mélancholie* and *Humoresque*).

VII. **BOSTON PUBLIC LIBRARY**

A. Music: manuscript of *Ballade A La Lune*. The identity of the hand has not been ascertained.

VIII. **UNIVERSITY OF NEW HAMPSHIRE**

A. Letters: two letters--of 15 June 1834 to a woman friend, probably in the United States, who is also a friend of Amy Beach; and undated, probably shortly thereafter, to Amy Beach.

IX. **EASTMAN SCHOOL OF MUSIC** (Sibley Music Library)

A. Letter: autograph letter, 12 June 1930, to David James.

X. **STANFORD UNIVERSITY** (Memorial Library of Music)

A. Miscellany: three first editions of Chaminade, each containing an inscription by the composer: in *L'Anneau D'Argent*; in *Les Heureuses*, inscription to Suzanne Astruc; and in *Scherzando*, Op. 10, inscription to Mme. Albert Schiller.

XI. **OTHER**

A. Programs: local concert programs in main public library of Philadelphia, Indianapolis, and possibly also in Louisville, Cincinnati, and Chicago.

Index

The prefix "W" refers to items in "Works and Performances," "D" to items in the "Discography," and "B" to items in the "Bibliography." Numbers without a letter prefix represent page numbers in the "Biography" and in "Appendix III."

About the Author

MARCIA J. CITRON is associate professor of musicology at Rice University. She is the author of *Letters of Fanny Hensel to Felix Mendelssohn* (1987) and has contributed essays on women composers to several scholarly publications, including *Women Making Music, Mendelssohn and Schumann Essays, The New Grove Dictionary*, and *The Musical Quarterly*.

Recent Titles in
Bio-Bibliographies in Music
Series Advisers: Donald L. Hixon and Adrienne Fried Block

Thea Musgrave: A Bio-Bibliography
Donald L. Hixon

Aaron Copland: A Bio-Bibliography
JoAnn Skowronski

Samuel Barber: A Bio-Bibliography
Don A. Hennessee

Virgil Thomson: A Bio-Bibliography
Michael Meckna

Esther Williamson Ballou: A Bio-Bibliography
James R. Heintze

Gunther Schuller: A Bio-Bibliography
Norbert Carnovale

Max Reger: A Bio-Bibliography
William E. Grim

Heitor Villa-Lobos: A Bio-Bibliography
David P. Appleby

Jean Langlais: A Bio-Bibliography
Kathleen Thomerson

Lowell Mason: A Bio-Bibliography
Carol A. Pemberton

Daniel Pinkham: A Bio-Bibliography
Kee DeBoer and John B. Ahouse

Arthur Bliss: A Bio-Bibliography
Stewart R. Craggs

Charles Ives: A Bio-Bibliography
Geoffrey Block